To Dons all the best!

Tom Kelly

Cashing In on a Second Home in Mexico

How to Buy, Rent and Profit from Property South of the Border

by Tom Kelly and Mitch Creekmore

Crabman Publishing • Rolling Bay, WA

Cashing In on a Second Home in Mexico
How to Buy, Rent and Profit from Property South of the Border

Produced by Crabman Publishing, Rolling Bay, WA 98061
Copyright © 2005 by Tom Kelly and Mitch Creekmore

ISBN 0-9770920-0-3

Cover and interior design © 2005 TLC Graphics, *www.TLCGraphics.com*

Cover photo: Villas Del Mar at Palmilla, a Los Cabos development by Hatfield Investments and Schnitzer Interests.

Printed in the United States of America

Publisher's Cataloging-in-Publication

Kelly, Tom, 1950 Oct. 8-
     Cashing in on a second home in Mexico : how to buy, rent and profit from property south of the border / Tom Kelly and Mitch Creekmore.
     p. cm.
     Includes bibliographical references and index.

     1. Real estate investment—Mexico. 2. Real property —Mexico—Foreign ownership. I. Creekmore, Mitch. II. Title.

HD328.K45 2005   332.63'24'0972
                       QBI05-600119

Table of Contents

PART THREE: THE MONEY PICTURE: EXPLORING MORTGAGES AND TAX RAMIFICATIONS

PART FOUR: HELPFUL SOURCES

About the Authors

Tom Kelly is a nationally syndicated newspaper columnist and radio talk show host. He served *The Seattle Times* readers for 20 years—several as real estate editor—and his work now appears in *The Los Angeles Times, The Houston Chronicle, St. Louis Post Dispatch, The Oakland Tribune, Kansas City Star, The Sacramento Bee, The Tacoma News Tribune, The Reno Gazette-Journal, Louisville Courier-Journal, Nashville Tennessean,* plus more than two dozen other newspapers.

In 2005, Tom's award-winning radio show "Real Estate Today" began its 12th year on 710 KIRO-AM, the CBS affiliate in Seattle and the state's largest station. The show is syndicated by Business Talk Radio to approximately 40 domestic markets and airs on 450 stations in 160 foreign countries via American Forces Radio.

He is the author of *The New Reverse Mortgage Formula* (John Wiley & Sons) and co-author of *How a Second Home Can Be Your Best Investment* (McGraw-Hill).

Tom was president of the Santa Clara University class of 1972. He and his wife, Dr. Jodi Kelly, an associate dean and professor at Seattle University, have four children and live on Bainbridge Island, Washington.

Mitch Creekmore is senior vice president and director of international business development for Stewart

Information International, a world leader in title insurance and other real estate information services. He joined Stewart Title Guaranty Company in 1994 and has been responsible for the development of the company's marketing strategy with implementation of the business plan for Stewart-Mexico. His primary effort has been to enlighten the legal and real estate community on both sides of the border about the availability and benefit of title insurance on Mexico land and how the land conveyance system in Mexico functions. He has been a licensed real estate broker for more than 20 years.

In 2003, he was appointed by Arizona Governor Janet Napolitano as co-chairman of the Real Estate Task Force on Mexico in participation with the Arizona-Mexico Commission. He gained approval from the State Bar of Texas and the Texas Real Estate Commission, as well as the Arizona Department of Real Estate and the California Department of Real Estate to provide a mandatory continuing education course for attorneys and real estate agents entitled "Acquiring Property South of the Border." He has authored numerous articles on the Mexican system of real estate conveyance, Mexico's foreign ownership requirements including Mexican land title matters, subdivision development procedures, escrow and tax considerations, *ejido* land and financing issues.

Mitch graduated from Louisiana State University in 1976. He has served as a captain on the Houston Livestock Show & Rodeo's International Committee, on the board of directors of the Houston Racquet Club and is an officer of Stewart Title Guaranty Company. He is a licensed private airplane pilot. Mitch has four children and lives in Houston.

Acknowledgements

T his book is dedicated to my parents—Bob and Jane Kelly— who bent over backward to provide seven children a delightful family home in which to grow, learn and love. I also am indebted to them for wonderful vacation memories in the sun.

My genuine thanks to all the Realtors and the many individuals from home building, mortgage lending, tax and accounting, printing, editing and distributing that have aided me for years in my newspaper writing and radio work and who also provided creative insights and useful information for this book. I have called upon them often and their patience, interest and kindness have been extraordinary. Leading this list are Sam Speigel, Linda Owens, CJ Yeoman, Miriam Lowe, Carol Weinrich, Heidi Henning, Tami Dever, Monica Thomas, Erin Stark, Christine Hrib-Karpinski, Laura Shelley, Debra Stevens, Jim Grogan, Joanne Elizabeth Kelly, Rob Keasal, John Tuccillo and Kevin Hawkins. I also am grateful to the numerous second home buyers and renters for sharing their stories.

—Tom Kelly

This book is dedicated to my late father, Dr. Tom Creekmore, a wonderful writer in his own right, who with his love and insight encouraged me to write about Mexico; to my loving mother, Leslie; to my siblings, Gary, Denise and Kevin; and to my children, Courtney, April, Tanner and Ashton.

I also wish to thank Stewart Morris, Sr. for his vision and wisdom of our international title business; Jeannie Osborne, a great boss, supporter and friend; Hector Barraza, my mentor and *compadre,* and Lic. Paco Manzo Taylor, a Mexican *notario publico* and historian and a wonderful teacher about Mexico.

—*Mitch Creekmore*

Preface

After nearly a decade of work in Mexico insuring real estate properties to foreign purchasers, the same issues always seem to surface regarding second home acquisitions:

- "If I buy a house in Mexico, don't I get a 99-year lease from the government?"
- "I understand that I can buy a residence in Mexico only if the title is vested in a Mexican corporation."
- "I didn't think Americans could own Mexican beachfront properties."

All of these suppositions are incorrect. This book attempts to help clarify and explain why Mexican real estate, when using the proper safeguards, can be a terrific, secure investment. It will also explore the purchasing mistakes of the past, summarize several of the attractive new locations that are luring foreign dollars and explain why Mexico is so eager to welcome second home buyers from outside its borders.

The worst thing a potential purchaser can do is to remain ignorant of the law and procedures involved in the conveyance of real estate in a foreign country. As we state several times in this book, Mexico is *not* the perceived "Wild West" where anything goes and the prevailing Mexican attitude is "trust me, *no problema.*" It is inherently important for non-Mexican buyers to understand that Mexico has formality of law with authorized regulation of real estate development procedures at all levels. This process is coupled with a statutory government framework for the legal conveyance of real property.

Great personal wealth has been attained through real estate ownership, but for most of us, it has been limited to investment in a primary residence. Although Mexican real estate also can be a viable investment venue, Americans have had a great deal more trepidation considering properties "south of the border." And for good reason—considering the history of some acquisitions.

Given today's investment climate, however, Mexico provides an attractive, alternative arena for potential investment. Real estate in Mexico should have a similar appreciation "upside" as does real estate in a U.S. development—coupled with the advantage of use and enjoyment of the property as a vacation residence.

—Mitch Creekmore

Many years ago, while searching for yellowtail tuna with a group of older fishermen off the warm waters of Ensenada, Mexico, I was drawn to the tiny cottages that dotted the dry hills above the sea. What a place, I thought then. Who owned those spots?

Sometimes, nobody really knew—including the folks who had houses there. For Mexican families, it often did not seem to matter. For U.S. citizens seeking an affordable alternative to outlandish U.S. waterfront prices—especially second home buyers and retirees—the property ownership question became a moving target.

Jack Smith, the late *Los Angeles Times* columnist, for years described his experience of building a weekend second home just south of Ensenada. His contractor, confidant and eventual longtime friend—the curiously wonderful Romulo Gomez—often frustrated and delighted Smith with his extremely casual *mañana* attitude toward property rights, construction and life in general.

("How will we get water?" Smith would ask Mr. Gomez. "The water will come. God will bring the water....")

Smith, who died in 1996, compiled his columns into the legendary book *God and Mr. Gomez,* a must-read for anybody building in a foreign country (or hiring a contractor anywhere). It also served as a reminder that Americans should understand the ramifications of obtaining an interest in Mexican property, especially near the water.

Many things have changed since Jack Smith acquired his Ensenada property more than three decades ago. This book is an attempt to explain some of those changes—how you can now hold title to wondrous little getaways near the coast, havens that few visitors frequented a few short years ago. It will also help clarify tax ramifications and provide tips on renting the property when you're too busy to enjoy the sandal life.

I wonder what Mr. Gomez would have accomplished with Internet access?

—*Tom Kelly*

This book is a guide to investigating, buying and renting property in Mexico. The rising cost of U.S. real estate, the want of a slower pace and warmer climate—especially for retirees—and the immense information library that is the Internet have contributed to the dreams and growing interest Americans have in Mexican property. Tales of friendly people, improved air travel and inexpensive living costs have awakened a dream in many people to find that treasure of a hacienda, fix it up and then enjoy long, leisurely seasons under the shade of an old tree or beach umbrella. And later, they see themselves whiling away their retirement in sandals and shorts.

We lay out the important considerations involved in buying and owning property in Mexico. These include the necessity of understanding your own motives, developing a long-term plan for your property, learning about the legal and financial environment in which you will be an owner and obtaining the necessary familiarity with the local culture and language so you can enjoy your property as you intend.

This book contains real stories of how real people attained their dream of owning Mexican property. It includes helpful maps of the most popular areas where Americans, and others, have purchased. It also includes preparation checklists, outlines of specific regions, helpful websites and English-Spanish language tips and terms.

More importantly, it will guide consumers through the variety of nuances brought by the language and customs of this incredibly curious and beautiful country. Now, it's time to start our journey.

The Mexican Getaway

Why a longtime lure is finally garnering second home buyers

The growth and popularity of Mexico's real estate industry has absolutely exploded compared to a decade ago when it appeared to be on a fast track to implosion. What went right? Did the enormous group of United States baby boomers simply return to their old spring-break haunts and begin buying beachfront memories? When did it turn the corner? Was it with the turnaround of the peso in 1996?

Does it still make sense to consider buying a getaway in a laid-back, it-can-wait-until *mañana* setting? Values in some Mexican markets have tripled in five years—far exceeding the rates of return in much of the U.S.—but will those numbers continue to rise?

This book is divided into four sections. The first deals with the Mexican landscape, both from the prospective of desirable geographical areas as well as how foreigners can safely own property. We'll share personal experiences from owners and residents. The second section discusses preparing and planning and helps you make the important location decisions about your investment: where to buy, what to buy and how to find and retain renters who will help offset your costs. The third section explores the evolution of mortgages in Mexico and offers creative alternatives to conventional financing and what to expect when the taxman comes knocking at your door. The fourth section provides resources, tips, terms and a English-Spanish dictionary of common real estate terms.

The next chapters will help you get to know some of the incredibly diverse and gorgeous new areas that are now driving the Mexican second home market, while encapsulating a few of the longtime favorites. Everybody's heard of the vibrant markets of Cancun, Los Cabos and Puerto Vallarta, but what about Arizona's favorite seaside destination—Puerto Peñasco—or Minnesota's new winter outpost—Manzanillo? There's a reason Alaska Airlines now has daily service to Loreto, the oldest permanent settlement and the first capital of Baja California.

This book also explains and clarifies many of the complexities of the Mexican real estate purchase, and it guides you through the maze of possibilities for renting out your second home in the sun. It will provide you with sources to buy, sell, rent and insure. It will also help you with important terms in Mexican real estate—and offer a few guidelines for Mexican social life.

Was it just a matter of time before foreigners would feel secure in holding a different form of title south of the border? Or was it the push by the Mexican government and private companies in the United States to clarify the rules of ownership while promoting exotic, new areas that potential second home buyers had never seen on the Mexican radar screen? Some attempts by nonnationals to own Mexican property created national disaster stories that have been well publicized. In recent years, headlines from *The Los Angeles Times, San Diego Tribune, Arizona Republic, CNN* and *The Wall Street Journal* chronicled stories about Americans losing their properties in Mexico. Sensational articles headlined "Paradise Lost" (*L.A. Times*, September 1995) and "Rocky Point, a Ramshackle Beach Town" (*Arizona Republic*, January 1996), told of the plight of unsuspecting American buyers who had been misled, misinformed and ultimately "cheated" out of the homes and investments they had made. Unfortunately, it was true. A U.S. and Canadian buying public was not yet educated to the beneficial and protective changes in Mexico's foreign investment law and local development criteria, nor was there an abundance of accessible information about the nuances of transacting real estate in this country. Unscrupulous sales people simply wanted the old times to continue. Moreover, U.S. title insurance companies were just beginning to develop after Mexico's peso devaluation in 1994. Instead, prospective buyers went to their favorite Mexican destination and had to rely on sellers, developers and agents in the local market who told them, "Trust us; that's the way we do business here."

It's simply not that way anymore. The business section of the *Houston Chronicle* featured a front-page article on December 28, 2004, written by Jenalia Moreno on Americans buying property in Mexico entitled, "American Invasion, U.S.-Style Real Estate." The article stated, "Mexican beach resorts are so popular with retired Americans, baby boomers nearing retirement age and even middle-aged couples wanting vacation homes that condominium and housing developments are often sold out before construction is complete."

So why the dramatic change from "Paradise Lost" to the "American Invasion"? Quite simply, Mexico's real estate markets have changed, real estate agents have adopted a mindset favoring security and disclosure for purchasers, and American buyers have become much better informed and educated. We also have seen the emergence of a U.S. transactional process utilizing extended title searches, issuance of commitments for title insurance, third-party escrow and closing services, and ultimately title insurance policies guaranteeing one's rights of ownership, whether fee simple in Mexico's interior regions or entitlement via the bank trust (*fideicomiso*, FEE-DAY-CO-ME-SO) or a Mexican corporation for foreign purchasers in the restricted zone. In all markets, what is equally important are the changes made by developers, sellers, real estate agents, and local and state governments in each locale. Significant strides have been made for the enhancement and protection of foreign real property investment. What is truly amazing is that these changes have occurred in the last three years. Here are a few reasons why.

- Mexico is deeply dependent on tourism and the investment of foreign capital into its real estate market. Americans have realized that rates of return and appreciation on acquired properties with our neighbor to the south exceed those in the United States. It's a simple case of supply and demand.

- FONATUR, the tourism agency of Mexico, has increased its efforts to promote and enhance the investment of real estate acquisitions by foreigners in the Republic of Mexico.

- The creation of the Mexican Association of Real Estate Professionals (AMPI) and MultiList Services in the markets of Cabo, Peñasco, Vallarta, Nayarit, La Paz, San Miguel and the Riveria Maya is helping to promote higher levels of professionalism and service in Mexican real estate markets.

- The creation of a Real Estate Task Force ad-hoc committee comprising real estate professionals on both sides of the border who are appointed by the respective governors in the states of Arizona and Sonora is shining an even brighter light on real estate practices in the Sonora market.

- The State of Sonora passed the first ever real estate agent registry law that also contains a continuing education requirement for those engaged in the sale of real properties in Sonora.

- The introduction of third-party escrow services and title insurance policies.

- With the continued emergence of U.S. lending companies that originate mortgages on Mexican residential properties, the market has become energized with pent-up demand for secured real estate lending. Mexican trust banks have been more willing to provide trust services to U.S. lenders at competitive rates.

- The growing amount of information offered through the Internet on developments, agents, listings and markets as well as educational information. Interested buyers are now armed with a wealth of knowledge about the Mexican real estate experience before they visit.

- Many agents in any given market are aware that the dynamics of transacting real property has changed. Some are still slow to come around and give up their "old school" ways, but many have realized that a sophisticated and better-educated buying public will demand greater transactional security and title certainty.

- Title insurance companies with established offices have come to the local markets with the concept of "title assurance" and coordinated title services similar to what a buyer would receive in the United States from a title insurance company. The markets have finally realized and embraced the fact that for Americans, the title insurance cost is the cheapest part of the transactional process when compared to other costs of closing. Most important, dealing with a U.S.-based title company in Mexico gives U.S. buyers a sense of confidence, reliability and security.

More big changes continue with Mexico's highway system. When the North American Free Trade Agreement (NAFTA) treaty was initiated in 1994, one of the stipulations was that all three parties (Mexico, United States and Canada) must comply with "international standards" to fulfill its objectives, including "geographical, technological or infrastructural factors." In a capsule, on all levels involving trade, Mexico must improve its roads up to international standards.

In Part I, we explain where, how and why second home buyers have purchased real estate in Mexico. There are simply too many cool hideaways and gorgeous towns to chronicle, but let's explore some of the most intriguing locations of a wonderfully diverse country. Some of these destinations already have been discovered yet others are just appearing on the radar screen.

PART ONE

The Variety of
Second Home Options

CHAPTER ONE

Top Ten Locations That Will Appreciate Over Time

New destinations, coupled with old standbys, will bring personal and financial dividends

Mexico has it all. From lush and tropical mountainous municipalities perched on brilliant bays, to miles of white sand beaches merging into iridescent azure water, to quaint European-style houses lining cobblestone streets in picturesque villages and towns, our Spanish-speaking neighbor to the south is abundantly rich in geographic and natural diversification. Mexico is a country that provides a panorama of stunningly beautiful landscapes and indigenous culture regionally seasoned by its history and native ancestry. Pyramids, volcanoes, caves, mountains, ancient ruins, waterfalls and underground springs provide a spectacular playground for those wishing to explore and experience its natural array of beauty. Hundreds of species of birds, animals, plants and flowers help create the majestic contrasts that make Mexico so incredibly appealing. Dry and arid desert terrain transcend to the humid jungle at opposite ends of the country, providing a definite appeal to certain types of inhabitants. These locales have also become the destinations for many a foreigner seeking a different clime and setting in which to reside or vacation. It is merely a question of what you like and where you want to be. Mexico is a country that offers something for everyone.

Forty-three percent of the land area of Mexico fronts on water. The coastlines vary in their topography and geographic presentation as a result of the terrain that lines the Pacific Ocean, the Sea of Cortes[1], the Bay of Banderas, the Mexican Caribbean and the Gulf of Mexico. Until the days of paved roads and aircraft, Mexico was not so much a united country as a loose federation of regions virtually isolated from one another by a rugged geography. In some areas, the mountain ranges were so impenetrable that neighboring towns were practically ignorant of each other's existence. Today modern communication systems leap mountains and find remote villages. Still, unifying characteristics in so large and varied a country will never be easy to find.

The topography along the Mexican Pacific Coast is remarkably similar to the shoreline from San Diego to Portland. The 1,100-mile stretch from Mazatlán to the Tehuantepec Isthmus is a changing landscape of shallow bays, sandy beaches and cliffs that plunge into the sea. The real difference lies in the cli-

---

[1] Both Sea of Cortés and Sea of Cortez are commonly used to reference the Gulf of California. Sea of Cortés is used in this book in honor of the original explorer of the region, Hernán Cortés.

mate: While the ocean in Portland could never be described as inviting and the winters are wet and cold, the sun shines upon the balmy Mexican Pacific nine days out of 10, year-round.

Because tourism is viewed by the Mexican government as an obvious road to prosperity and a vital generator of the country's gross domestic product, the creation and expansion of luxury vacation resorts along the Pacific Coast as well as along other Mexican shorelines have become a major investment strategy. The obvious potential for foreign capital to flow south of the border, however, remained practically unexploited until very recently. Americans and Canadians, obvious urbanites to be sure, view tropical beaches as places of leisure and relaxation, seldom remembering that until a few decades ago the tropics—especially backwater areas like Acapulco—were synonymous with endemic disease and mortality rates. Today, the tourist advertisements of luxuriously grand and appointed hotels lining Mexico's beaches belie the fact that until the 1950s, these beautiful coasts were deserted, except for a few small villages whose only interest in the sea was as a reliable source of food. It wasn't until 1970 that a paved road stretching the length of the Baja peninsula's rugged terrain was finished.

Most of Baja California remains untouched and unknown to man, like some areas of the Yucatan Peninsula and most of the mountain regions of the Sierra Madres. Yet the various climates and geographical environs coupled with the proximity of the sea have combined to create a strange but surprisingly beautiful landscape. Increasingly larger amounts of money are being invested to develop the coastlines of Mexico where fine sand, balmy waters and abundant sea species are regarded as self-evident reasons to turn these areas into the 50-yard line for new tourist and investment activity. Economic ambitions are being balanced against the ecology of Mexico's abstractly beautiful and unique environment creating a vast playground and investment opportunity for all of North America. Established or up-and-coming, here are the 10 places to be down the road:

Manzanillo, State of Colima

Surrounded by two volcanoes, El Fuego and El Nevado de Colima, Manzanillo provides an escape to hidden paradise. It is a land of ancient wonder and mystique. In search of Chinese treasure in the Pacific, Hernán Cortés and his minions were among the first to visit the area now known as Manzanillo. Navigator Alvaro de Saavedra discovered Manzanillo Bay in 1527 and named it Santiago de la Buena, or Santiago's Bay of Good Hope. Cortés twice visited the bay to protect his galleons from Portuguese pirates. It became a departure point for many important expeditions.

In 1825, the port of Manzanillo opened, so named for the abundant groves of manzanillo trees that were used extensively in the early days of shipbuilding. The small municipality became a city on June 15, 1873, and in 1889, the railroad was completed to Colima. Other amenities, such as electricity and potable water, were soon introduced and by 1908, President Porfirio Días inaugurated the railway linkage to Guadalajara designating Manzanillo as an official port of entry. In more recent years, the harbor has been modernized and deepened, allowing access to all major shipping lines around the world. As the largest port on the western coast of Mexico, the Port of Manzanillo can admit ships of more than 30,000 tons.

Manzanillo is a city commonly known as "heavenly paradise." With geographic coordinates similar to those of Hawaii, the climate is tropical and the temperature rarely varies between 75 and 85 degrees Fahrenheit. Forest and mountains sit upon the ocean's edge overlooking the horizon. Among its many splendors are whale watching, hiking, biking, tours, golden sand beaches, golf, sport fishing, water sports and snorkeling. Manzanillo has been regarded as the "Sailfish Capital of the World" made famous by the fishing tournaments held in November and February, with prizes worth thousands of dollars. In the early 1980s, the popular movie *10* that featured Bo Derek and Dudley Moore was filmed on local beaches.

Unlike other tourist destinations in Mexico, Manzanillo presents a casual, relaxing atmosphere in addition to its many activities. Time simply seems to move slower in the mixture of pleasure and natural wonder. A variety of landscapes such as transparent lagoons, hidden grottos, mountains and beaches all await your arrival. Many tourist areas in Mexico are geared toward adults only. Manzanillo is different. Friendly people and a family atmosphere make this a destination appropriate for all ages. With an unending amount of activities for both the young and old, everyone will find it easy to enjoy themselves. Furthermore, Manzanillo has been classified by the Mexican government as one of the safest places to live in the country and has one of the lowest rates of crime and unemployment.

Loreto—State of Baja California Sur

Why is Loreto headed in the right direction? FONATUR, the Mexican tourist development agency, has finally seen the light and is developing this Sea of Cortés location so retiree snowbirds, second homeowners and vacationers will have an attractive new option to the towering beach concrete of some of the country's more popular hotspots.

Loreto, known for its famous fishing and boating, was among five Mexican communities selected by FONATUR in the 1970s for tourism expansion. The others are Cancun, Los Cabos, Ixtapa-Zihuatanejo and Huatulco. Huatulco, at the foot of the Sierra Madre del Sur Mountains on mainland Mexico, is the least known of the FONATUR Five. While it does not have the number of high-rise hotels found in Cancun and Ixtapa, it offers moderate hotels, all-inclusive resorts and the usual golf, water sports, shopping and dining.

About 700 miles south of San Diego, Loreto is the closest of the five communities to the United States. Loreto has an airport, also built by FONATUR, making the community accessible by air from San Diego, Los Angeles, Phoenix and Hermosillo.

FONATUR is now actively putting its development dollars into the infrastructure of this quaint town that served as the first capital of "the Californias." Unlike the high-rise condos of Los Cabos, Cancun and Ixtapa, however, the emphasis in Loreto will be community villages with dwellings of four or fewer stories designed to blend in with the Baja landscape plus shops, restaurants, bike lanes and sidewalks that encourage foot and pedal power rather than a consistent reliance on the automobile. Ordinances in the Loreto area prohibit the street and beach hustling of trinkets, timeshares, T-shirts and other dream-interrupting memorabilia present in so many Mexican tourist towns.

While some longtime Loreto fans and resident expats dread the thought of any major development near this special place,

FONATUR appears committed to an actual environmentally sensitive environment in its fifth and final targeted tourist area, situated about 300 miles north of Cabo San Lucas. FONATUR approached the Trust for Sustainable Development (TSD) in Victoria, British Columbia, a company with a track record of planning and delivering projects with positive social and ecological impacts. The "sustainability" philosophy is an approach to development that improves livability while preserving natural resources and ecosystems.

What took so long for Mexico to consider an alternative to the high-rise concept? One answer is clear and present: money. Los Cabos—Cabo San Lucas and San Jose del Cabo—became much more popular than expected, forcing FONATUR to funnel most of its available funds to that area for roads and services. Why jump over easy dollars (Los Cabos) to get to perhaps more difficult dimes (Loreto)? FONATUR rode the glitz horse for as long as it could before taking on a new focus. "FONATUR has always believed that Loreto would be the easiest area to develop for tourism," said Jim Grogan, one of the principal partners of the group developing the Villages of Loreto Bay. "Loreto is the closest to the United States of Mexico's five designated tourist areas, giving it easier access for people from the states."

Zihuatanejo/Ixtapa—State of Guerrero

Local legend says the Tarascans built a royal bathing resort on the Las Gatas Beach in Zihuatanejo Bay. That was sometime around 1400. The azure waters of Zihuatanejo attracted attention long before Columbus. By 1500 the Aztecs ruled the coast from the provincial town capital at Zihuatlán, the "Place of

Women" (so named because the local society was matriarchal), not far from present-day Zihuatanejo, having pushed out the Tarascans. A few months after Hernán Cortés conquered the Aztecs, he sent an expedition to explore the "Southern Sea" in hopes of finding a route to China.

In 1522, Captain Alvarez Chico set sail and explored the little bay on the Costa Grande. His Aztec guide told him that this place was known as Zihuatlán. When Chico described the little bay to Cortés, he tacked on "nejo" to the name giving rise to what we know today as Zihuatanejo. Acapulco became Spain's sole port of entry on the Pacific by royal decree in 1561. As a result, all other ports on the Pacific slumbered for hundreds of years with the exception of the occasional galleon or pirate caravel. It was not until the early 1960s with the arrival of the highway from Acapulco that Zihuatanejo finally awoke. No longer isolated, the headland-rimmed aqua bay attracted a small colony of paradise seekers.

In the late 1970s, the little municipality had only grown to 5,000 inhabitants and was still quite "sleepy." Then there came the change. FONATUR, Mexico's agency for tourism development, decided Ixtapa, Zihuatanejo's neighbor five miles to the north, was a perfect site for a world-class resort. Known for its brilliant white sand beaches (Ixtapa means "White Place"), investors in participation with FONATUR, developed the infrastructure, drainage, roads and utilities in order to support the development initiative. After the jetport was built, the inseparable twin resorts of Ixtapa and Zihuatanejo began attracting a steady stream of Mexican, Canadian and American vacationers.

Zihautanejo Bay would be beautiful even without its beaches. Ringed by forested hills, edged by steep cliffs and laced with rocky shoals, there are five main beaches on the bay. Playa La Ropa (Clothes Beach) is the favorite resort beach, a mile-long crescent of yellow-white sand with gentle surf. It got its name centuries ago when apparel from a galleon wrecked offshore floated up on shore. Playa Madera (named Wood Beach since it was once a loading point for lumber) and Playa los Gatos (Cat Beach) are also popular tourist destinations when in Zihautanejo.

There are 10 distinct beaches in Ixtapa. From Playa Hermosa to Playa del Palmar, these beaches have been the center for investment money. The confidence that was placed in this area seems justified. From the super-luxurious Clifton Westin Brisas Hotel to "Billion-Dollar Beach," Ixtapa offers an array of broad yellow-white sand enclaves with gentle surf to long stretches of open ocean shoreline to outer beaches that have powerful rollers good enough for surfing, boogie boarding or body surfing. Playa del Palmar is Ixtapa's main beach. It offers the locals and visitors a more intense stretch of wild surf. Other popular surfing spots are near Playa del Palmar, Playa Quieta and Playa Linda. Scuba diving is also a rewarding experience throughout the various beach areas including Isla Ixtapa.

Todos Santos—State of Baja California Sur

The author John Steinbeck once wrote about the region, "A dream hangs over the whole region, a brooding kind of hallucination. The very air here is miraculous, and outlines of reality change by the moment." Founded by Jesuit missionaries in 1724 and blessed with *pozas* (natural springs) fed by runoff from the nearby Sierra de la Laguna Mountains, Todos Santos thrived for more than a century as a fishing, farming and sugar cane center. Located on the Pacific Ocean and straddling the Tropic of Cancer, Todos Santos is one hour north of the bustling Cabo San Lucas where fishing and agriculture still remain the primary way of life. Because it is located between mountains, an ocean and the desert, the differences in mood and climate are extraordinary. Local residents and visitors get to experience a break from the heat because of Pacific breezes uncommon to Cabo San Lucas.

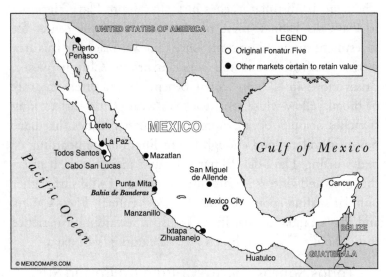

This quiet and serene municipality did not earn a spot on the gringo map until the early 1980s. With a strong New Mexico influence, Todos Santos has become home to an eclectic cadre of artists, painters, sculptors, Hollywood creative types, intellectuals and surfers willing to drive a mile or more on unmarked, teeth-rattling roads to reach beaches where pelicans often outnumber boards. Today, expats make up about 10 percent of the community's 5,000 residents. They've opened fine-art galleries, stylish restaurants and retreats. And they're proud that rosemary focaccia, weekly dharma talks and expensive canvases coexist with unpaved streets, mangy dogs and a wake-up call of trucks as they wind through town.

Todos Santos is also home to the legendary rock 'n' roll hit "Hotel California," by the Eagles. No matter that the Hotel California was a $2.50-a-night "flea-bag dive" where intrepid backpackers were lucky to find a working toilet, vanloads of gullible day trippers make the short trek to Todos Santos to see the landmark hotel that had been shuttered for the past four years. Two Canadians recently acquired the hotel and they plan to target Hotel California to a more discerning crowd. "There's a place where legend becomes reality, and this one has taken on a life of its own," said John Stewart, one of the owners. "It's perfectly conceivable that the song and hotel are connected. There's a magic and an energy in this town that goes way beyond whether it was written here or not." Of all the rumors and shifting realities in Todos Santos where demand for real estate has been extremely strong since the terrorist attacks of September 11, the Hotel California–Eagles connection has remained the most persistent. Was the area clearly made famous by the hotel and the Eagles? Who knows for sure. Still, most visitors remark "it's laid back and in the middle of nowhere. It must be the place."

Mazatlán—State of Sinaloa

Mazatlán stretches for 15 miles southward along sun splashed beaches that host more than one million visitors each year. Known as the "land of the deer," the coastline is a combination of beckoning islands, blue lagoons and golden beaches that have given this city the title of "Pearl of the Pacific." By

Mexican standards, Mazatlán is not an old city. Most of its public buildings have been standing for less than 100 years. Located just below the Tropic of Cancer, Mazatlán was first discovered by the conquistador Nuño de Guzmán around 1531 as he burned his way through Sinaloa. It was not until 1602 that the small village of San Juan de Mazatlán, 30 miles to the south of present day Mazatlán, was even mentioned. Legend has it that English and French pirates used the hill screened harbor as a lair from which to pounce upon the rich galleons that plied the coast. Although pirates were gone by 1800, the legends persist of troves of stolen silver and gold buried in hidden caves and under windswept sands along the coastline.

From 1876 to 1910, the Mazatlán citizen gained a much needed spell of prosperity under dictator/president Porfirio Diaz's "Order and Progress" initiative. The railroad was built, the lighthouse and port were modernized and the cathedral was finished. Education, journalism and the arts blossomed. In the early 1890s, the Teatro Rubio was completed becoming the grandest opera house between Baja California and Tepic. Then, during Mexico's revolution of 1910–1917, Mazatlán suffered much destruction. After order was restored in 1920, the city soared to a decade of prosperity followed by years of deflation and depression after the 1930s. It was not until the sixties and seventies that Mazatlán experienced its "discovery." With the renovation of the port and the construction of new highways, the city limits were expanded to the north from the old port town. New hotels sprang up giving rise to a new "Golden Zone" tourist area, which coupled with Mazatlán's traditional fishing industry, provided thousands of new jobs for an increasingly affluent population. Some three-quarters of a million inhabitants now populate Mazatlán.

The center of Mazatlán is denoted by the towering double spire of the Catedral Basílica de la Purísima Conception (Immaculate Conception Cathedral). Begun in 1856 by Bishop Pedro Loza y Pardave, the cathedral was constructed on the filled lagoon site of an original Indian temple. The cathedral could not be completed until 1899 because of Mazatlán's turbulent history and did not become a basilica until 1937. Two blocks behind the cathedral is the colorful Mercado Central (central market) and the tantalizing aromas of all the wonderful fruits, vegetables and food sold there. The central plaza is nearby and offers an array of small sidewalk cafés on the plaza's north side as well as indoor restaurants. A little farther to the west from the central market is the *malecón* (seawall) and Av. Olas Altas (high waves). This café-lined stretch of the boulevard and the adjacent beach was at one time the tourist zone of Mazatlán. Extending several shoreline blocks from the Monumento al Venado (Monument to the Deer), it is a relaxing area to pause and soak up the flavor of old Mazatlán.

As the *malecón* moves northward from the downtown area, a curving white ribbon of sand becomes the Golden Zone out to Punta Camarón. This shoreline stretch is denoted by a cluster of high-rise hotels. Offshore from Punta Camarón are three islands—Chivos (Rams), Venados (Deer) and Pajaros (Birds). The three islands when viewed on the horizon seem to float like a trio of sleeping whales. Mazatlán also offers a variety of beautiful crystalline beaches starting from Av. Olas Altas out to Punta Camarón and onward to the area known as Zona Dorada. The lineup of successful hotels immediately north of Punta Camarón testifies to the beauty of these shining strands with gentle rolling waves and glowing, island silhouetted sunsets giving rise to the label of the "Golden Zone" in Mazatlán. The Zona Dorada is truly a magical tourist destination. Mazatlán is also home to two well-known resort residential developments at opposite ends of the municipality, El Cid on the north and Estrella del Mar to the south. Both projects offer excellent championship golf courses and the opportunity to acquire beachfront lots, single-family or condominium residences.

La Paz—Baja California Sur

La Paz is the capital of Baja California Sur, the center of government, commerce, education, health care and environmental research for the entire region. Named the "City of Peace," La Paz was among the first missions in all of California. It has a rich history, delightful people, delicious spicy food, perfect weather and an easygoing lifestyle.

Hernán Cortés was the first explorer to arrive in what is now known as La Paz during the 16th century. He named it the Villa de la Santa Cruz and after several years, Cortés finally abandoned his attempts to conquer the peninsula because of a lack of food and water and the occasional ferocious attacks by the natives. California resisted the conquerors except the missionaries and their spiritual force. It was not until 1596 that Sebastian Vizcaino, while circumnavigating the peninsula on exploratory expeditions, renamed the municipality La Paz. Throughout its history, La Paz has endured numerous conquerors, pirates, missionaries and entrepreneurs, creating a flowery past full of risk, daring and love.

The famous French diver and ecologist Jacques Cousteau baptized the Sea of Cortés as "The Aquarium of the World" because of its countless species of marine plants and animals.

Dotted with underwater mountains and canyons, this incredible sea creates a unique ecosystem that circulates huge amounts of nutrient-enriched water, producing seasonally heavy plankton blooms, which in turn contribute to the massive diversity of tropical and pelagic fish found throughout its waters. With three major warm-water lagoons, the Sea of Cortés hosts resident pods of various species of sea mammals including the gray whale calving migration, sperm whales, orcas, humpback whales, blue whales and fin whales, all often visible when sailing in these rich waters. Colonies of sea lions and gigantic pods of dolphins, huge manta rays, massive whale sharks and impressive numbers of sharks, especially hammerheads, coupled with the sea's vegetation and other species of fish, have given La Paz the reputation of being a world-class scuba diving destination. There are more than 25 first-class dive spots around the many islands surrounding the Bay of La Paz, Espíritu Santo and Cerralvo.

The surrounding desert is an equally intriguing, unique and beautiful ecosystem that provides boundless surprises. For centuries, its flora and fauna have evolved endemic characteristics because of their relative isolation. Elephant trees and thorny chollas, primitive cirios and strange looking valleys of cardon are part of the 4,000 different plants that make up the spiny green carpet on the sandy earth. Many resident birds and migratory species are found here as they winter and pass by on their migration to southern locations. Desert bighorn sheep, foxes and coyotes are abundant as well.

Just south of the city, at the edge of the Tropic of Cancer, stands the Sierra de la Laguna. This mountainous mass, declared a biosphere reserve in June 1994, rises to an elevation of almost 2,200 meters (almost 6,600 feet). Its climate and vegetation change dramatically relative to the elevation from brushwood and semi-arid vegetation at lower elevations to pines and piñon-oaks and, at the highest attitudes, sudden streams flowing into majestic crystalline pools. La Paz, which is one of the few places in the world where the desert literally collides with the sea, also offers modern tourist facilities and a high standard of living. Two new master-plan developments are now under construction. Paraiso del Mar (Paradise of the Sea) is a 1,500-acre tract that will encompass 600 acres of condominiums, town homes, single family detached houses, casitas and villas, hotel, spa and retail services. The development will also have a championship golf course and incorporate environmental and ecologically controlled development considerations. All in all, La Paz is a great locale for anyone wishing to live or visit an adventure with safety and comfort.

Huatulco—State of Oaxaca

Oaxaca State is located in the southeast portion of Mexico and has more than three million inhabitants. Huatulco is on the coast in the southern part of the state situated 277 kilometers from Oaxaca City, the capital of the state. In the Mizteca language, Huatulco means "the place where wood is adored." The handicrafts of Huatulco, as well as the State of Oaxaca, are considered to be some of the most beautiful and majestic in all of Mexico. Fantastic animals carved in wood, known as *alebrijes*, are common to this region and demonstrate the ability and talent of the local artisans. This small municipality (only 18,000 in population) also boasts a pristine coastline and near virgin spots characterized by the nine Bays of Huatulco. The bays, named

Conejos, Tangolunda, Chahue, Santa Cruz, the Órgano, the Maguey, Cacaluta, Chachacual and San Augustin, make up this marvelous Eden on the coastline of Oaxaca. The nine Bays of Huatulco and their crystalline waters invite tranquility to a destination not plagued by mass tourism. Huatulco has an average temperature of 28 degrees Centigrade (88 degrees Fahrenheit), making it an ideal locale for bathing suits, sandals and staying close to the water. There are approximately 2,220 rooms, ready to receive guests, who stay for an average of four nights.

Many years ago, the Bays of Huatulco were a refuge for pirates and voyagers, as well as a rest stop for exhausted galleon crews coming from the Far East. Centuries later, a group of fishermen established a small village called Santa Cruz—a place where time appears to have stood still. In a little more than a decade, the three towns of Tangolunda, Santa Cruz and Crucesita all emerged, and Huatulco went from a remote wilderness with no electricity, running water or sewage system to having one of the most advanced, environmentally friendly public systems in Mexico. Visiting the nine Bays of Huatulco is considered the ultimate activity. The beaches surrounding the bays are virtually deserted and only accessible by water thus giving the visitor the ultimate private experience in snorkeling or diving in the bays' underwater parks and *bufaderos*. Huatulco also has a cruise pier that can serve two cruise ships simultaneously and safely disembark up to 7,000 passengers. The Marina Chahue has 88 slips for 27- to 75-foot boats. FONATUR has created a master planned concept for the development of Huatulco and its bay system that will eventually offer several thousand new hotel rooms, golf courses, restaurant and retail services, residential infrastructure and subdivisions for the development of condominiums, townhouses, single-family residences and time share operations. It is also envisioned that Huatulco will have a centrally located retail mall with approximately 200,000 square feet and a new yacht club in Chahue.

Puerto Peñasco—State of Sonora

Located at the northeast corner of the Sea of Cortés and just 66 miles from the Arizona border, this Sonoran municipality started as a fishing village in the 1930s. It gradually grew into one of the major shrimp-producing locales in the Mexican market. During the Prohibition era in the United States, an enterprising businessman by the name of Johnny Stone visited Puerto Peñasco. He quickly realized the potential of this village to attract wealthy Americans who wanted a place to vacation and fish. Stone drilled a well for water, then built the town's first hotel and opened for business. The notorious Al Capone, who was among the first clientele, brought friends along to enjoy the climate, drink, gamble and deep-sea fish. It was not until many years later that Americans discovered Puerto Peñasco as an alternative for retirement and vacation. Whether you lived in Phoenix or Tucson, you could drive from either city within four hours to this small beach town. Affectionately dubbed Rocky Point by Arizonans, it was a true "drive-in destination in Mexico." More important, Rocky Point became Arizona's beach. It was indeed much closer than San Diego.

Puerto Peñasco is surrounded by the Sonoran desert on one side and the Sea of Cortés on the other. Unique ocean conditions in this municipality create extreme tides of up to 23 feet between high and low. It is not uncommon for the water to recede at low tide over a thousand yards along the beach and even further, sometimes over a mile, in Rocky Point's estuaries adjacent to the Sea of Cortés. As a result, the marine life is unique and so are the beaches. Swimming in Rocky Point is safe and emulates lake conditions with no riptides and very calm water unless it becomes windy. It is one of the few places in the world where you can watch the sunrise and the sunset on the same ocean horizon. Rocky Point is sunny almost year-round and receives very little rainfall.

Puerto Peñasco has become one of the hottest real estate investment markets in Mexico. Even though Rocky Point does not have an international airport like other Mexico beach destinations, it has experienced tremendous growth and new infrastructure development over the past five years. During this period of time, more than $500 million have been invested in the Puerto Peñasco residential and commercial markets. The fact is, Arizona is land-locked and Rocky Point has long been Arizona's favorite beach playground. In the area known as Sandy Beach, a 5-kilometer stretch from the Peñasco marina out to the Cholla Bay subdivision, as many as 10 new residential projects have been constructed or are under construction now. The developments include condominiums, villas, casitas, penthouses and detached residences, all situated on the beach. The Las Palomas master planned development includes a seaside golf course among its 2,000 planned residential units. Other residential projects including new retail and commercial developments are planned for Sandy Beach.

Puerto Peñasco is not just Sandy Beach. The municipality has approximately 30 kilometers of coastline. Several single-family subdivisions have been developed over the past 15 years south of town. The Las Conchas development has more than 600 homes constructed, with more houses and small neighborhood enclaves on the horizon. Residential construction and single family lot sales continue to flourish all the way out to the Mayan Palace development, a timeshare, condominium and residential lot project. Other subdivisions dot the coastline in between offering interested buyers a variation in development type and price point. Not only has Rocky Point nearly finished its $3.5-million revitalization of its municipal airport, but Governor Eduardo Bours of Sonora has approved construction of a $45 million international airport for Puerto Peñasco. With greater accessibility from across the country, Rocky Point will attract the major hotel chains it has lacked over the years because of its "drive-in" reputation. Once called "a ramshackle beach town," it has truly emerged as a tourist and retirement destination for many southwestern residents of the United States.

San Miguel de Allende—State of Guanajuato

Juan de San Miguel, a Franciscan monk, founded San Miguel de Allende in 1542. By the 1770s, San Miguel had reached a population of 30,000 inhabitants. Many major cities in the United States, such as Boston, New York and Pittsburgh, weren't as large as San Miguel at that time. The town reached its glory during the Spanish colonial period. Two events keyed the popularity—the public hanging of Ignacio Allende's head in Guanajuato from 1811 to 1824 and the subsequent Mexican War of Independence. Today, San Miguel de Allende is a National Monument and was declared so by the Mexican government in 1926. This small municipality of 80,000 retains a rich colonial charm with its cobblestone streets and beautiful Spanish colonial mansions, many of which have been restored to their former splendor. No neon here, no steel and glass eyesores, no traffic lights. All new construction must conform to stringent colonial architectural controls.

The *jardin*, as it is known and called by the locals, is the main plaza and the center of the historic district, serving as a hub for sightseeing and a respite for the weary. On many mornings, the resident Americans occupy the "gringo bench," reading their newspapers. Ornate wrought-iron lamp posts and manicured laurels shading the wrought-iron benches complete the French aura of the *jardin*. Often in the evenings, Mexican mariachis are playing in the band kiosk highlighting the plaza. Adjacent to the *jardin* is the Church of St. Michael the Archangel. Although the church could pass for a cathedral, it is simply a parish church *(parroquia)*. La Parroquia towers over the *jardin* and the town. While the church was built in the 17th century, the distinctive façade was added at the opening of this century. The multi-towered, neo-Gothic façade is undeniably noncolonial. Although some residents decry the departure from the traditional styles and groan about the corruption done to the colonial charm of the town, the *parroquia* has become the visual symbol of San Miguel de Allende.

La Parroquia is not the only church worth visiting. The seemingly constant tolling of bells confirms that San Miguel is a city of churches. The Church of San Francisco, notable for its uniquely Mexican Churrigueresque façade, the Oratorio de St. Felipe Neri, the favorite of San Miguelians, and the Church and Convent of La Concepcion, once the largest complex in San Miguel, all are located in close proximity to the *jardín*. Visitors have to walk but a few blocks to visit these wonderful and historically rich churches, each with its own story and baroque-style architecture. There are a number of interesting houses near the *jardín* that also merit a visit. The House of La Canal, across the street, is now a bank, but it is a striking example of an 18th-century nobleman's residence.

The Inquisitor's House, the home of a commissioner of the Holy Office, is noted for its delicate wrought-iron balconies and a French influenced façade. Adjacent to the Parroquia is a mid-18th century house with a baroque facade that is now a museum. It was owned by a hero of the War of Independence, Captain Ignacio Allende y Unzaga, namesake for San Miquel de Allende. The lovely country mansion of Don Tomas de la Canal is famous today as the Allende Institute. It was founded in 1938 by Sterling Dickinson, the first prominent American to settle permanently in San Miguel, and has become a prestigious art and language school. Today, San Miguel de Allende is a center for the arts, with two major art institutes, numerous galleries and too many artists-in-residence to count. Attracted by this atmosphere and the incredibly gentle year-round weather (average temperature is 75 degrees Fahrenheit), there is a very sizable foreign community that makes San Miguel a very cosmopolitan town. The residential real estate market has been robust over the past five years as a result. And despite all this, it's still quiet and tranquil and still without a single traffic light. That's San Miguel!

Bahia de Banderas/Punta Mita—State of Nayarit

Nayarit is the neighboring state to the north of Puerto Vallarta, Jalisco. Its capital city is Tepic, located 104 miles (167 kilometers) north of Vallarta in a fertile valley that has become Nayarit's center of commerce and government. The Huichol

Indians named the capital, which means "place between hills."
Its history dates back to 1160 A.D., when it was believed to be
a stopping ground for Aztecs on their way to the Valley of
Mexico. Several archeological sites have been discovered in the
larger Tepic area. With a population of 200,000, it has become
known for its modern urbanism, grand architecture and for
being the main trade center for the Huichol Indians, who
bring their beautiful handicrafts from their remote mountain
villages to sell in local stores. Nayarit has an abundance of once
pristine beaches that have slowly been developed into spectacular resorts and residential communities. The state, with its
magnificent coastline of white sand beaches, still boasts being
a destination of great surf and a laid-back lifestyle.

Bahia de Banderas (Bay of Flags) is a horseshoe-shaped bay
that may have been formed by an ancient volcanic crater. It is
the largest natural bay in Mexico and the second largest in
North America—surpassed only by Canada's Hudson Bay. It
measures 20 miles across with more than 40 miles of coastline.
It is also one of the deepest bays in the world with depths of
up to two miles. The waters of Banderas Bay are protected
from the inclement weather of the open seas because it faces
west and is framed by the Sierra Madre mountain range.
Because of its extensive coastline, Bahia de Banderas has
become home to some of the most extraordinary and spectacular developments in all of North America.

Nuevo Vallarta is a planned resort-residential community 15
minutes by car north from the Vallarta airport in the state of
Nayarit. Originally begun by the federal government over 10
years ago, it has become home to two "mega" developments,
Paradise Village (which has a marina and an indoor air-condi-

tioned mall) and the Mayan Palace. There are several large planned developments with another 10 to 12 hotels and time-share projects all located in Nuevo Vallarta. Many of the hotel developments feature an "all inclusive" concept and offer a variety of amenities, water and sports activities and nightly entertainment. Many of these projects are selling villas, casitas and condominiums as well as various timeshare/vacation ownership products.

The Punta Mita master-plan development is a 15-minute drive north from Nuevo Vallarta. This 1,500-acre resort and residential project features a Four Seasons hotel and private beach club with a Jack Nicklaus golf course. Developed by Grupo DINE of Mexico City, Punta Mita has various residential subdivisions of beach front, estate and golf course lots, villas and casitas and has sold land for development to other U.S. and Mexico residential developers. Currently, five other residential projects are under construction, including a new five-star hotel within the gates of the Punta Mita planned development.

South of Punta Mita is the municipality of Bucerias or affectionately known as "place of the divers." This old-fashioned Mexican town is 12 miles north of the Vallarta airport and enjoys a five-mile stretch of white sand beaches that is the longest along the entire coastline of Banderas Bay. Its long shallow shoreline is perfect for body surfing, boogie boarding, surfing and shell collecting, and this small locale has become popular with Canadians and many North Americans. Bucerias has plenty of local color with its many shops and town square market. Literally dozens of open-air restaurants line the beach on one of four main streets that run for miles parallel to the water. Just north of Bucerias is Cruz de Huanacaxtle, a tranquil town settled in the 1930s by the Chavez family and home to the beautiful and peaceful La Manzanilla beach. A few kilometers further north are the municipalities of San Francisco (also known as San Pancho) and Sayulita. Both are sleepy little villages in the jungle seemingly untouched by time and technology where the general attitude is *mañana*, no need to rush. The tranquility and untamed natural beauty of these two areas has attracted many northerners and they have become favorite retirement and vacation spots for many naturalists. These destinations have also become hot spots for many surfers venturing south in search of quiet and peaceful beaches that feature warm water and great waves.

How do you acquire a piece of one of these places, or other magnificent settings, that are so numerous in Mexico? In the next chapter, we explain how to safely purchase real estate south of border and define the highly controversial and misunderstood "restricted zone."

CHAPTER TWO

Safe Avenues
for Acquiring Your
Dream Location

Dynamic, misunderstood fideicomiso *unlocks
the door to "restricted zone" parcels*

As we mentioned in the Introduction, purchasing real estate in Mexico has changed dramatically over the past decade—especially for foreign, or non-Mexican, nationals. Beginning in 1994, the federal government of Mexico liberalized ownership provisions of all property within the constitutionally protected area known as the "prohibited zone." Prospective buyers outside of Mexico's borders seeking to buy tourist (housing developments, condominiums and timeshare projects), rustic, industrial or urban property can now enjoy greater legal freedom and ownership rights as mandated and protected under Mexico's new foreign investment law. Why didn't activity immediately boil over with Americans and Canadians seeking a calming, warm, relatively inexpensive retreat far from the chaos of their big-city existence? As we explore in other chapters, the devaluation of the peso, the lack of attractive, dependable mortgage money and the inability of lenders to foreclose proved to be huge chuckholes on the road to second home sales south of the border. Improvements to these challenges, coupled with the positive push by the Mexican government to promote investment and tourism, plus improved transportation, roads and infrastructure make the Mexican real estate big picture appear more like today's paved highway compared to the dusty, treacherous Baja road of yesteryear.

In Mexico, as in the United States, federal, state and local laws administer the transfer of real estate property rights. Foreign nationals wishing to acquire property are subject to permission and registration with Mexico's Department of Foreign Affairs. This federal agency is responsible for awarding the lawfully required permits and authorizations to purchase land in the Mexican Republic as well as to acquire real estate properties.

Buying south of the border, however, is not like buying property in the United States or Canada, and purchasers must always remember that the process is different than purchasing another house in their neighborhood. Even if you believe you are a savvy real estate person, take off your domestic blinders and prepare to look through a different set of glasses. The Mexican legal system is not the same as its American equivalent. That is not to say that real estate transactions (*operaciones*) in Mexico are totally different or more complicated than in the United States, but more awareness, street sense and patience usually are needed.

In a nutshell...

What is the "restricted zone"? As defined under the Mexican Constitution, the restricted zone is the area 100 kilometers from any Mexican border, and 50 kilometers inland from any coastline. Because it is so long and narrow, the entire Baja peninsula is considered to be in the restricted zone and the Mexican bank trust (*fideicomiso*) is required for any non-Mexican acquiring property for third-party residential use.

What is a *fideicomiso*? The *fideicomiso*, or trust, is not only one of the most misunderstood legal instruments but also one of the most dynamic. The *fideicomiso* is the vehicle used by the government to exercise its discretionary power permitting foreigners to acquire ownership rights to real estate within the "restricted areas" of Mexico, granting the trustee (a Mexican bank), legal title to the property for a determined period of time.

The parties to a *fideicomiso* are:

- The settlor (Seller—*fideicominte*)
- The trustee (the Mexican bank—*fiduciario*)
- The beneficiary (buyer—*fideicomisario*)

As trustee, the Mexican bank acts on behalf of the foreign beneficiary in any and all transactions involving the property held in *fideicomiso*. However, the beneficiary retains the use and control of the property and makes the investment decisions regarding it. The beneficiary has the right to use, mortgage, encumber, improve, lease without limitation and sell *without restrictions* and to pass the property to named heirs. In essence, the beneficiary has the same absolute rights to use, benefit and enjoy the property as if it were in fee simple (direct) ownership.

Fee simple purchase. Foreigners may directly acquire property within the restricted zone, providing it is to be used for commercial activities. In other words, the usage must be industrial or retail (bed and breakfast, boutique hotel, restaurant, etc.) in order to qualify as nonresidential. Residential properties in the interior of Mexico (outside the restricted zone) may be purchased by foreigners in fee simple title with registration of their ownership to the Ministry of Foreign Relations.

Foreign Investment Law. In effect since December 28, 1993, this law has been a major step toward bringing ownership of Mexican real estate in line with other industrialized countries. It allows fee simple (direct) ownership of nonresidential properties in the country's restricted areas, provided that such property is owned by a Mexican corporation and that it is intended for commercial purposes. There are exceptions, such as the master trust provision. The Foreign Investment Law also extended the duration of the *fideicomiso* term for third-party residential properties from 30 to 50 years, with a renewal upon request by the party having an interest in the property.

Already in a trust. When a property has already been placed in a Mexican trust, *fideicomiso*, the transaction most likely to be entered into would be an Assignment of Rights (*cesion de derechos*), because the buyer in essence, is acquiring the seller's rights to the *fideicomiso* that holds title to the real property.

The worst thing a purchaser can do to remain ignorant of the law and procedures involved in the conveyance of real estate in a foreign country. It is inherently important for non-Mexican buyers to understand that Mexico has formality of law with authorized regulation of real estate development procedures at all levels, and this formality is coupled with a statutory government framework for the legal conveyance of real property. Despite the perception, Mexico is no longer the "Wild West" where anything goes and the prevailing Mexican attitude is "trust me, *señor, no problema.*"

Jay West, a real estate broker, is a past president of the Los Cabos chapter of Mexican Association of Real Estate Professionals (AMPI—Asociacion Mexicanas Professionales Inmobiliario, A.C.). AMPI is a professional organization recognized by the National Association of Realtors and its international sister organizations. West has been frequenting Los Cabos since 1988 and moved there in 1995 to lead Cabo Realty (*www.caborealty.com*). In the past, "people were selling dirt and condos with no questions asked by either side," West explains. "Many buyers, including me, learned the hard way. No more. Today it is different."

Foreign purchasers should be acutely aware of the same basic issues that any prudent buyer would study before acquiring real estate. Additionally, they should not depend on the seller for information or advice about the property because there is no way of knowing whether it is correct. They should obtain the status of the title to the property by requiring an in-depth title search. They should be knowledgeable of the type of contracts to be utilized for a purchase-sale agreement (*compraventa,* or more often *contrato de promesa defideicomiso*) and preparation of the deed (*escritura publica*) by the notary public (*notario publico*) in Mexico. They should be aware of earnest money deposits and escrow considerations, and ultimately, a buyer should have an understanding of the actual conveyance method in Mexico and how legal title or beneficiary trust rights are established and a *fideicomiso* is vested and recorded for foreign purchasers.

Does the seller have legal title?

The first thing a buyer must consider is whether the seller of the property has legal title to the property, and if so, whether the property can be legally transferred. Although this seems to be a logical and foregone precaution, there have been many documented transactions in which foreigners thought they had acquired real estate only to find out later that the seller was unable to transfer legal title. Very simply, the seller didn't own the property or had not completed the required development procedures for the conveyance of the real estate. A good example would be agrarian land (*ejido,* explained in Chapter 4) not properly regularized, or the conveyance of a condominium unit that does not have a recorded condominium regime (*reg-*

imen de condominio) or even the sale of a lot or house in a residential subdivision (*fraccionamiento*) that does not have the required and published state/municipal development approvals. In any of these cases, the result is that the purchaser has paid money for the acquisition of the property but cannot receive legally recorded title or beneficiary interest in a Mexican bank trust.

How do I confirm that a seller has the right to sell?

An adequate title search of the property should be performed.

A buyer should always ask the seller for a copy of the *escritura* vesting title to the real estate.

The buyer should request a copy of the lien certificate (*certificado de libertad de gravamen*) on the property that should indicate the owner of record, surface area and classification of property type, the legal description and whether there are any liens or encumbrances filed of record against the property.

The buyer can also request a certificate of no tax liability (*certificado de no aduedo*) from the local taxing authority.

The *notario publico* is responsible for the title search in Mexican transactions. The notary typically only examines the current deed and a current lien certificate resulting in the possibility of a short or incomplete title history of the property. Today, there are U.S. title companies, as well as Mexican companies, that facilitate the title examination process on a more in-depth basis and issue either a Commitment for Title Insurance on Mexico Land or a title report from the Mexican company. A foreign purchaser always has the option of hiring Mexican counsel to provide a legal opinion on the status of title as well.

Contracts and agreements

Most real estate transactions in Mexico have at least two contracts: First, an offer and acceptance (*oferta*) and/or a promissory agreement (*contrato de promesa*), and second, a purchase-sales agreement (*contrato de compraventa*). The first two agreements are preliminary agreements containing the basic transactional information. They are not the instruments by which title to the property is transferred to the buyer. The second contractual document is the agreement to be protocolized by the *notario* that will transfer title to the buyer. This document may have several different forms: a real estate trust agreement (*contrato de fideicomiso*), a reserve title agreement (*contrato de compraventa con reserva de dominio*) or an assignment of real estate trust rights (*contrato de cesion de derechos fideicomisarios*).

The Civil Code defines an agreement (*convenio*) as an accord (*acuerdo*) between two or more persons to create, transfer, modify or extinguish obligations. Specifically, the Civil Code defines a contract as an agreement that produces or transfers obligations and rights. In general, real estate contracts in Mexico must be "protocolized" before a notary public, and to be binding on third parties, they must be filed with the public registry of property. Once there is a written acceptance to the offer, it is recommended that the buyer's attorney draw up the sales contract or promissory agreement. Since this agreement is the single most important document the buyer will execute with the seller, and the agreement's contents will determine the terms and conditions of the transaction, the buyer should insist that his attorney perform this responsibility.

Major differences between U.S. and Mexican transactions

There are many aspects of Mexican real estate deals that are very similar to transactions closed in the United States. It is easy to presume that the basic terms and principles with which a purchaser is familiar in the U.S. also hold true in Mexico. However, a foreign buyer is much better off assuming nothing. Two such terms that are not equivalent are escrow and earnest money deposit. In the United States, an escrow or title company, or a person legally empowered to act as an escrow agent, will serve in the capacity of handling escrow functions and earnest monies. In either case, the company or individual who carries out the escrow procedure is licensed and empowered by law to do so. They are legally responsible to see that the agreed-upon conditions of an escrow agreement are met before any funds are released. This is not the norm in Mexico. Historically, foreign purchasers have given an earnest money deposit as contractual consideration to the seller. In many cases, the real estate agent or broker involved in the transaction has served as an escrow agent. Real estate brokers are not licensed in Mexico and typically do not set up separate accounts for earnest money deposits. The *caveat* here cannot be expressed strongly enough: If a foreign buyer is willing to give earnest money to the seller or the real estate agent in the transaction, be prepared not to get it back! Read more on this in Chapter 3.

In the past few years, Mexican escrow companies and financial brokerage companies have added the service of utilizing U.S. bank accounts for earnest money deposits. A foreign buyer should always exercise caution and use common sense when it comes to the company chosen to shelter a portion of the funds earmarked for their dream getaway. As is often said, "Don't leave your brains at the border!"

The role of the *notario publico*

Ultimately, foreign buyers get to the point where they are ready to have the transaction consummated and take title to the property. In Mexico, all real estate transactions and the legal conveyance of any type of property involve the participation of the *notario publico*. Although their title translates to "public notary," the *notario publico's* responsibilities greatly exceed the formalization of signatures.

Appointed by the governor of the state and the executive branch of the federal government for a particular state district, *notarios* are attorneys who must pass two extensive examinations to receive their lifetime appointments. In a typical transaction, they will prepare the deed of conveyance subject to the purchase-sale agreement. The *notario* brings buyer and seller together for the formalization of the property transfer and they authorize the appropriate signatures upon execution of the *escritura*. Finally, after the property transfer has been formalized, the *notario* will record the *escritura* with the public registry of property where the property is located. Prior to the closing, the *notario's* additional duties include: (1) to examine the documents of the selling party to ensure their accuracy and legitimacy, (2) to verify title, and (3) to search the public records to determine the status of the seller's title to the property and the existence of liens against the property. The *notario* is also responsible for the collection of all applicable property taxes, capital gains taxes and government transfer taxes. As a representative of the state, however, the *notario* does not insure title to the real estate nor does he or she have any legal responsibility for title defects. In short, a purchaser cannot seek restitution against a *notario* in the event the purchaser suffers a monetary loss because of a title defect unless fraud, misrepresentation or gross negligence could be proven in a Mexican court of law.

What about buying property in the restricted zone?

Title to all real estate in the "restricted zone" for foreign purchasers can only be legally vested and recorded in one of two ways: (1) in a Mexican bank trust (*fideicomiso*) for all residentially declared property, or (2) in a Mexican corporation for all nonresidential real estate. There is no in-between choice or gray area concerning foreign acquisition in the restricted zone (50 kilometers along Mexico's entire coastline, 100 kilometers along all of Mexico's natural borders and all of Baja California, as per Article 27 of the Mexican Constitution). Foreign nationals can be the sole and exclusive stockholders of a Mexican corporation that holds fee simple title to nonresidential property in the prohibited zone.

In any type of real estate acquisition in Mexico, non-Mexican purchasers must always register their ownership interest with the Secretary of Foreign Affairs and must waive their rights to foreign government intervention in the event of a property dispute. This is known as the Calvo Clause, which is constitutionally mandated, and is contained in all bank trust agreements. It should be noted that Mexican banks, acting as trustee for a foreign buyer in a *fideicomiso,* make no warranty or guarantee of the title to the property in the trust nor do they provide any restitution in the event of a title defect. Foreign buyers should always be advised to consult U.S. or Mexican counsel regarding real estate transactions. Potential purchasers also can contact U.S. title companies to assist them in answering questions about conveyance issues, title searches and title policies for a prospective property as well as escrow account considerations. And one important warning: If you are told by a seller or agent that "this beautiful piece of land on the border" or "this lovely house on the beach" does not need to be in a corporation or in a trust, or it does not need to be closed by a *notario,* walk away immediately…and very quickly.

Most purchasers who contemplate buying a house in Mexico now are aware that Mexico has a restricted zone. However, many purchasers are not aware of the Foreign Investment Law of Mexico (FIL) originally established in 1971, amended to the New FIL in December 1993 and ultimately amended again in October 1998. This FIL, discussed in an earlier section, is known as the *Reglamento de la Ley Inversion Extranjera y del Registro Nacional de Inversiones Extranjeras.* Relative to properties within this restricted area, the amended Foreign Investment Law's intent is to clearly and narrowly define what is residential property, what properties must be in a *fideicomiso* (Mexican bank trust), and what properties are considered nonresidential, and therefore, can be purchased by foreigners in a Mexican corporation.

What constitutes a residential or nonresidential property?

For the purpose of the terms set forth in Article 5, Title Two of the Law, real estate used for "residential purposes" shall mean any real estate destined "exclusively for residential use of the owner or third parties." The following activities, without limitation, shall be deemed real estate held for nonresidential purposes: (1) those destined for timeshare use, (2) those destined for any industrial, commercial or tourism activity that may simultaneously contain a residential component, (3) real estate acquired by credit institutions, financial intermediaries and auxiliary credit organizations to recover debts owed to them and in the ordinary course of business, (4) real estate used by entities in the course of their business consistent with sale, development, construction, subdivision and other activities included in the development of real estate projects, until these are sold to third parties, and (5) generally, real estate destined for use in commercial-, industrial-, agricultural-, cattle-, fishing-, forestry- or service-related activities.

What if there is a dispute on the nature of property use?

When in doubt whether real estate is deemed destined for residential purposes, the Ministry of Foreign Relations shall resolve the matter in 10 business days from the date the party consults the Ministry on the subject. If, at the end of 10 business days, the Ministry fails to respond, the use in question shall be deemed for nonresidential purposes.

Further, Article 6 of Title Two specifies that when in doubt on whether real property is located within or outside the restricted zone, the Ministry of Foreign Relations, in consultation with the National Institute of Statistics, Geography and Data Processing, shall decide as appropriate. Finally, Article 7 of Title Two provides the notification procedure that interested parties must give to the Ministry of Foreign Relations, that is, (1) the location and description of the real estate, (2) a clear and accurate description of the uses to which the real estate in question is destined, and (3) an ordinary copy of the public instrument, known as an *escritura,* that records the formalization of the acquisition.

How do I really own my property?

When you condense and boil down all of the language and definitions of law, coupled with the resulting legal effect that must be understood, what does a foreign purchaser really glean from this information? Simply, that Mexico's Constitution and Foreign Investment Law are very specific regarding foreign acquisition of real estate—particularly in the restricted zone. Most importantly, foreign buyers of Mexican properties must realize that title to real estate in the restricted zone can only be vested in one of two ways: either in a 50-year renewable Mexican bank trust (*fideicomiso*) or in a Mexican corporation that can solely and exclusively be owned by one or more foreign stockholders with no Mexican ownership participation. We simply can't state this enough: There is no gray area concerning Mexico's constitutional or Foreign Investment Law. The title to houses on the beach, villas, condominiums, townhouses or single-family lots within Mexico's restricted zone can only be in conveyed into a *fideicomiso* with foreigners having renewable beneficiary interest when the property is intended for third-party residential use.

The assertion by some that title to residential real estate can be vested in a Mexican corporation for foreign ownership purposes simply is not correct unless the residence is intended solely as a commercial enterprise (bed and breakfast, boutique, hotel). However, all other real estate, nonresidential in nature, can be conveyed to foreigners in fee simple provided the title is in a Mexican corporation whereby foreigners can have exclusive ownership. Most important, whether title is vested in a *fideicomiso* or in a Mexican corporation, all of these properties can be insured by a U.S. contract of indemnity more commonly known as a title policy. For example, Stewart Title Guaranty de Mexico, plus other title companies, can provide owner's and lender's policies for guaranteeing ownership rights in Mexican real estate.

CHAPTER THREE

Clarifying the Deal:
More Than *No Problema*

*Sometimes an alarming methodology
en route to ownership*

R eal estate deals in Mexico close when the buyer and seller execute the deed of conveyance, money changes hands between the parties and the deed is then recorded in the public records. Simple and logical—except it really isn't that easy in Mexico. For more than the past decade, a cowboy attitude and transactional manner has pervaded Mexico's residential beach market. This alarming methodology is nonstandard by foreign expectations and puts foreign buyers at risk when purchasing residences in the "restricted zone" of Mexico. Amazingly, the comment given to foreigners desiring to buy in Mexico is, "That's the way we do business here."

Beware...of the absence of licenses

❊

Now, repeat for clarity: "There are no real estate licenses in Mexico." Agents south of the border do not have/need/own a license to sell property.

Potential second home buyers and investors have come flooding into Mexico armed with information and virtual portfolios. Even first-timers have expectations and a notebook filled with data. Although many individuals claim to be real estate professionals, don't expect to find folks resembling your home-town Realtor in every office.

Even though there are competent, ethical individuals in all regions, it's always wise to ask if your chosen representative is a member of the National Association of Realtors (NAR, *www.realtor.com*) and the Mexican Association of Real Estate Professionals (AMPI, *www.ampinacional.com*). In addition, find out if he or she is a supportive member of local multi-listing services (MLS) and can help guide you through the maze of the unfamiliar Mexican transaction.

Use this person, and ask questions. Lots of questions.

The following scenario is typical regardless of the geographic locale and doesn't seem to vary much between Los Cabos, Puerto Vallarta, Puerto Peñasco or the Cancun corridor. Let's say a foreign buyer, Fred Fairway, identifies a house, condo, villa or lot on the beach he's been targeting for years. Fred, like many others, does not do more than a cursory research and employs the services of a local real estate agent in the beach area. The agent informs Fred that in order to get the process started, an initial deposit is going to be required. The deposit may range from $1,000 to $5,000, and Fred makes the check out to the agent or to the seller. Most of the time, the deposit goes directly into the bank account of the agent and is not tied to an escrow agreement with a third party acting as the escrow agent. When Fred disputes his property boundaries and seeks to recover his deposit, he soon discovers that his hard-earned cash has become nonrefundable because it was not tied to an escrow agreement. Keep in mind that when you write a check and hand it over in Mexico, the chances of recovering it are reduced dramatically without an escrow agreement.

One of the critical pieces of the closing puzzle is the letter of intent, or the contract stage. The customary process in Mexico ultimately leads to an arrangement between the parties known as a Promise to Trust Agreement, although there may be other proposals or simple contracts prior to this final document. Upon execution of the Promise to Trust between the parties, the buyer is invariably required to pay the seller 100 percent of the agreed purchase price. Since the seller has agreed to convey the property and authorize the Mexican bank acting as trustee for the *fideicomiso* to transfer the beneficiary interest to the new purchaser, he or she is therefore entitled to all of his or her money. Real estate agents in Mexico will tell foreign purchasers the closing of the transaction occurs when the Promise to Trust Agreement is signed. Caveat emptor, nothing has closed! Let's explore what has transpired and what needs to be done in order to have a legal and "protocolized" beneficiary interest established on the real property under Mexican foreign investment law.

What has happened in the deal... and what still needs to happen

Fred, the buyer, has given the seller all of the money contemplated in the transaction and yet he does not have a trust permit required by Mexican law to be issued by the Ministry of Foreign Affairs in order to establish his beneficiary interest. Fred does not have the *escritura publica* (public deed) prepared by the public notary in Mexico. The notary must be authorized by the trust bank to proceed with the transfer of the beneficiary interest via the public deed and which the notary must draft to process the transfer

No property appraisal has been prepared, yet an appraisal is a requirement under Mexican federal statutes for tax purposes in order for the *fideicomiso* to be established. There is no lien certificate from the public registry that would indicate any liens or encumbrances on the property and is a required element of any real property conveyance. Fred really doesn't even know if the seller has good title to the real estate in question. Why? Because Fred has never been presented with a copy of the deed that vests the title to the seller. The public notary, at this point, has yet to begin the required title search of the property. Fred merely has received verbal assurances from the seller and the agent that there are "no problems" with the title.

Primary awareness issues and concerns

The sale of real property between Mexican nationals is a fairly simple and expeditious transaction via a *compraventa*. They are not concerned—nor do they have to be—with Mexico's foreign investment laws. This is not the case, however, when they sell to foreign purchasers in the restricted zone. Their attitude is, "Why should I wait for my money just because you have to get a bank trust? That's your problem; just pay me." This attitude has been pervasive because some—not all—real estate agents support that philosophy and push what can be a premature transfer of funds. Let's face it: The sooner the seller receives all of his or her money, the agent gets paid the commission. Why should the agent be concerned with whether the buyer gets his or her *fideicomiso* established once the agent has received the commission fee due from the seller? Besides, many agents will tell purchasers nothing can, or will, go wrong. Sadly, this is simply not true.

Let's sample some of the more obvious "what ifs." What if the seller dies before the conveyance? What if there are title defects or undisclosed lawsuits, maritime matters or lien issues? What if an agent, who receives the money via a deposit, doesn't give the seller all that he or she expects? Then who will execute the deed? What if there are unexpected problems with obtaining a trust permit or *notario* problems? Or what if the seller has sold the property twice, unknown to you or the agent? The simple truth is you have given the seller your money with little or no chance to get it back,—other than a lawsuit in Mexico.

How do I protect my real estate investment?

In every real estate deal, buyers have choices. There are many properties for sale in Mexico, and emotion should not, and cannot, overcome the reality of insurmountable challenges. Buyers need to be smart and educated about the deal, deposits, title and conveyance matters. Many real estate developers sell their property with a percentage down at the time of the Promise to Trust Agreement, with the balance paid when the public deed can be executed establishing the trust. Other U.S.-based developers, and more and more real estate agents, are utilizing third-party escrows in the United States to protect foreign buyers. Full disclosure of potential issues is becoming more prevalent. Any property in Mexico can be researched and a title investigation can be done in order to issue an Owner's Policy of Title Insurance. Purchasers can obtain insurance—and be assured they are heading down a safe road—when they release their money to the seller upon execution of the *escritura publica* and the issuance of the *notario's* preventive notice to the public registry of property. At the end of the day, foreign buyers have a right to a transaction process that ultimately protects their investment and minimizes their risk. Those who participate in the sale of real estate in Mexico must strive to protect that which "feeds and prospers them." When they don't, purchasers should walk away and buy elsewhere.

Summarizing closing costs

It is common practice for the buyer to pay the transfer or acquisition tax as well as all other closing costs, including the notary fees and expenses, and the seller pays capital gains tax and the broker's commission. Since January 1, 1996, the federal law regarding the real estate transfer tax, which was two percent for the entire Republic of Mexico, was modified in order to allow each of the Mexican states to determine its own tax. The range may be from one percent to four percent of the tax appraisal value, which is generally less than the sales value. The rest of the closing costs, which exclude the property transfer cost, may vary from three to five percent of the appraised tax value or more, depending on the particular state. These percentages are applied to the highest value of the following: the amount for which the property is sold, the value of the official tax appraisal, or the value designated by the property assessment authorities. Most real estate companies in Mexico charge a brokerage commission of 5 to 7 percent, based on the actual sales price of the property. However, different area broker rates reflecting higher broker expenses may be found, such as in resort areas.

Based on the present tariff, the bank charges the person desiring to set up a real estate trust, or *fideicomiso*, an initial fee of approximately $500 for drawing up of the original trust agreement and establishing a trust, plus a percentage according to the value of the property. In addition, the bank charges an annual fee, depending on the value of the property, to cover its services as a trustee.

Learning a lesson the hard way

Is it so difficult to buy and sell property the correct way in Mexico? When are sellers and agents going to realize there is a safe and secure manner in which to protect a buyer's money in the conveyance of real property rights? How many Americans need to lose hard-earned investment dollars in the acquisition of property in Mexico? As we've stated before, "If a buyer is willing to give earnest money to the seller or agent in a real estate transaction, be prepared not to get it back!"

The good news is that there are companies in Mexico that have changed their corporate policy when handling buyers deposits, and more of Mexico's real estate firms are coming around to this protective procedure as a company requirement.

For example, on December 1, 2003, the *Gringo Gazette* published an article highlighting the risks of relying upon a local Los Cabos company to provide escrow services. Chris Snell, president of Snell Real Estate, wrote the article, "Separating Fact From Fiction—Third-Party Escrows," The article alleged in part that one of Snell Real Estate's agents deposited a customer's money with Los Cabos Escrow Services. The agent for Snell Real Estate failed to follow Snell Real Estate policy, and consequently the customer's money was lost when the owner of Los Cabos Escrow Services fled Mexico with more than $750,000 of U.S. "escrowed" deposits from a variety of pending deals. Snell Real Estate, acting in a responsive fashion, reimbursed its customer's money and established a new escrow account with Stewart Information International. (This is not the first time money has been stolen from U.S. purchasers in this particular market. It has happened twice in three years. As mentioned previously, it's not about a country or an ideology; it's about people and the illegal acts they do for money.)

The Snell case is one good example of professionals providing the service promised to the customer. This has been happening for years in Mexico—agents and brokers who are relentlessly committed to using escrow services provided by a neutral third party and providing title insurance policies on the properties they represent. However, it can also be a hard lesson to learn for both an innocent purchaser and any agent. The simple solution is do not get involved in real estate transactions without establishing a secure escrow for the purchase of real estate in Mexico. Using a neutral escrow agent acting in accordance with an executed escrow agreement—in addition to purchasing title insurance—is the most secure means of protecting your real estate investment south of the border.

The escrow agreement is negotiated and mutually agreed upon between the parties. It is a "stand-alone" document that instructs the escrow agent how the money is to be received, held, administered and ultimately disbursed. The escrow agent is required to comply with the terms of the escrow agreement and follow the disbursement instructions provided by the lender, purchaser and seller. Furthermore, when such services are provided by U.S. title insurance companies, the escrowed funds are deposited into a U.S. federally insured depository bank that offers the possibility of opening a money market interest-bearing account, which will benefit such parties designated in the escrow agreement.

CHAPTER FOUR

Understanding the Nuances of *Ejido* Land

*Specific parcels have been the focus
of confusion and outrage*

For years foreign purchasers have been persuaded to "purchase" *ejido* parcels or beach front lots without fully understanding that they can't legally own *ejido* property nor can the *ejidatarios* (those individuals who have the beneficiary interest in the land) legally sell it. Hence, all potential buyers of Mexican real estate should know the difference between private property and land described as *ejido*.

An *ejido* is an old communal farm formed when the *campesinos* (farmers) of every village in Mexico were given property to form a co-op. The Constitution of 1917 proclaimed that all land in Mexico would either be *ejido* (communal) or owned by

Mexican nationals. The *ejido* is owned by no one and worked by everyone—not unlike a huge community "pea patch" in the United States that no single person owns yet many use as a garden to grow flowers and vegetables for whatever reason they please. However, in most cases, the *ejido*-cultivated land is divided into separate family holdings, which cannot be sold, although they can be handed down to heirs.

Article 27 of Mexico's Constitution allows the federal government of the United Mexican States to create agrarian lands for the benefit of their citizens. With its constitutional inception in 1917, Mexico began the process to provide *campesinos* a beneficiary interest to land owned by the government. Entitled under *La Ley Agraria* (the Agrarian Law), these government parcels, known as *"ejidos"*, are recorded with the *Registro Agrario Nacional* (National Agrarian Registry) in Mexico City. The ejidatarios can live, farm, homestead and construct dwellings on the property but they do not own it. Under Agrarian Law, the *ejidatarios* cannot sell, lease, subdivide, joint venture, contribute, mortgage or encumber the property. As mentioned, they have the use and benefit of the land, but they do not have title to it.

In 1992, recognizing the inherent value *ejidos* presented because of their geographic, border or coastal location, coupled with the development potential they created, the Mexican government enacted a Constitutional Amendment in order to "regularize" agrarian lands. Under the auspices of the Ministry of Agrarian Reform, the Mexican government could now provide a process of legal entitlement converting the *ejidal* regimen to one of *regimen de domino pleno o privado* (regimen of full dominion or private land). In other words, *ejidatarios* had the right to take the land that they didn't own and convert it to private property thereby allowing them to benefit monetarily from the ensuing regularization process. Unfortunately, there have been several highly publicized cases and examples of Americans, Canadians and other non-Mexicans buying *ejido* land that has not been properly regularized. Purchasers have paid significant amounts of money for a home or a building lot on the beach with the promise that they would receive a bank trust, only to find out years later that the land had not been properly privatized. The end result is that the purchaser cannot have a legally recorded and recognized beneficiary interest to the property in a Mexican bank trust (i.e., title vested in a *fideicomiso)* nor can the purchaser have a valid lease as a legal alternative to use the property.

How do I know if *ejido* land has been properly privatized?

As mentioned, Mexico is not the "Wild West" that some foreign purchasers believe it to be. With formality of law, as in other real estate matters, regularization of an *ejido* is a legal process requiring time, procedure and lots of patience. The ultimate goal is to get private title to each parcel that can then be conveyed to a trust or Mexican corporation for the benefit of non-Mexican purchasers. However, there are a number of steps along the way that potential buyers should be aware of for *ejido* land to be privatized.

In order to begin the regularization process, the *ejidatario* needs to have (1) certificate of agrarian rights, (2) certificate of common parcel rights, and (3) an agrarian tribunal order or resolution.

The following questions should also be asked:

- Can the *ejidatario* provide certification with documents or testimonies that he or she is in quiet and public possession of the property? That as owner, he or she has title to it and that there are no pending legal actions against the property?

- Can the *ejidatario* provide a plat or other acceptable plans that define the parcel with a metes and bounds description and the total area of the land?

- Has the *ejidatario* petitioned the general assembly of the *ejido* to request approval to convert the *ejido* parcel to one of full dominion?

- Did the general assembly of the *ejido* agree, resolve and record in the minutes of the meeting that the *ejidatario* is allowed to convert the parcel to full dominion?

The regularization process has a series of steps, much like the number of steps needed in the typical foreclosure sale of property in the United States. Notice must be given and timeframes closely followed.

Why does the regularization process involve so many steps and take so long?

The *ejido* itself is normally a large tract of land that is utilized by all of the *ejidatarios* for their sustenance. Managed and operated in a similar fashion to that of a farm cooperative, the *ejido* has no land subdivision or individual parcels. Subdividing the *ejido* into *parcelas* is what the regularization process accomplishes. Typically, the privatization of *ejido* land can take 6 to 12 months to complete, but it could easily take longer. Although this time period appears lengthy, keep in mind that there are many individuals involved who must come to a unified and collective decision to privatize the *ejido*. Negotiations within the *ejido* on whether to privatize or not could take several months.

Then, even when an *ejidatario* or a group of *ejidatarios* wants to sell, lease or joint venture their particular private parcels to a third party outside the *ejido*, they must offer a first right of refusal to all of the other *ejidatarios*. This process, known as *derecho al tanto* usually means that the *ejidatarios* must give notice to the *comisariado* (president) of the *ejido* of their intent to sell, lease or joint venture. The president should provide a public disclosure of the intent and if, after 30 days, there are no purchasers or objections, the *ejidatarios* may proceed.

Does the regularization process really work?

There are many examples of *ejidos* being properly regularized and the subsequent wonderful developments that have come from these once government-owned lands. Whether in Puerto Peñasco, Los Cabos, Puerto Vallarta, Mazatlán, Guadalajara, Reynosa, Querertaro or many other cities in Mexico, residential, resort and industrial developers on both sides of the border have undertaken the process to successfully privatize *ejido* property knowing the inherent value of the future project. Buying land that was entitled as an *ejido* can be a safe and prosperous personal or business venture. The key is to make sure that the land has been fully privatized or is in the process of regularization. And to be certain, purchase an Owner's Policy of Title Insurance for your property. A title insurance policy, issued on Mexican land, can insure that the land is not *ejido*.

With the title insurance policy in hand protecting your ownership rights, you'll probably sleep better at night.

Famous case brings loss of dreams—and money

If there were ever a "black eye" on the face of Americans attempting to obtain Mexican real estate, it had to be the seaside development known as the Baja Beach and Tennis Club, located in the municipality of Punta Banda near Ensenada, Baja California, Mexico. National newspaper stories told the tragic tale of Americans who lost their homes because of a Mexicali tribunal court ruling that overturned the ownership of the land. The tribunal ruled that property was not an *ejido* and was, in fact, private property owned by the seven plaintiffs in the lawsuit. After the ruling, many Americans could not pay the price set by the owners and had to vacate their beautiful homes.

The case was disturbing and incredibly sad and still waves red flags when any *norte americano* considers a purchase south of the border. All non-Mexican nationals must understand that Punta Banda was not the norm but an aberration in a country that during the past decade has made significant changes to its foreign investment laws. Mexico has a genuine desire to promote, enhance and protect foreign investment in its real estate sector.

Punta Banda should clearly signal that in any country—including the United States—title discrepancies exist, lawsuits get filed and in some rare cases, buyers lose their property. "Catastrophic failure of title" doesn't happen often, but in the case of Punta Banda, it clearly occurred. In order to be an educated and prudent buyer, it is extremely important to understand the issues concerning the Punta Banda case and owning residential real estate in Mexico. Americans, Canadians or Europeans should not fear buying property in Mexico. Owning a house, a condo or residential lot on the beach can be a secure, legally entitled, publicly recorded and hopefully, profitable investment. However, any foreign purchaser should know Mexico's laws concerning foreign ownership of residential real estate. Buyers should always seek advice about title matters on a prospective acquisition from competent sources.

The American residents at Punta Banda were victims of possible fraud and misrepresentation concerning the Ejido Coronel Esteban Cantu's ability to enter into lease agreements for lots within the development known as the Baja Beach and Tennis Club. However, it would also appear that many of these same individuals were naïve and "threw caution to the wind," ignoring the warnings and disclosure that the ownership of the land was in dispute and there was pending litigation to resolve the title matter. Some of the residents have publicly stated they knew there was a possible title problem yet still proceeded to invest in the construction of a home. Furthermore, the plaintiffs in this case had given public notice that the *ejido* did not own the property, that the land was in fact private and that no one should build on it. In the end, the American lessees must have determined that it would work out to their benefit and they would trust in the assurances they had been given by the developer, Carlos Teran del Rio, and the Ministry of Agrarian Reform. As we know now, the catastrophe did happen, overturning the ownership of the land in favor of the seven plaintiffs who filed the original lawsuit in a Mexicali tribunal court!

In light of Punta Banda, why should foreigners not fear buying real estate in Mexico? Quite simply, when the Americans at Punta Banda entered into what they perceived were valid lease agreements for their lots years ago, title assurances and the ownership protections that exist today were not readily available. Comprehensive title examinations complete with a Mexican legal opinion on the status of title can be rendered by Mexican counsel on any property with no geographic or property type prohibition. Copies of all of the documents in the chain of title can be obtained from the public registry of property for any given parcel or residential unit. Lien certificates, land use permits and subdivision authorizations are examined in the process when a U.S. title insurance company is requested to issue a Commitment for Title Insurance on Mexico Land. Purchasers of Mexican real property can now receive Owner's Policies of Title Insurance that can be issued on both sides of the border from various companies to both U.S. and Mexican buyers.

Most title insurance policies today are U.S. contracts of indemnity guaranteeing ownership rights as vested in a *fideicomiso* (bank trust) for residential property acquired by foreign buyers in the prohibited zone, or for properties held in a Mexican corporation for nonresidential purposes, i.e., industrial and commercial. Mexico is not at all unlike the United States in that there is a definitive legal framework for the ownership of land by foreigners known as the New Foreign Investment Law (December 28, 1993) and as mandated under Article 27 of the Mexican Constitution. Moreover, there is formality and compliance in the development of real property. Regulatory statutes and procedures are mandated on a state-by-state basis and require a series of official approvals, permits and authorizations coupled with public disclosure and written notification by the governing public agency.

What is unfair about this terrible event is the negativity the resulting evictions created. Many Americans believed this was Mexico's fault and the country is not to be trusted. This is simply not true—nor is it just. Although there is blame to be shouldered by some unscrupulous Mexican officials and government personnel, some of the blame rests on the Americans who believed "it can't happen to me." They were not prepared to walk away from a potentially bad deal and figured that it was too good to pass up. When contemplating acquisitions in any foreign jurisdiction, all potential buyers must use the same prudent logic and business acumen utilized in buying property in our home country. Be knowledgeable of the relevant issues concerning the property and use all the available tools. And, don't forget that the property can probably be insured with a title insurance policy enforceable under U.S. jurisdiction, guaranteeing your ownership rights.

In the next chapter, we take a peek at some of the places people have chosen to enjoy and invest in Mexico. From small *casitas* on the beach to huge developments on a hillside overlooking the Pacific, to inland communities of expats, it's time to sample a few pieces of an exquisite real estate menu.

CHAPTER FIVE

Sharing the Stories of People and Places

Personal experiences detailing who stayed where and why

A memorable stay at La Ventana Bay

T he laid-back lure of Mexico's beaches, forests, deserts, people and culture has been capturing visitors and second home buyers for decades. Not only is land plentiful, exotic, captivating and beautiful, but it is also typically more affordable than most of the property found in America's getaway areas. In fact, many second home researchers predict it mostly likely will become the Florida of the Baby Boom Generation. When a specific interest comes in a terrific place with sunshine and a bargain price, it's difficult to pass up. Just ask Jerry Kerr; he came to Mexico for the wind—and the visit turned into a lot more.

Kerr knew he wasn't a high-end resort player who wanted a high-rise condo, nightclubs and California-like price tag. A little $140,000 casa in the middle of nowhere that was walking distance to the water and could accommodate family and friends was the ticket. The longtime alumni director at Santa Clara University—about an hour's drive south of San Francisco—was born and raised on the popular piece of land just south of "The City" known as the peninsula. He had been involved with the university for such an extended period of time—first as a student then as an administrator—people in the community wondered if he had been at the school longer than the Jesuit fathers who founded California's oldest institution of higher learning in 1851.

When Kerr finally retired, he was healthy and active, and still "not even close to 65." One of the activities that kept him moving and fit was windsurfing in the frigid waters of San Francisco Bay. It was also the activity that brought him and his wife, Jean, to buy a parcel of land on an eastern cape of the Sea of Cortés at Ventana Bay, where the clear, warm, turquoise water is always 20 degrees warmer than San Francisco Bay and the consistent winter breezes lure windsurfers and kiteboarders from around the world. Ventana Bay looms just east of the tiny village of La Ventana, 40 miles south of La Paz, the capital of Baja California Sur and home to 200,000 residents, supermarkets, hospitals, banks, cultural events and an international airport.

"If not for windsurfing, we would have chosen elsewhere," Jerry Kerr explains. "That place could have been Kihei on Maui, but the last I looked you couldn't drive to Hawaii."

And the Kerrs have driven to Ventana Bay from San Francisco Bay. Their 1997 Toyota Corolla is now their Mexican vehicle, but

Jerry says it will not be necessary once their casita is finished above Ventana Bay. He can easily take a taxi from the La Paz airport to his second home, then either walk or bicycle to a local grocery for most of the shopping. There's no need to pack his windsurfer on the car's roof racks because the beach is a short nine-iron shot away. Visitors to La Ventana, and its slightly larger neighbor the sleepy town of El Sargento, typically travel by plane from the states to either the La Paz or the Los Cabos International Airport. Alaska Airlines, American West, Continental, American Airlines and Delta fly into the Los Cabos

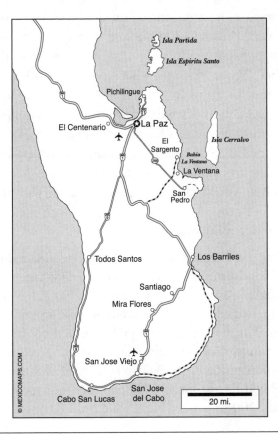

airport, bringing scores of visitors to the twin towns of Cabo San Lucas and San Jose Del Cabo. Aero California has two flights daily into La Paz, with more air service reportedly on the way. Although the drive from Los Cabos to Ventana Bay is significantly longer at 2 hours 30 minutes, the scenery is magnificent.

The Kerr's building plans rolled in stages as they became more understanding of what could be possible given zoning, location and budget in their Baja setting. They purchased a small lot in the La Ventana Bay community from Bill Edsell, a Canadian transplant and the energy behind La Ventana Bay. Edsell grew to love windsurfing on the many lakes surrounding Kelowna, British Columbia, and then spent time in one of the most popular windsurfing areas in the world—the gusty Columbia River Gorge—that separates Oregon and Washington. In the early 1980s, Edsell made a trip to Mexico to find a location for a windsurfing school and stumbled upon a terrific possibility at Los Barrilles, a wonderful spot on Baja's eastern cape. In 1996, property became available a few miles north in an area designated as the El Sargento Annex of La Ventana Bay. After four years of paperwork and permits, Edsell finally broke ground in 2000, beginning with a small resort plus 12 adjacent building lots.

The Kerrs, Baja regulars since 1994, had visited Edsell's first Mexican windsurfing spot at the Los Barrilles and then heard through sailing grapevine that "Mr. Bill," as Edsell is fondly referred to, had relocated to an interesting site 45 minutes south of La Paz. They visited in 2001 and were sold on the ideal setting for windsurfing, kayaking and snorkeling, as well as the wonderful reception of the Bahian families of El Sargento. They paid $39,000 for the lot in 2002 and soon began construction of a small, 300-square-foot casa (one bedroom with bath and closet) and a 1,000-square-foot outdoor patio and kitchen. The bedroom is highlighted by a 15-foot rotunda built with individually carved and set bricks and provides a sense of greater space. In 2004, they enclosed the patio and kitchen to form a large kitchen/family room and extended the patio. The next stage will be an additional bungalow at the rear of the 0.4-acre lot so family and friends can have a separate and independent space. The unit will be connected by a walkway and could also provide rental income when Edsell's resort becomes overbooked.

"The considerations in building center upon lifestyle," Jerry said. "Most of our time is spent outdoors and the need for a lot of interior house space is not a factor. A large outdoor patio and cooking area are musts. Breakfast on the deck in the morning, a *cerveza* or two in the evening—it's always pleasant to be outside with the warm breezes and a view of the placid sea."

The couple has been extremely pleased with the quality of workmanship. They said the contractor and his crew, hand-picked by Edsell, are very proficient and cooperative and work extremely hard. Edsell acts as building site administrator when the Kerrs are not around. They also found Edsell's experience with house placement, making the most of view and privacy, to be invaluable.

What did all this cost? The Kerrs purchased a view lot, not a beachfront parcel. They now have approximately 900 square feet inside and 1,200 square feet of patio outside. Initial construction costs ran $60,000 and the additional casita will cost $30,000. When furniture, kitchen fixtures and other appointments are added to the mix, the Kerrs total investment will be $140,000—for a warm spot, walking distance to favorite activities that even allows their grown kids their own space. The community is not dependent upon utilities other than a weekly garbage pickup; it has has solar energy, trucked-in water and the resort has wireless Internet service. All construction in the area requires architectural plans by a certified architect and must pass La Paz county codes. The Ventana Bay Resort also has its own codes, covenants and restrictions. In addition, residents benefit operationally as some owners share common costs, such as year-round gardening.

Safety is one of the major benefits of the community. Unlike single vacation homes, the La Ventana Resort area is gated and fenced on all sides—not protection from vandalism but to prevent the neighboring cattle from invading the property and munching the vegetation. "Vandalism and theft are not a concern," Jerry said. "In fact, our home and well-being are much safer in Mexico than in California."

The Kerrs' long-term plan is to spend most of the winter in Baja. They have paid off the loan they took out on the land and paid cash for the building and improvements. Part of the couple's master plan was to convert some of their previously saved retirement assets into a vacation home in order to have use of the facility plus a more favorable investment for future appreciation. Compared to the sliding conventional financial markets in 2000–2002, it appears to have been a wise decision.

"Although our goals of buying and building were fairly simple, our experiences have broadened our perspectives," Jerry said. "Even without windsurfing, a stay is so very much worthwhile. There are many other sports and activities. The pristine beauty of the land and sea, combined with the congeniality of the people and good weather, make for a true holiday. If you're interested in good nightlife, it's not the place for you. But the good, simple life? Make your reservations."

A trip across the border to the dentist...

*Bruce Stampley, a freelance writer, shared a
common concern with others wishing to spend
time in Mexico: medical and dental care.*

It's just a short run to the Third World. Twenty-five
miles in fact. That's how far it is from Deming, New
Mexico, to Palomas, Mexico. Deming sits quietly
along Interstate 10, 50 miles from Las Cruces and
about a hundred miles south of Tucson, Arizona. In
fact, Deming's claim to fame is that it is a great spot for
snowbirds (for those of you that do not speak
Travelese, snowbirds are migratory folk who seek out
warm climes in winter) to escape the frigid Minnesota
winters and that Palomas, Mexico, is so close. Being
close is important to travelers and residents alike.

When I first heard of inexpensive dental treatment in
a little clinic in Palomas, my mind conjured pictures of
a Mexican *dentista* in a blood-stained apron yanking
teeth out with water-pump pliers and no anesthetic. As
I have been an uninsured victim of the robbery that is
health care in America, I decided to see for myself. My
imaginary dental clinic could not have been farther off
the mark.

Palomas looks like many of the lesser known border
towns. It is slightly unkempt, with pot-holed streets,
houses that have no color and dogs of dubious ances-

try roaming around. They are, however, friendly dogs and Palomas "feels" okay. There is no sense of needing to look over your shoulder that is common in so many border towns. On my first trip, we elected to leave The General, my trusty Ford Expedition, on the American side and walk across the border. It is only two blocks to the clinic. We later found that it is perfectly safe to take your vehicle across. Just make sure you have no firearms aboard and you lock the car securely.

The Fierro Clinic is well known to folks who live in the boot heel of New Mexico. Dr. Fierro has been practicing dentistry in Palomas for many years. He is well regarded in both the *gringo* and Hispanic communities, and over the last few years, his *clinica* has blossomed into a full-fledged dental hospital, with oral surgery and full periodontal care available.

As the demand for less costly health care has grown, many Americans have looked to the south for a way to stretch their medical dollar, and the Fierro Clinic is a prime example of the quality of care that is available to those who choose to look. There are 11 dentists at the clinic. Every one of them, all Mexican nationals, trained in dental schools in the United States, or at the internationally known university in Guadalajara. The clinic is a shining example of modern sterility, high-tech equipment and sparkling cleanliness. The staff all speak some English and if one hits a linguistic snag, Vivian, the doctor's secretary, is fluent in both Spanish and English and is always available to untangle the problem. The clinic opens at 8 A.M. and closes at 6 P.M. There are no appointments. It is first-come, first-served, so get there early if you want to spend some part of your day playing in Palomas.

The clinic offers a full range of dental services from cleaning and deep scaling to crowns and bridges and all sorts of appliances. They also offer laser whitening, which my wife found to be wonderful. The clinic accepts some insurance, but if this is an issue, call them before you make the trip. Remember that although America runs on credit cards, much of the world still uses cash, so plan your foreign travels accordingly. If you need a prescription for pain medication, there is a *pharmacia* right across the street where you can also stock up on nonprescription pharmaceuticals for about a third of what they cost in the States.

There is also a modern vision center where you can have your eyes examined by an American-trained optometrist for much less than in the States and still have your glasses in two hours. I had a complete eye exam done and got a six-month supply of disposable contacts for less than $120.

Then there is the famous Pink House Restaurant and Bar, which is purported to have been a bordello in times gone by. Used by famed *bandido* Pancho Villa as his headquarters for the only foreign invasion of the United States in history, the Pink House is now a great eating spot and shopping mecca for travelers. The margaritas are great, and the salsa is very *picante*. Just down the street at the Hotel Santa Cruz, the Veracruzano-style seafood is excellent.

To give one an idea of the economic gulf that separates American dental care from that of Mexico, I give you this comparison. I required a full set of X-rays, a deep scaling, a thorough cleaning, a small permanent bridge, and eight crowns. The estimated cost of this project? My American dentist, a wonderful person, smiled and said, "Ten thousand dollars." The Fierro clinics quote? Two thousand U.S. dollars. Much more doable on an underinsured writer's pay.

Pancho Villa State Park is a good place to overnight with your RV, and the little town of Columbus on the American side has a couple of decent motels if your dental care needs more than one visit. Dr. Fierro is in the process of building "Hotel Fierro," reminiscent of a La Quinta, right around the corner from the clinic to accommodate the needs of people whose treatment plan requires they stay overnight.

Loreto: Development takes a different route

Tom McClintock, a food service executive from the Seattle area, is not unlike many potential second home buyers. Pushed along by a dramatic event, he and his family have been forced to reconsider the way they live their lives. In McClintock's case, the event was heart attack on a dark February night. His master plan no longer includes adding sales clients and territories. Instead, he scheduled a mid-year 2005 retirement and plans to sell his primary residence to purchase a summer cabin in Alaska and a winter home near Loreto (*www.loreto.com*), a small fishing village on the Sea of Cortés that features friendly locals, terrific food and near-guaranteed sunshine.

"It's relatively close to our friends and family, and it's not as expensive as some other resort spots in Mexico with a lot fewer people," McClintock explains. "We know there's a risk in everything we do, yet Loreto appears to be headed in the right direction. I am lucky that I can even think about the possibilities; a lot of people simply can't."

Aero California and Aero Mexico have nonstop flights to Loreto from San Diego, Los Angeles and Phoenix. Other cities in the Southwest are expected to follow suit. Alaska Airlines announced its new Loreto service in early 2005. Why do Alaska Airlines and other companies believe that Loreto warrants new service, especially given the difficult times ahead for the airline industry and general economy? Loreto's infrastructure—including streets, sidewalks, water and wastewater systems, and telephone lines—will be installed and maintained by FONATUR for at least 25 years. The agreement includes 350 home sites already fully serviced by utilities and streets. Part of the Loreto deal is that FONATUR did not want to duplicate the high-rises of Cancun or create similar housing and transportation challenges as found in Los Cabos. Members of FONATUR had done all of the heavy lifting for a potential Loreto development. Roads were in, water was on the way, but how do you limit the region to an alternative of small Mexican villages rather than erecting more huge concrete condominiums?

David Butterfield, president and founder of Trust for Sustainable Development (TSD), has taken many of the ideas that worked in Canada to the Villages of Loreto Bay, a $2-billion, 8,000-acre planned community 5 miles south of Loreto that eventually will include 5,000 homes on 3 miles of coastline and in the foothills of the Sierra de la Giganta Mountains. TSD was the primary force behind Shoal Point, a former Chevron bulk oil plant fronting on Victoria, British Columbia's Fisherman's Wharf. The former "brownfield" site is now a $110-million landmark residential and commercial development with 161 residential units and 50,000 square feet of commercial space dedicated primarily to marine-oriented and technology-based businesses. Shoal Point is an energy efficient development with a blend of older architectural style and state-of-the-art materials and technology.

The project (*www.loretobay.com*) will harvest more potable water than it consumes, create more energy than it uses and enhance the habitat it occupies. "What we've begun creating is a series of walkable seaside villages," says Butterfield, who is focusing on second home and retirement buyers in Canada and the United States. The first of nine residential stages, with homes priced between $200,000 and $1 million, opened in November 2004. Neighborhoods are limited in size so that a majority of the population is within a five-minute walking distance of the planned village center.

Jim Grogan, an Arizona attorney and developer who is also chair of the Arizona Tourism and Sports Authority, said one of the keys to the development has been the ability of foreign citizens to hold title to Mexican property. "Loreto Bay offers title insurance for every property it sells," Grogan said. "This ensures the marketability of your title and gives you no-fault recourse in the event of problems. The carrier shoulders the potential risks and indemnifies against losses or damages arising from title defects. That can't be said of all real estate in Mexico."

As discussed in Chapter 2, the laws of property ownership in Mexico have changed, allowing non-Mexican citizens to have property rights similar to those in the United States and Canada. The Mexican Constitution, however, prohibits direct ownership of real estate by foreigners in what has come to be known as the "restricted zone." The restricted zone encompasses all land located within 62 miles of any Mexican border and within 31 miles of any Mexican coastline. In order to permit foreign investment in these areas, however, the Mexican government created a special trust in 1972, known as the *fideicomiso*. Since foreigners are not able to enter directly into contracts to buy coastal real estate, they must have a bank act on their behalf—similar to a trust established to hold property for minors. The bank, as trustee, buys the property for the foreign buyer, and then has a fiduciary obligation to follow instructions given by the buyer. The buyer retains and enjoys all the rights of ownership while the bank holds title to the property. The buyer is entitled to use, enjoy and even sell the property held in trust, at its market value, to any eligible purchaser. The trust lasts 50 years and is perpetually renewable.

Loreto Bay, with the help of FONATUR, obtained a master trust on the entire 8,000-acre property. The plan calls for 5,000 of those acres to remain as a nature preserve and also includes the expansion of an estuary. According to Grogan, the 8,000-acre development will have a series of nine phases. Phase One is right on the beach. Housing options include $2-million dollar beachfront homes, single-family courtyard homes starting at $150,000, three- and four-bedroom courtyard homes priced between $200,000 and $650,000, and smaller "live-work" residential units in a town center, and condominiums. The residences are not fractional ownership or timeshare properties, but Grogan said his company would manage and rent the properties for the owners when the homes are vacant.

Grogan's homebuilding experience includes serving as president of GW Holdings, a diversified real estate investment company that included the Rocks, a private residence club with 40 fractional ownership homes in northeast Scottsdale. Grogan also was senior executive vice president and general counsel at UDC Homes in the 1990s; before that, he was the managing attorney at the Phoenix law firm of Gallagher and Kennedy. In 1998, after UDC was sold to Shea Homes. Grogan became president and CEO of Samoth Capital Corporation, a Canadian company specializing in real estate lending, hotels, master-planned communities and multifamily projects. In July 2000, Grogan was named by then-Governor Jane Hull to the Arizona Tourism and Sports Authority, the public agency created to promote tourism and design and build a $353-million multipurpose convention facility and NFL stadium in Maricopa County. The board later elected Grogan its chairman.

According to Grogan, the first targeted sales regions will be the western United States and British Columbia. The potential market includes second home and retirement buyers. One 18-

hole, public golf course has been operating for years along the Sea of Cortés, and there are plans to add two more as the community develops. Loreto Bay officials have been meeting with Troon Golf in Scottsdale, Arizona, about managing the future courses, said Tim Schantz, Troon Golf's executive vice president of acquisitions.

Butterfield, the driving force behind the development of the Villages of Loreto Bay, said the project matched all the criteria he was looking for in a development, including affordability. The range of housing includes everything from detached bungalows to huge waterfront homes and apartment condominiums. "I was just looking for a semiretirement place in the sun where I could be warm, swim in the sea, live in a beautiful home, eat fabulous food, take care of my health and continue learning," Butterfield said.

In keeping with the mandate of his company, Butterfield has established sustainability targets:

- To produce more energy than is consumed through the use of solar and other photovoltaics (PV) technologies that use semiconductor technology to convert sunlight directly into electricity.

- To produce more potable water than is consumed to enhance vegetation and to facilitate the "recharge" of an existing aquifer and desalinization processes.

- To improve biodiversity through the restoration of overgrazed lands and the creation of an additional estuary system.

Bill and Barbara Gibson were among 10 couples from Calgary, Alberta, who joined the Butterfields on one of the initial charter flights to the Loreto Bay site. They ended up purchasing their piece of sun and surf. Gibson, vice-president of Blast Promotions, Inc., in Calgary, says he had followed the progress of Shoal Point in Victoria and knew the business background and success of the Butterfield group.. "When we got there, we had a lot of questions because all we were looking at, really, was a piece of dirt," says Gibson. The Gibsons were looking for a winter escape, but also viewed Loreto Bay as an investment property. The couple purchased a $250,000 courtyard home in the Casa Bohemia portion of the first phase of the development, an area Gibson says will be used as a focal point for the marketing of the overall complex.

Prior to opening the project to the public, Butterfield took Mexican President Vicente Fox on a tour of the proposed development, and he also sat in on planning meetings with various officials. "When we decided to go ahead with this, we figured there had to be thousands of people looking for the same thing," Butterfield said.

From hoop dreams in Minnesota to dream homes in Manzanillo

If you've planned a lunch with Bob Koens and the subject turns to basketball, you might as well plan on delaying any afternoon appointments. However, if the conversation somehow leaps to sunshine and warm water, don't plan on making it home for dinner. Koens, a native of Santa Maria, California, moved to the Twin Cities years ago to become an assistant basketball coach at the University of Minnesota. After years in the college game and even more in the private business sector, he's now taken a team approach to not only establishing a 530-acre, $400-million community of Midwest second home buyers in Manzanillo, Mexico, but also to a sister city arrangement between St. Paul and Manzanillo. The governor of the state of Colima, the Mexican region that encompasses Manzanillo, even made a trip to St. Paul at the request of "Ambassador Bob."

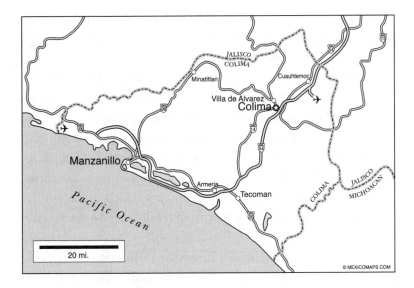

"All of these Midwest snowbirds have been heading to Florida or Arizona, but some of these people can no longer afford Florida or are looking to something different," Koens explains. "We are going to provide that in Manzanillo. For the same time it would take you to drive to a lake cabin in northern Minnesota, you can fly to Manzanillo and be on the beach."

Manzanillo, now larger than Puerto Vallarta with a population of 130,000, is also growing more popular on the commercial front. View homes appreciated approximately 30 percent from 2003–2005, and its port business has surpassed Veracruz, making Manzanillo the largest port in Mexico. Expansion is also underway to make the port even larger and deeper to accommodate bigger ships, heavier traffic and even more foreign and Mexican companies whose business interests center around cargo movement. Several cruise ship lines are now making Manzanillo one of their main stops.

The progress and improvements don't stop at the port. Downtown, *El Centro,* has gotten a face lift. A new central plaza, or *jardín,* with rose gardens, sculptured topiary trees, giant sailfish sculpture and two-mile boardwalk along the ocean highlighted by palm-tree lined beaches make visiting the downtown area a pleasant experience. Electricity has been moved underground, and a Moorish-style facade offers visitors a shady place to walk while they peruse the many shops and restaurants. Frequently there are exhibitors (most recently from Oaxaca) with a variety of items to sell, from jewelry to clothing to native liqueurs. City Hall has also been renovated, and parking, though still a problem, has been expanded. The streets have been widened with interlocking paving stones, a traffic circle helps direct the traffic flow, and non-skid tile graces the sidewalks in the main shopping district. The are two new hospitals with intensive care wings, several private clinics, two major supermarket department stores, affordable quality dental care, a variety of restaurants and bars, clean unpopulated beaches and the best climate year-round in the world. In Colima City, just an hour away, there's a Sears, City Club, Wal-Mart, Sam's Club, McDonald's, Domino's Pizza and Office Depot. The pace is slow, and the people are friendly.

"Manzanillo is without a doubt a beautiful place," says Koens. "The temperature is perfect and the beaches are spectacular.

Even though you are able to find beaches and beautiful places all over the world, it is the people that really make Manzanillo a marvelous and special place one would not want to leave. The people are friendly and very welcoming."

It was the people and weather that lured Koens' in-laws to Manzanillo, about 145 miles south of Puerto Vallarta, more than three decades ago. The family would gather south of the border for special holiday vacations and his mother-in-law, Ardis Peterson, became active in the community and with cultural events. Each time the family returned to the Twin Cities, more people would ask about the draw of the area and the possibility of buying property there. In 2001, Koens had considered building a series of condominiums adjacent to the Karmina Palace, a popular destination resort on the shores of the Pacific Ocean. While doing research on the waterfront parcel, a larger hillside property piece that the Mexican government had ordered to be liquidated became available by private offering to approved investors. Koens and his associates raised the capital to buy the 530 acres that they plan to turn into Las Cascadas de Manzanillo, five-star gated community, featuring winding cobblestone streets, waterfalls and lagoons and a golf course. The development group said it envisions three to five hotels and hundreds of housing units, including condominiums and single-family houses. Some of the homes, hotels, restaurants and shops will circle a natural lagoon that will be opened up to the ocean. The property's rising elevations feature ocean views from virtually every vantage point. Critics of the development plan contend the natural environment will be destroyed by all the building. The new owners counter the objection by saying they will be bringing in more fresh water for wildlife and vegetation, plus rejuvenating a lagoon, now used as a dumping site. By opening up the lagoon to the ocean's tides, it will be replenished daily with fresh sea water.

"The area means too much to too many people—including me," Koens said. "There is no way we are going to take anything away from the beauty of the land or the environmental sensitivity of the property."

Choosing safety when there are other options for sun

Susan Dearing has lived in Manzanillo for more than 15 years. She operates a scuba shop, writes guidebooks about the area and oversees two helpful websites, *www.gomanzanillo.com* and *www.divemanzanillo.com*. She believes one of the most important reasons North Americans move to Manzanillo is the low crime rate. Not only does the state of Colima have the lowest crime rate in the country, but Manzanillo has the lowest in the state. Hearing those facts piques the interest of many foreigners, who could find sun and warm water just about any place in Mexico.

"A few days ago, I was—as usual—in a hurry, and shopping at Soriana supermarket," Dearing says. "After receiving an emergency call from my office, I quickly checked out, threw the groceries in the car and raced back to the store. An hour later, I noticed my purse was missing. All credit cards, debit card, prescription glasses, cell phone, passport and other I.D. were in the bag—in short, my life! It was more than two hours before I could get back to Soriana, and no purse. I tried calling my cell phone. No answer. About an hour later, I tried again. A man answered. He was a taxi driver, and he said I had left my purse in a cart outside in the parking lot. He had it and offered to meet me back at the Soriana lot. When my purse was returned to me, everything was there, including the money. If you want to meet nice, honest, people, you'll find them here. That's why I've stayed in Manzanillo so long. There are more special people here than anyplace I've ever lived."

Lisa and Juan Martinez were living out the American dream in Florida, working hard, making lots of money and feeling the stress. Finally one day, Juan sat Lisa down, and said, "We can't go on like this. We have everything we ever wanted, but no time to enjoy it. Something needs to change."

Soon they started looking for a new lifestyle, and safety and security for their children. Juan was searching for a new business opportunity and included Mexico as a possibility. He found the Hotel La Posada in Manzanillo, which was in an area that was known for being one of the safest in all of Mexico and a good place to raise a family. Lisa and Juan were a little worried because they were leaving everything they had ever known, and investing all their money—and the rest of their lives in an unknown, unproven hotel, not to mention a foreign country. But since moving the Manzanillo, the couple has never looked back. They say they are healthier, happier and closer than ever and would not change their life for any amount of money. Their girls are in a bilingual school, they participate in local activities (swimming, dancing, etc.), they have a wonderful, tranquil beach to frolic on and there is plenty of "family time." And the hotel business is thriving.

Although property values have risen more than longtime residents thought possible, the area is still more affordable than in other areas with a large foreign population, such as Cancun,

Acapulco or Puerto Vallarta. Although the focus is always waterfront or view parcels, Manzanillo has gated communities, such as La Punta and Club Santiago, offering amenities such as golf and tennis. There are also several major spas and health clubs, and a variety of water sports activities available, including deep sea fishing, scuba diving and snorkeling. Manzanillo's twin bays offer two, five-mile stretches of unpopulated beach for walking or jogging, and there are areas for bird watching, hiking and camping. Other beaches nearby are good for beach-combing, surfing and sunbathing.

Out of the restricted zone: Lake Chapala draws retirees to Mexico's interior

Lake Chapala is the largest natural lake within the Republic of Mexico, but certainly not the best known destination for travelers from the United States and Canada. Most tourists headed for a week of Mexican sun, fun, tequila shooters and ocean-side sunset bars and discos have never heard of the "other" paradise in the country's central highlands.

More than three hours from the nearest sandy beach resort, Lake Chapala has been a destination for foreigners since the 1920s, when the artsy crowd—including a Russian ballerina, composers, musicians and writers such as D. H. Lawrence—began discovering the peaceful quiet and friendly villagers. In the intervening years, waves of foreigners—many of them retirees—have arrived to settle for a moment or a lifetime in one or another of the string of small fishing villages along the 60-mile-long lake's north shore. The influx of residents steadily increased, culminating with a deluge of expats who have flocked into the country since the 1994–1995 peso crisis (peso devaluation). Lake Chapala, sometimes known as Lakeside, is now home to more U.S. and Canadian citizens than anywhere else outside their home countries.

Some promoters tout as the area's best calling cards its nearly perfect year-round climate and economy that allows retirees live a better lifestyle than they could at the same rate back home. Yet 15-year resident Judy King tells many of the tour groups and newcomers to whom she speaks each year *not* to move to Lake Chapala for either the weather or perceived financial benefits. Both of these factors can disappoint newcomers, according to King, even though the area has an average temperature of 72 degrees. It's always best to target personal comfort.

"One year could have a really chilly January or a hotter than normal May," said King, formerly of Denison, Iowa, and who now hosts an informative website (*www.mexico-insights.com*) and offers orientation seminars for consumers considering the Lake Chapala area. "Local legend claims Lake Chapala as the 'second best climate in the world.' While we say that it only rains at night, there are years when tropical storms and hurricanes on the coasts of Mexico can pull the clouds into this central area. We don't get the storms' damage, but those systems can force clouds into our area, and we will see rain during the daytime for a few days."

Even *AARP The Magazine* touted the Lake Chapala area (entire article reprinted in this chapter) as one of the great places in Mexico for U.S. retirees, but those who relocated to the area believe the headlines and eye-catching kicker lines in the article gave those still north of the border a false impression. King estimates there are 5,000 to 7,000 foreigners living full-time on the North Shore of Lake Chapala. That number balloons to about 15,000 in the winter months, and another 2,000 to 3,000 come in the summer months to escape the heat and humidity of Texas, Florida, the coast of Mexico, California, Nevada and Arizona.

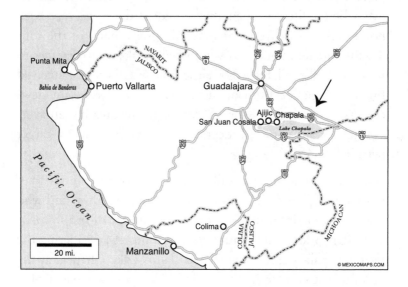

If people move here thinking they are going to live cheaply or live like kings on just their Social Security check, they are going to be disappointed, according to King. The peso has been much stronger against the U.S. dollar in recent years, and that means fewer pesos in the expats' pockets when they change their retirement dollars. While the exchange rate is not as beneficial as it was in the late nineties, many of those who have moved to Lake Chapala still feel they have a better lifestyle than they could back home. Although the cost of purchasing a home is high, and few mortgages are available at Chapala, the low cost of property taxes (under $300 a year for the vast majority), car insurance, labor for repairs, household help and medical and dental care, most newcomers in the area believe they live more comfortably here than they could back home.

Although many still state the climate and economy as their reasons for relocating to central Mexico, that can't be the only reason why are so many retirees—and those still in their forties and fifties—are flocking to the shores of the lake. It doesn't take much more than a cursory look around the area to realize that this small pocket offers goods, services and activities not readily available in other areas.

The enterprising Mexican businesses that have taken the phrase "build it and they will come" to heart are growing and flourishing with the area. A good example is Superlake, the market located on the busy highway in tiny village of San Antonio Tlayacapan. This store has grown in 10 years from a tiny fruit market to a major influence in the area by importing and stocking foreign grocery items.

Francisco "Pancho" Paz grins shyly as he confirms that surprising bit of news: "We bring a 48-foot trailer of goods every month from Texas and now have regular customers who come from Guadalajara, Puerto Vallarta, San Miguel Allende and other parts of Mexico to shop here."

The Paz family has listened to the wish lists of area residents and the shelves are full of gourmet mustards, exotic bottled salad dressings and wonderful specialty oils and vinegars. Long before a cake mix was produced in Mexico, Superlake carried many of the brands from north of the border. Others have taken a note from the Paz plan for success. Manuel has expanded his original small newsstand in Chapala to a chain of three magazine and book stores. He now sells newspapers, magazine and *The New York Times* best selling paperback books that are flown in from the United States. Even hardware stores are jumping on the bandwagon, and with NAFTA making more U.S. brands and goods available in Mexico, the stock of other local stores is gradually changing to reflect the tastes of Lake Chapala's minority expat population.

The foreigners who have relocated to Lake Chapala are certainly the vast minority in the area—recently about 5 to 10 percent of the population along the north shore, depending on the time of year. These foreign residents at Lake Chapala aren't the same vacationers who arrive to party on the beach for a week or two before dashing back to the frozen north. Lake Chapala doesn't have the franchise-chain bars and flashing discos that appeal to spring-breakers.

The retirees at Lake Chapala are constantly in motion with their talents, work experience and time. More than 90 English-speaking events are planned each month for clubs, groups, concerts, events and other activities. There are several dozen groups and organizations raising money to help the original residents of the area. The foreigners are reaching out to assist the children of the area obtain an education. Although Mexican law requires children to remain in school through sixth grade, the reality is that many families just can't afford to pay the fees, books, uniforms and transportation costs to keep their kids in school. Thousands of Lake Chapala students benefit from expat fundraisers and programs.

Other good works initiated by relocated retirees include help for deaf, handicapped, crippled and ill children. There are homes for indigenous elderly Mexicans who are without the normal family system that cares for its own. Volunteers teach classes in English and computer skills, tutor children after school, staff and stock three area children's Spanish language libraries and attend to the plethora of services at the Lake Chapala Society.

The LCS boasts the largest membership of any foreigner's organization at Lake Chapala and in Mexico—now with more than 4,000 members. Visitors and members flood the LCS grounds every day, dropping in for blood pressure, hearing, vision, skin cancer and other free or low-cost health screening and testing. At the backbone of the organization is the library, with more than 35,000 volumes in English.

There are clubs and groups to suit the interest of every new-comer—from quilters to bird-watching enthusiasts, and bridge or cribbage players to classical music concerts and the little theater productions. Residents can go on fishing expeditions, golf, play tennis, volleyball, softball, rugby, soccer, hike or ride horseback—or do nothing at all but enjoy life under the warm and friendly sun.

What is the big draw for Lake Chapala? "Here we don't have to reinvent the wheel," said King. "Everything folks like to do back home, including watching any U.S. or Canadian television station is available, right here. Then if people want more, they're just a short drive from Mexico's second largest city, Guadalajara. There's another whole level of shopping, museums, galleries, malls, restaurants and activity there.

"Visitors who are checking out the area are sometimes cynical; they want to know the bad side of the area. They can't believe it's this close to perfection. But Mexico isn't for everyone.

There are people who shouldn't try to move here—they just aren't suited for it, emotionally or financially. Still, for people who are willing to adjust and adapt, this can be their own little slice of paradise."

La Vida Cheapo by Barry Golson[1]

For 600 bucks a month, retirees in Mexico can live in a three-bedroom home, with a gardener. For a cool thousand...well, you won't believe it

Guadalajara

On a balmy afternoon in Guadalajara, my wife, Thia, and I are relaxing with Janet Levy in the garden of her rented stucco home in a quiet, leafy part of the city. A former assistant to the chief executive of a Washington, D.C., nonprofit organization, Levy, 69, settled in Guadalajara in the early 90s - and life since then, she says, has been nothing less than grand.

For starters, there is her standalone three-bedroom house with a maid's room, the kind that might rent for $2,500 a month in an upscale D.C. suburb. "I pay $600 a month," she says. "And that includes the gardener." Levy points out that Wal-Mart, Costco, Sam's Club and Blockbuster all have stores in Guadalajara, Mexico's second-largest city, with a population of five million. So when she's not puttering in her garden, Levy can indulge in American-style shopping.

Levy is also keen on Mexican health care, which, as we find, is a popular topic among expats. Though U.S. citizens living in

[1] Reprinted with permission from AARP the Magazine, March-April 2004

Mexico are not covered by Medicare for doctors' visits and medical services (unless they travel back to the U.S.), the national insurance program is available to foreigners and costs about $300 a year. There is private insurance as well, at prices considerably cheaper than in the U.S., though costs have been rising.

As for hospitals, Levy informs us that Guadalajara boasts several excellent facilities, including Hospital San Javier (which has a branch in Puerto Vallarta), Hospital del Carmen and Americas Hospital. The custom in Mexico is for a family member or friend to stay at the hospital with the patient. Many doctors speak English, but most nurses don't, so some Americans take a Mexican friend who can translate.

Levy says Americans she knows, many on modest incomes, pay for medical expenses out of pocket, because fees and lab costs are so reasonable. They'll use insurance only for major procedures. "I've had back surgery and my gall bladder out, and the care was excellent," she says. Virtually all drugs except controlled substances are available without prescriptions. "I pay $40 an office visit," Levy says. "And did I mention how nice it is to sit and really talk to a doctor?"

Why are we in Guadalajara? Well, after 30 years with only a few weeks off each year, my wife and I both suddenly found ourselves between jobs. Ordinarily, I'd have done what I've done in the past — immediately hit the pavement in search of work. But this time it struck me: What's the hurry?

So, while we're not ready for retirement ourselves, having just skittered past the midpoint of our 50s, we thought we'd use the extended downtime to travel and check out possible places to settle.

We had another reason for traveling south of the border: to see what it would cost. According to my research, something like half of the people in my generation haven't saved enough to retire comfortably. Meaning, if we hope to kick back in the lifestyle to which we've become accustomed, one of three things will have to happen. We'll have to either a) save a lot of money fast or b) win the lottery.

Or alternatively, we could move to Mexico. I'd read a few of those how-to-retire books that claim you can live in Mexico on $400 a month, with all the frijoles you can eat, and my skeptical reaction was, "Oh, really?" So I checked some other sources and found that, while our own lifestyle would take a considerable hit if we tried to get by on $400 a month, the cost of living well in Mexico can be quite low indeed. Our curiosity was piqued.

As for the language barrier, I retain a ragged fluency in Spanish, having lived in Mexico for a few years as a child. Thia speaks only the Spanish she's picked up from restaurant menus. In other words, we were about as proficient as most American couples considering a move to Mexico. We charted a course through a "retirement belt" that stretches from central Mexico to the Pacific coast and is an increasingly popular destination for thousands of Americans seeking to settle in sunnier climes and less expensive venues. The plan was to meet, chat with and generally poke our noses into the lives of retirees.

We make Guadalajara our first stop because the State Department estimates that more than 50,000 Americans live in the area. We find a lot to like about what guidebooks call the "most Mexican of cities," not least of all its graceful architecture, matchless Orozco murals, and extremely friendly and accommodating citizens. We spend several days sightseeing, listening to street corner mariachis, and antiquing and boutiquing in the arts-and-crafts suburb of Tlaquepaque. We eat well, with dinners for two—including appetizers and a cocktail apiece—rarely topping $25.

We are surprised to learn, therefore, that the majority of American transplants no longer settle in Guadalajara proper. Instead, retirees generally head south to the Lake Chapala area, about 45 minutes away by car. "The city once was a draw for retirees, but no more," says Michael Forbes, a trim, transplanted Brit in his 40s, over a breakfast of *huevos rancheros*. Forbes is the editor of western Mexico's most widely read English-language weekly newspaper, *The Guadalajara Colony Reporter*, and has witnessed the routine: "People come down and look around, but 95 percent of them head elsewhere. Lake Chapala, with its year-round temperate climate and all those like-minded people, can seem like a paradise."

Levy disagrees. She likes Guadalajara's many fine museums, the symphony, the big-city life. "I'd get bored at Lakeside," she declares, using the name Americans have given the large expatriate colony around Lake Chapala. "Why, there are people there who never even come into Guadalajara." This is the first volley we witness of the popular retirement sport—putting down where other retirees live.

We decide to scope out Lakeside for ourselves.

Guadalajara scorecard (on a scale of 1 to 10):

- Looks—7 (lovely downtown)
- Charm—6
- Culture—9

- Shopping—10
- Medical facilities—9
- Other Americans—2 (not so many as we expected);
- Wow factor—wonderful nighttime plaza life.

Thia's review: "Big city, love the shopping, but not being able to speak Spanish can be frustrating."

Barry's review: "Nice place to visit, shop, and see doctors, but not to live in."

Lakeside

We pack our bags and taxi south to Lake Chapala, a $30 ride. The view as we approach is breathtaking—a 50-mile-long lake, no urban haze, all sun and hills and marshes. Idyllic, but looks can be deceiving: the lake is polluted by industrial waste upriver. Where once there was fishing and water sports, the lake is now a view, nothing more. There have been ongoing efforts to clean it up, including a hands-around-the-lake protest several years ago, but significant results seem a long way off.

The retirement zone comprises two communities along the lake, a few miles apart: the funky, more Mexican village of Chapala, where gringos and locals live mostly side by side, and Ajijic (pronounced ah-hee-heek), where many Americans and Canadians live apart from the natives in pricey gated communities. Ajijic straddles a highway strip whose shop signs are half in English, half in Spanish, but the town does have its Mexican charms: A few blocks in from the main highway, for instance, you'll find small plazas, quaint churches, and solemn donkeys pulling carts.

Our guide at Lakeside is Ruth Ross-Merrimer, 69, an irrepressible dame with a sardonic wit. A Californian who worked in documentaries, Ross-Merrimer has lived here for 20 years and has reported on the social scene for several local English-language publications. She has also self-published a novel called *Champagne and Tortillas*, which pokes satirical fun at a retirement community not unlike Lakeside. She can be tart about the goings-on around the lake, but also boasts about the amateur theater, the October concerts and the opera season, as well as the charity work done by the gringo population, which includes a large number of Canadians. "Some people do live in gated bubbles," she says at the lively Ajijic Grill, where we meet. "But most had enough of an adventurous spirit to move to Mexico in the first place. They were doers, and they pour a lot of that energy into local charities. It's either that or Margarita City."

Whether you move to Guadalajara, Lakeside or elsewhere in Mexico, Ross-Merrimer advises, be prepared for culture shock. "The two cultures have opposing attitudes toward wealth, death, time, and taxes," she says. "Americans tend to flaunt their wealth. Mexicans shield it, sometimes behind walls with spiked glass. Americans consider death the end of life; Mexicans consider it a part of life. Americans obsess about time; Mexicans are casual about it—and that's understating it, honey. Americans pay their taxes without protest; Mexicans put them off or ignore them."

Thia and I meet a wide range of retirees over the next several days. We see gorgeous homes, landscaped with all of the dazzling garden foliage the climate encourages ("Stick a clothespin in the ground here, and it'll grow," says Ross-Merrimer). And although we didn't collect data in a formal way, we were struck by how consistently retirees spoke of the reasonable cost of living in Lakeside compared with where they'd lived before. Here are a few of the comments we recorded. On housing: "A house that costs $600,000 in Phoenix might cost $300,000 here." On taxes: "Real estate taxes in a New York suburb can run $12,000 a year for a house this size; here they're $67." On utilities: "Gas and electricity are $600 a month in Chicago; here it's $100." (Electricity in Mexico is expensive, but at Lakeside, there's little need for air conditioning.) And finally, on amenities: "A maid in New Jersey, if you can afford one, can be $100 a day. Here, it's $5 to $10 a day."

In Lakeside, as in other Mexican retirement havens, you can live as cheaply or as extravagantly as you've a mind to. Karen Blue, who at 52 "chucked corporate life" in San Francisco's Bay Area to settle in Ajijic in 1996, runs seminars for newcomers to the area with her business partner, Judy King, 59, who unlike Karen needs to work for a living. They also host a helpful subscription website for people thinking of moving to the Chapala area.

Blue and King join us for lunch to talk about life in Lakeside for those without fat pensions or golden parachutes. Our first question: "Can Americans live comfortably here on their Social Security checks?" The answer is an unqualified yes.

"Truth is," says Blue, "there are lots of respectable homes you can rent for about $600, and then you add maybe $100 for a gardener and maid—which makes for a very competitive housing package, no matter what your financial circumstances." Adds King: "I actually know a fair number of people who do it on less than that. They've looked around, gotten a decent little place for $350. They may not go out to eat much, they eat more tacos than steak, but they have a very nice life here. So yes, you can live here on your Social Security check."

On our last day in Ajijic, we gather at a lush garden home with several transplanted residents, including retiree John Bragg,

69, and his wife, Mary, 57, Californians who moved to Mexico 11 years ago. I mention to John that we are planning to visit legendarily arty San Miguel de Allende next. "Oh, I'd never live in San Miguel," says Bragg, engaging in the ever-popular sport of bashing other retirement havens. "The town is filled with Texans. You can't even go to a bar and hear any Spanish. Some blond lady's gonna come up to you and say, 'Y'all must be new in town. Wouldn't you lahk to go on a house tour?'"

As it happens, one of the first people we'll meet in San Miguel is a lady who runs—you guessed it—house tours.

Lakeside scorecard:

- Looks—7 (for the vista)
- Charm—4 (some nice plazitas)
- Culture—5 (October concerts and ballet)
- Shopping—2 (but Guadalajara, 9, is not far)
- Medical facilities—2 (ditto)
- Other Americans—9 (lots of them)
- Wow factor—all sorts of personal services, from tai chi classes to assisted living facilities.

Thia's review: "No need to worry about speaking Spanish here, but kind of suburban."

Barry's review: "Nice folks, but not where I'd settle. Can't get over that pretty lake no one swims in."

San Miguel

The colonial silver town of San Miguel de Allende is the crown jewel of central Mexico. It boasts cobblestone streets, pastel-washed doors, art galleries nestled in every other nook, an enchanting main plaza known as El Jardin, and the Parroquia, a spired, fanciful-gothic confection of a church located in the center of town, whose bells toll at utterly unpredictable hours.

Although somewhat remote (the nearest airport is in León, an hour and a half away), this town of 70,000, which is home to an estimated 2,500 American retirees, scores high on the jet-set buzz meter. Little wonder. The restaurants are first-rate, shopping is an extreme sport (the streets are packed with art galleries and shops selling ceramics, folk art and antiques) and the music spilling from the town's restaurants and cafés sometimes suggests a university town on perpetual fiesta.

We meet Jennifer Hamilton, a 62-year-old Audrey Hepburn look-alike, in her airy, elegant apartment just off the Jardin. Another transplanted Californian, who has lived in San Miguel for 12 years, she gives tours of San Miguel's fanciest homes, a Sunday afternoon event that draws as many as 400 gawkers at a time.

While Hamilton enjoys talking about the multimillion-dollar mansions up in the hills, she also speaks frankly about the drawbacks of San Miguel not described in the travel brochures. "It's not a little village anymore," she says. "The streets are crumbling from the weight of the tourist buses. Good homes are expensive; utilities go up every month. I'm worried that the town will price itself out; I don't want it to become only for the very wealthy and the Mexican poor. There are still tin hovels tucked between fabulous homes. Water's giving out, too. Something will have to be done." She pauses, smiles. "But I still tell people to come down here to live. There's so much to do here!"

The town's chief arbiter and critic, Archie Dean, agrees. Author of the indispensable *The Insider's Guide to San Miguel*, the 66-year-old Dean is a gangly, fedora-wearing, knapsack-carrying New York State native who spends his days walking the streets, stopping at restaurants and cafés to sample fare for the next edition of his book. When he arrived in 1990, he says, San Miguel was a relatively primitive town where phones were scarce and shopping limited. "Now we're all connected," he says, referring to cybercafés, cable TV piped in from the States and direct-dial long-distance phone calls. He contradicts the notion that only rich retirees can afford the town. "There are apartment rentals at every price, from $300 to $5,000. You can live well for as little as $700 a month. And I know a lot of people living here on modest fixed incomes."

For those expats possessing the wherewithal, San Miguel's cosmopolitan charm and arty ambience can also translate into opportunity. On the leafy patio of the Casa de la Cuesta, a charming bed-and-breakfast a few minutes from the plaza, we chat with owner Bill LeVasseur, 59, a former advertising executive who lived and worked in Mexico when he was younger and returned with his wife, Heidi, an artist, in 1994. Owning a B & B was not in their plans. "We were retiring," he says, "not thinking about a new business or anything."

Nevertheless, the LeVasseurs crunched their numbers and decided that the home they'd begun building in San Miguel could be enlarged and turned into a home away from home for tourists. LeVasseur says that an income of $50,000 a year assures a retiree of a good life, "including eating out two or three times a week." The couple have three grown sons in the States, and in addition to traveling back home themselves, occasionally they send "plane tickets for the kids and grandkids" to come to Mexico.

The LeVasseurs tell us they considered retiring to other places in Mexico but decided San Miguel was the place for them.

"Sure, some people like their condos in Puerto Vallarta, but the heat there in the summer is unbearable and they've got mosquitoes as big as blackbirds. They've got McDonald's and Taco Bells, and we sure don't. Life is more authentic here." Sounds like our cue to move along—to Puerto Vallarta.

San Miguel scorecard:

- Looks—10
- Charm—7 (points off for the traffic and McMansions)
- Culture—10
- Shopping—8
- Medical facilities—6
- Other Americans—7 (more points subtracted for some obnoxious wealth flaunting)
- Wow factor—a world-class language school, ditto the restaurants.

Thia's review: "I'm leaving my heart here and coming back someday."

Barry's review: "Love it too, but I'm not a mountain guy. I like the ocean."

Pacific Coast

We won't tarry long in Puerto Vallarta here because we didn't tarry long there. Guidebooks extol its blend of old-Mexican charm and jet-set beach glamour. There's a large, active American retirement community in Puerto Vallarta, an international airport 20 minutes from downtown and plenty of the amenities that spring up around a modern resort. Still, there's a touch of Las Vegas to Puerto Vallarta. It's a matter of taste, I suppose, but after four days we decide to move up the coast, where we hear life is a little less frantic.

We wander some 25 miles north of Puerto Vallarta to the village of San Francisco, known to locals as San Pancho. There, we are the guests of Bill Kirkwood and Barbara Hart-Kirkwood. Ex-Silicon Valley fast trackers who'd vacationed in the region for two decades, Bill, 54, and Barbara, 52, moved permanently to San Pancho two years ago along with another couple, their close friends John Levens, 56, and Judi MacGregor-Levens, 55. Together, the couples built Casa Obelisco, a striking 5,300-square-foot open-terrace Mediterranean house with a mosaic dome perched above a splendid beach. The two families live in separate wings and this year began to rent out extra bedrooms as a bed-and-breakfast. While there, Thia and I luxuriate in the canopied beds, checking our shoes in the morning for scorpions.

Bill and Barbara's tales about house building, making new friends and adapting to Mexico's what-will-be mentality are upbeat and cheery. But outspoken Barbara, the kind of gal who'd give you the straight dope about anything (including her "terrific" $3,500 face-lift in Mexico), faults a "certain lawlessness" in her adopted country. Though they always feel personally safe, she says, fighting the mordida (bribes) system is useless. Despite ostensible reforms under President Vicente Fox, traffic cops must still be paid off. "Taxes are absurdly low, and so is a policeman's pay," Barbara explains. "How else can they make ends meet?"

They say many friends come to visit, look at properties and get the itch. "Then, at the last minute, they back down," says Barbara while fixing an *adios* sunset drink for us on their rooftop. "Why? Fear of the unknown. In the States, you know there's always a fix; here, it's often fix-it-yourself. You've got to have that spirit."

Which brings us to the final leg of our own quest. A couple of miles south of San Pancho, 40 minutes north of Puerto Vallarta, lies the village of Sayulita, estimated population 1,500. Thia and I stumble upon it while in search of an early breakfast one Sunday morning during our stay at Casa Obelisco.

At first, Sayulita seems a slightly grungy place, with no paved roads and with chickens and dogs running loose. But strolling down to its gently curved beach, sitting down to watch pelicans dive-bomb for their breakfast in the surf, we know we've found someplace special. The village, ringed by soft hills, has no traffic lights, paved roads or ATMs—and just one grocery store worthy of the name. (There are, however, three Internet cafés.)

We quickly get advice from fellow beachcombers: "You have to go to Rollie's." We are directed past the little town plaza near the beach, up a dirt street just past the butcher shop. Across the street, beneath a plain awning, is Rollie's, the town's leading breakfast establishment. The place is packed, and there's a line out the door. Proprietor Rollie Dick, a crinkly-eyed gent of 64, runs the short-order grill; his wife, Jeanne, 59, waits on tables. From time to time Rollie strolls out to sing for the patrons and waltz a delighted lady customer around the tables.

The amateur-theater ham from Salinas, California, is Sayulita's biggest booster and its gringo godfather. After closing time at noon, in the Dicks' apartment above the restaurant, Rollie explains how a retired school principal (Rollie) and a teacher (Jeanne) landed in this tiny town beside the Pacific.

It happened, he says, while they were on a vacation five years ago. They fell in love with Sayulita, and before leaving, Rollie asked the woman they were staying with to contact them if a property that matched their limited resources came on the market. Like so many others approaching retirement, Rollie had toyed with the idea of opening a restaurant. When word came that a building was available in Sayulita, the Dicks decided to take the chance.

The Dicks paid $50,000 in cash for a three-story building with a welding shop on the ground floor that Rollie converted into the restaurant. "You had to have vision," he says. "Plus, property taxes are only $32 a year." He lived there for nearly two years on his own, understanding little Spanish, waiting for Jeanne to retire and join him.

Later in the afternoon, on a stroll through town, Rollie expands on How Things Are Done Down Here. "There is, absolutely, a mentality here of living in the now, not worrying too much about the future. And you know what? It's wonderful! We made the decision that we were going to live here as guests of Mexico and do things their way."

The next day, Thia and I go looking for a piece of land of our own in Sayulita.

True, we set out merely to chronicle our journey, not to put down a stake. We're not retiring yet. But what can I say? We found a lovely little parcel above the village. We paid cash for it and got some papers in return.

Will we build there? Will we become expatriates? Will it all turn out all right? That's another story.

Pacific Coast Villages scorecard:

- Looks—9
- Charm—10 (those sunsets!)

- Culture—0
- Shopping—1 (but both villages are within 30 miles of Puerto Vallarta)
- Medical facilities—2 (but again, there's Puerto Vallarta)
- Other Americans—7 (laid-back, quirky)
- Wow factor—that surf, for beginners and hot dogs alike.

Thia's review: "Ideally, it would be four months here, four in San Miguel, four in New England."

Barry's review: "Three words—*que sera, sera.*"

Barry Golson is the former executive editor of Playboy *and* TV Guide *and former editor-in-chief of Yahoo! Internet Life.*

Mar de Cortés: More boats as second homes?

A second home is not just about single-family dwellings. According to your friendly U.S. Internal Revenue Service, a second home can be a boat or recreational vehicle as long as it has sleeping, cooking and bathroom facilities. You can also deduct the mortgage interest on a boat or RV as long as they are used as security for the loan. While boats and RVs have been extremely popular in Mexico for decades, the boat and yacht component is really on the upswing because the country believes it has found a way to further promote tourism (Mexico is now ranked 10th worldwide) and make a buck at the same time by appealing to visiting watercraft enthusiasts. Originally, the marine plan was called the Nautical Ladder (*Escalera Nautica*), a series of 27 marinas constructed on both sides of Baja California and on the mainland of Mexico. The chain, seeking to lure the 1.6 million boaters in the U.S. south-west plus others, was scheduled to start at Punta Colonet, a small cove 120 miles south of Tijuana on the northern coast of Baja California, then extend down to and around the cape at the tip of Cabo San Lucas, up the Sea of Cortés (Gulf of California) then down the Pacific Coast to Huatulco. It was the biggest tourism project of the Vicente Fox administration and its road has not been smooth and comfortable. Not unlike the old Baja Highway, the Nautical Ladder project has endured huge chuckholes and detours, shortcuts and blowouts. Heading into President Fox's final year in office, the effort was trimmed considerably and renamed the Sea of Cortés Project, or *Mar de Cortés*. The entry port now appears to be the existing marina at Ensenada plus key rungs of the remodeled ladder at Cabo San Lucas, Puerto Peñasco and Nuevo Vallarta.

The most interesting piece of the Sea of Cortés Project puzzle is a "land bridge" across the Baja peninsula, from Santa Rosalillita on the Pacific to the northern end of Bahía de los Ángeles on the Sea of Cortés. This would allow skippers to trail their boats across the peninsula rather than sailing all the way around it to reach the Sea of Cortés.

The original Nautical Ladder was hit by rising fuel costs, environmental concerns and initial investor skepticism. President Fox, who ended a 71-year rule of the Institutional Revolutionary Party (PRI) with his victory as a democrat in 2000, clearly wanted a marine project completed before his one-term, six-year run was up in 2006. The Sea of Cortés Project appeared to be that attempted compromise. In addition, Fox wanted to push through the idea of making Punta Colonet a major commercial port rivaling Los Angeles and Long Beach. The plan is to have Punta Colonet serve container ships by 2012, offering an alternative to Asian traders.

At the time the Nautical Ladder was first announced, environmental groups—especially those focused on the land and waters of the Sea of Cortés—questioned the scope and goals. John McCarthy, director general of FONATUR, the organization assigned the task of luring not only vacationers but also huge dollars from international investors seeking to develop a variety of real estate possibilities, said at the time that environmental measures would be in place. "We know there has been plenty of discussion over the years in regard to the Escalera and the environment," McCarthy said. "We are taking careful steps to make sure everything is done correctly. Environmental studies are taking place and we will always ensure the safety of the land and sea. We want to develop to conserve. The goal is to create a way to enhance nautical tourism. We want to make it easier for people to sail or yacht to Mexico and know that we have marinas available to help facilitate safe navigation, and to make entry and transit into the region a simple process."

The plan, part of improving tourist infrastructure, is going forward because of the intriguing possibility of *norte americano* dollars at every rung of the ladder. FONATUR plans to franchise the marinas with early investment forecasts reaching a total of $2 billion in five Mexican states. The marinas will include everything you would find in a master-planned community, including major single-family homes and condominium projects, restaurants, shops, moorage and fuel. The plan is to space the marinas approximately 100 miles apart so boaters can have a safe harbor on each day of a trip.

FONATUR's goal is "to be a leading institution in the promotion and development of diversified tourist projects according to global trends, with a business structure that promotes the involvement in projects based on sustainable regional growth,

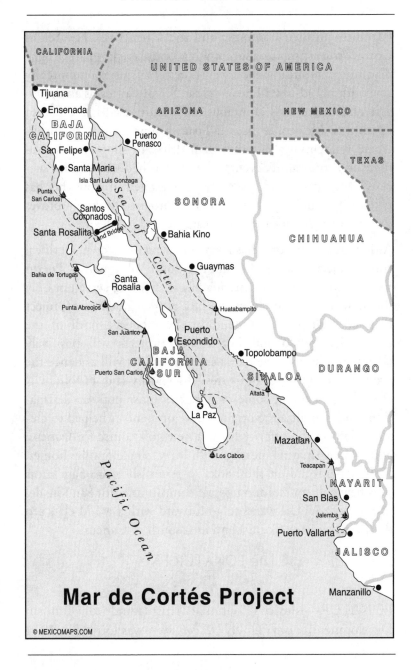

Mar de Cortés Project

© MEXICOMAPS.COM

guaranteeing their economic and social benefits." The Sea of Cortés Project's sustainable growth promise is a key part of large developments already underway. Loreto Bay, just 15 minutes by car south of old-town Loreto on the Sea of Cortés, is an 8,000-acre environmentally conscious community that is the first of its kind in Mexico. It features Spanish homes built in clusters where residents walk, rather than drive, to shopping, restaurants and community events. "Loreto has had tremendous success," McCarthy said. "We are very excited at how this has taken off so quickly. This particular project absolutely proves that a North American project can succeed in Mexico."

Although Loreto town has a small marina of its own, a critical rung project will be 30 minutes south of town at Puerto Escondido, a huge, picturesque bay that would serve not only the new Loreto development but also a 5,000-acre project planned near Puerto Escondido. "We believe both of the Puerto Escondido and Loreto Bay projects will positively change the lives of the locals and our efforts will enhance the eco balance in the Sea of Cortés," McCarthy said. FONATUR also plans to revisit some of Mexico's most popular destinations and revitalize the original developments it helped to create. High on the priority list is a new golf course for Cancun and a new marina nearby with new single-family homes. Similar plans are on the books to refurbish Cabo San Lucas plus new golf courses and upscale communities for San Jose del Cabo. FONATUR wants to go forward with a world-class eco destination in the Costa Maya area south of Cancun.

The FONATUR Five

FONATUR—Mexico's National Trust Fund for Tourism Development, *www.FONATUR.gob.mx*—was formed in 1974

to boost foreign revenue, spread the country's wealth more evenly and create jobs and raise the population's standard of living by establishing large-scale tourism developments in specific areas of the country.

Over the past 30 years, FONATUR has created and actively promoted five Integrally Planned Resorts (IPRs) that have become the backbone of Mexico's tourism industry. These resort destinations, which include Cancun, Ixtapa, Los Cabos, Loreto and Huatulco, have proven themselves to be more successful than many of the country's other destinations, garnering average hotel occupancy rates of approximately 65 percent and capturing approximately 55 percent of the country's foreign revenue from tourism.

FONATUR now has plans for several new projects. The Costa Maya Integrally Planned Tourism Project (ITP) is moving forward on the jungled coast south of Cancun, the Nayarit IPR is underway north of Puerto Vallarta and the Mar de Cortés Project is under study on the upper west coast of the mainland and along the east side of the Baja Peninsula.

Following is a capsule look of FONATUR's five initial areas.

Huatulco

Bahias de Huatulco is the most recent tourist destination to be developed by the Mexican Government on 22 miles of bays on a spectacular coast. Verdant jungles crawl out of the hills to mesh with white sand beaches and clear protected coves for miles in all directions. The weather is warm and the sky is clear, and the Pacific Ocean is warm all year long. Because Huatulco is a relatively new destination, most of the hotels and infrastructure are new as well. In an effort to make Huatulco more of an eco-friendly destination, the Mexican government has set aside

40,000 of the 52,000 acres in the area as an ecological reserve. Environmental groups are keeping a close watch on Huatulco and its tourism progress. Huatulco is quite removed from the pace often experienced at some other Mexican resorts.

State of Oaxaca, Mexico
Year established: 1984
Approximate number of rooms: 1,200

The beauty of the Bays of Huatulco is unmatched in Mexico and assures it as a destination without crowds and overdevelopment.

Web site for further information: *www.mexicoexpo.com.*

Los Cabos

Cabo San Lucas is where the Transpeninsular Highway ends. For most of the past 100 years, Cabo San Lucas was a small, quiet fishing village. Even when John Steinbeck chartered a boat out of Monterey to visit Baja in the 1940s, there was very little going on in the sleepy town. The 200-foot arch at Land's End was there marking the end of the Baja Peninsula, but back then it wasn't famous. With all of its natural beauty, resources, great weather and refreshing ocean temperature, it was inevitable that Cabo would eventually experience significant growth in tourism (two million Los Cabos visitors each year) and in population (now more than 25,000 residents).

State of Baja California Sur, Mexico
Year established: 1976
Approximate number of rooms: 8,500

Using Cancun as an example of over-development, the growth of Cabo San Lucas and San Jose del Cabo is of lower density and more eco-friendly.

Web site for further information: *www.caboexpo.com.*

Loreto

Loreto is the original capital of all of the Californias. The seafront Malecon (Paseo Lopez Mateos) has been completely rebuilt, and now features grass, palm trees and a seaside walkway complete with newer (2004) sitting benches right at the edge of the Sea of Cortés. Many additional improvements were made in 1997 to celebrate Loreto's 300-year anniversary and the international airport just south of town allows visitors to arrive in Loreto in less than a two-hour flight from Los Angeles and Phoenix. A nice marina has been built on the north end of town, which is now the focal point for most of the fishing out of Loreto. A good launch ramp can handle almost any size boat, although larger vessels should avoid the ramp at low tide. The hurricane in 2003 moved some of the big marina boulders around but the marina still functions well. Just south of Loreto is the newly developing Nopolo tourist area, offering golf, tennis, and custom homes in a very relaxing environment. The Camino Real Hotel is the newest addition to this resort area.

Loreto has always been popular with the fishing crowd. Kayakers have discovered the waters off of Loreto, and divers are becoming increasingly common in town. The waters off of the local islands have been set aside as an Underwater Natural Park. For serious sailors, the natural harbor 10 minutes south at Puerto Loreto (more commonly known as Puerto Escondido) is a great place to hole up during bad weather, or as a great destination in and of itself. The offshore islands of Isla Coronado, Isla Carmen and Isla Danzante each offer hidden coves and sandy beaches.

State of Baja California Sur, Mexico
Year established: 1976
Approximate number of rooms: 450

FONATUR's smallest project with future expansion planned for residential development, commercial centers, and marina development.

Web site for further information: *www.bajaexpo.com*.

Ixtapa

Ixtapa and Zihuatanejo are two very different Mexican cities located within 20 minutes of each other on Mexico's jungle western coast, about two hours north of Acapulco. Although both cities share a common airport, about 340 days of sunshine each year and the lush backdrop of the Sierra Madre mountains, that is where most of the similarities end.

Zihuatanejo was the first of the two towns to become established in this part of the Mexican coastline. The large and protected natural harbor was the perfect location for a port and fishing village, and the history of this bay is varied and colorful. Before the Spanish colonized Mexico, this large bay was used as a beach retreat by the Tarascan kings who lived nearby. Although most of the tourist shops, markets and restaurants remain near the water, the town itself has escaped the confines of the bay and the sprawl has moved into the nearby hills. Still, Zihuatanejo offers a charm very much unlike its nearby neighbor, especially along the southwestern shores of its harbor.

Ixtapa is located north of Zihuatanejo up the coast about five miles. Designed by the Mexican government and FONATUR as a tourist destination, Ixtapa looks more like a modern Mexican resort than its southern neighbor. High-rise hotels line the beachfront, and a host of restaurants and bars catering to tourists front the main street. Don't expect a town square; this is a resort, not a Mexican town or village. Most tourists stay in Ixtapa because of the number of hotel rooms and then head over to Zihuatanejo for a daily excursion of shopping and sightseeing. Those looking for more of the original flavor of Mexico often choose to stay in Z-Town, making excursions over to Ixtapa.

State of Guerrero, Mexico
Year established: 1974
Approximate number of rooms: 3,700

Developed next to the existing fishing village of Zhuatanejo, this destination offers old world charm and modern tourism facilities.

Web site for further information: *www.mexicoexpo.com.*

Cancun

Cancun is one of the Caribbean's most popular destinations. Great weather, white sandy beaches, lush green jungles and clear ocean waters combine to make this a desirable for a variety of age groups.

State of Quintana Roo, Mexico

Year established: 1974

Approximate number of rooms: 27,000

This island sand bar covered with tropical jungle and lined with white sand beaches is FONATUR's most successful project.

Web site for further information: *www.cancunexpo.com.*

Individual second home markets are as varied in Mexico as the backgrounds of the people who seek them. In Part II, we explore some ideas and over some strategies on how to best prepare to buy, enjoy and profit from your special retreat.

PART TWO

Preparation, Planning and Renting Strategies

CHAPTER SIX

Make Sure Your Dream Meets Up With Reality

Second home or strictly investment,
your property needs solid fundamentals

There are certain basics to consider if you are going to make the most of your Mexican home investment. It's easy to lose money on an emotional whim. Blue, warm water and picturesque mountains have ways of working wonders on the mind during a long holiday weekend to "just check out the opportunity." Suddenly, your promise of "honey, we won't be writing any checks this trip" turns into torrid excitement and visions of *cervezas* by the pool from November through March. Lots of people can lose money in real estate—even in appreciating Mexican locales—so let's try and do the most to protect your hard-earned cash.

Making a profit anywhere—stocks, bonds, commodities, real estate, sales—requires basic understanding and research. Regardless of what you read in the newspaper or see on television, there is no secret sauce that will absolutely guarantee big-time revenue and success. Your return, however, will be gauged differently if you decide it is only for personal use and not necessarily for investment income. How can you put a price on experiences and memories? For now, let's review some basics, explored later in detail, that are often overlooked in an emotional decision.

Mexican home... primarily as a second residence

Picking your place. The three most-used words in real estate—location, location, location—are repeated for a reason. If the property will be solely a personal residence, will its style and layout hold its appreciation over the long-term? Then think resale: If you had to sell if five years down the road, what would lure the next buyer? Finally, if you had to rent it out, is this the type of property that could definitely catch your eye and possible rental dollars? What appeals to just you may not appeal to the rental pool you will depend upon for consistent income.

Picking your community. Even if the house is perfect, is the neighborhood one that beckons late afternoon walks and friendly shopping? Do you think most of the people you know would like it, too? Remember, you can always add a bedroom or convert a patio space, but the area is set. Again, play the dual role of renter and retiree. If the parcel will eventually serve as your retirement residence, you need to choose a place where you will be comfortable later in life.

Finding the cash. One of the biggest changes that have occurred in the Mexican real estate market over the past five years has been the introduction of financing. And as lenders make more funds available, costs and interest rates will fall. The lower the cost of financing, the greater the cash flow and the higher your return on investment.

Tax is a benefit, but... While mortgage interest is deductible on second homes, it's usually not wise to buy a home solely for tax reasons. If your Mexican property eventually becomes your primary residence, you can sell it after two years and pocket $500,000 of gain (married couple) or $250,000 (single person). Sale of an investment property would not qualify for such a generous tax treatment.

Who's minding the store? Before you invest in real estate, you must decide how you will handle management. Having tenants, short- or long-term, will require that the property be managed effectively. It's a business, unless you will be the only occupants. This means maintenance and improvement, as well as simple rent collection. You will either do it yourself, or you will hire others to do it for you. Management is a cost and will diminish your cash flow. Either you will spend your time to do it, or you will pay someone else. Choosing the more cost-effective approach will affect the return on your investment.

How much can you handle? Real estate that will ultimately prove a good investment because of price appreciation might be a challenge every month because of negative cash flow. You are responsible to paying for and maintain your property regardless of whether or not the property is generating revenue. Before you invest, you need to create and hold a cash reserve to cover those weeks when the house is not rented, when the rent is late or when the toilet needs repair.

Second home viewed through an investor's eyes

Any investment needs to be evaluated for its total rate of return over its holding period relative to alternative investments. The holding period is completely under your control. You might decide to buy a second home as a prelude to retirement—vacation in it now, live in it later. Or your second home could be the stepping stone investment that appreciates and provides the downpayment for a third or fourth vacation rental. The alternatives against which you compare a real estate investment are also subjective. Consider how you would use the money if you didn't buy that second home.

The total return to your investment in real estate is not subjective. Rather, it has several very specific components. If you are evaluating the potential return from a second home, some of these must be estimated. It's usually wiser to be conservative in making these assumptions. The components of total return that affect your profitability are:

Cash flow. Rents provide a stream of income to sustain the expenses of the house and provide profit. In evaluating the investment, you need to adjust your projected rents in two directions. Each year, the rent should be adjusted upward for any increases because of inflation and improvement of market conditions. The weekly rental income might need to be lowered during slow periods. Talking with other owners or property managers in your market will enable you to get a good feel for what rent levels are and what vacancy rates you can expect.

Potential appreciation. Over your ownership period, the house will change in value—hopefully for the better! With the way Mexican properties have been appreciating, there's a good chance the value will increase over time. You have control over when you will sell the property, and thus, you can time the market to ensure the best chance of a capital gain. It is rare that investment property *must* be sold, so you can continue to rent it out during slow sales periods and wait for a better time to sell.

Managing, maintaining and renovating. There are expenses attached to owning investment or personal real estate. On the investment side, these need to be offset against cash flow and appreciation in calculating your return on investment. Any expenditure on a rental property to maintain or improve it is an expense that will diminish your near-term return. Also, any outside management expenses reduce cash flow to you. That doesn't mean you should let the property run down or quit your day job to manage it. Two things need to be emphasized here.

First, major changes (repair or remodeling) in the property can be depreciated over an extended period of time. Thus the amount deducted each year is only a portion of the total expense.

Second, your estimate of repair and renovation expenses is sensitive to your chosen holding period. A roof replacement might be of concern if you are planning to own the home for 30 years, but not if your time horizon is five years.

Tax considerations. If your Mexican getaway is your primary or secondary residence, the interest you pay to finance the purchase of the house is tax deductible. Because you benefit from this, it represents part of the positive return from your investment. Conversely, rental income is taxable to you and is thus reduced by whatever your marginal tax rate is. Finally, tax schedules will govern the allowable depreciation deductions for major home repairs and renovations. IRS schedules will provide most of the information you need to factor in the tax considerations of real estate investments.

Compare and contrast. You need to adjust your return for the time value of money. In other words, if your rental house yields a return of $10,000 in three years, you need to determine that amount back to today's dollars used elsewhere to see how much it's really worth. Using the return on an alternative investment—perhaps a bank account or certificate of deposit—is usually a good assumption.

All of these considerations can be plugged into a formula that will enable you to get a good estimate of what return you can reasonably expect on your real estate investment. That formula looks rather complicated but merely does what we described above. In fact, most advanced hand calculators have the formula already plugged in. All you need to do is put in your assumptions, and you can get an answer that will guide your decision. Check out some of the real estate calculators on the Internet to help you along your way.

Turning the possibilities of a Mexican second home purchase into reality is a straightforward process that requires both thought and work. It should be done jointly by everyone who will participate in the dream house. If you want to include children, close friends and other family members, that's fine. But only if they will have some responsibility—either physical or financial. Planning with people who will eventually lose interest in the property or give up their stake in it will likely leave you stuck with their tastes and thus dissatisfied down the road with what you have.

Take time to picture your place

Whoever participates in the decision-making, the best process of picturing your Mexican second home involves creating the most detailed picture you can. If at the end of the process, you can engage all your senses—touch, sight, smell, taste, hearing—in envisioning your dream house, it will seem more real to you and it will motivate you to proceed with confidence. As you develop the vision, remember that the controlling factor is not whether it exists, but rather whether you can fully envision it. Creating that kind of vision involves the following steps.

Begin by setting a time frame. When will you want to reach the goal of your Mexican second home? Do you want to wait until retirement to take up residence, or will you want to use it, at least part-time, well in advance of that? How long do you intend to live there? Answering these questions will not only help you envision the dream location, but also set the timetable for the financing process that will enable you to reach the dream.

Move a little deeper into the process by looking at the things you enjoy now in your leisure time. These will make up the bulk of your activity in the dream location, so the location ought to accommodate them. If you enjoy reading, cultural plays and lectures, then a larger community will be best. Access to golf, fishing, sailing or hiking will dictate a more specific resort community. Don't worry about whether your tastes will change because you will be revisiting the master picture often. You might want to add and subtract activities to account for new interests and limitations. Going through this step will enable you to define the type of location that will best suit your needs.

Next, focus in on the type of house you want. How much room do you think you need? If you are planning on sharing the home with family and friends, more bedrooms and more living space are needed than if you plan to be there with only your immediate household. How much time do you want to spend dealing with care and maintenance of the property? If you choose a more developed area, would you rather garden or have the time to play golf? Focusing on these decisions will help you choose the type of house as well as the type of ownership that best suits your vision.

Get more detailed. Think of the configuration of your Mexican *casa* and the amenities you want in it. Should it be single level or multilevel? Will you want it "wired" so you have access to the Internet? (This is also important in the interim if you are looking to rent out your investment property.) What type of appliances do you want in the kitchen? Do you want the potential for wheelchair accessibility? In other words, design in your mind the perfect house and then visit it often. The more familiar you become with the house, the more you will want to be in it.

Revisit the vision. Your tastes might have changed, and your family situation might be pointing you in a different direction, both in the near- and long-term. Go through the process again with your current status. You're doing this to remake the vision, but you're also doing it to assess your progress along the road to your dream. As you look at your vision again in light of the changes that have happened to you, also look at your financial position and determine whether your current holdings are on the right track. Is investment in a second home in Mexico a better proposition now than it was at your last review? Do you need to be in a different location to take advantage of population shifts and appreciation differences? Answering these questions will provide a valuable "midcourse" correction to your progress.

These are the steps in the visioning process. Creating a vision enables you to have a specific orientation, and having that orientation forms your decision making when it comes time to roll the dice. In the next chapter, we explore in more detail how to plug in the financial numbers to make your Mexican getaway come true.

What exactly is FM status?

Mexico has crafted several different immigration designations and most of the major ones are part of the "FM" family. Most are for nonresidents who plan to stay fewer than six months.

The FM-T may be easily and continually renewed by simply leaving Mexico within the allotted six-month period, and then reentering.

The FM-3 is designed for persons who want to live at least part-time in Mexico but do not necessarily intend to make it their permanent home. To be granted an FM-3 status, you must prove you have sufficient resources to be financially independent, or meet certain requirements to be able to work or own a business in Mexico. FM-3 *rentista* status has monthly income (from Social Security, investments, etc.) guidelines. If the applicant owns property in Mexico, the amount of income required is reduced by nearly one-half. An individual with FM-3 status is allowed to own foreign-plated vehicles and operate them in Mexico.

The FM-2 status is designed for those who intend to permanently reside in Mexico with requirements only slightly more stringent than FM-3 status. After five years of successfully meeting FM-2 requirements, an individual may apply for *inmigrado* status, which includes most of rights and privileges of a Mexican citizen. However, *inmigrado* status does not carry the right to vote and does not require the holder give up native citizenship. Holders may freely work and remain in Mexico without annual renewals.

There are restrictions on bringing and keeping foreign cars in Mexico. A valid driver's license is all that is required to legally operate a car or truck. Typically, holders of FM-T and FM-3 immigration status are allowed to drive and keep foreign-plated vehicles for the length of time indicated on their visas. A permit can easily be obtained and renewed through the *aduana* (customs agents) at the border. A copy of the FM visa should be carried in the car at all times for verification. Skilled Mexican mechanics for maintenance and repair are available in every town but always ask local friends and sources for referrals.

It's time to focus on what assets you can tap to make your Mexican property a reality. Is there a stock that old Uncle Charley handed to you as a kid that's now in a safe deposit box somewhere? Is there equity in the one rental property you own with your brother? In the next chapter, we ask you to dust off your financial memories and documents to determine what's possible.

CHAPTER SEVEN

Key to Your Profit Center: Finding the Right Path

Calculating your discretionary income guides property focus

Now that we have an idea of what makes up the big picture, where do you start along the path to your Mexican getaway? Learning where to start depends on knowing what you can obligate to your investment. If you seek second residence solely for your use or part-time rental, there are two ways for determining how much you can afford. The first is the asset method. Start by taking stock of your present wealth. Create a balance sheet of your assets and liabilities. Don't forget to include the equity in your primary residence, even though you may be dead-set against borrowing against the roof over your head. Homes are no longer cumbersome and illiquid assets, thanks to the integration of home equity lending with other financial opportunities.

If you have recently gone through a refinance or have children heading off for college, you know all about filling out forms provided by mortgage lenders and university entrance officials. You know the drill—list all of your debts including credit cards, cars, boats, mortgages and anything else you view as a "minus" on your financial chart. Balance these against all of your assets, including your savings, individual retirement accounts, home value, stocks and bonds and other assets. The net of these two numbers will give you your net worth and be an indication of the amount you have available to transfer into your Mexican investment. Record this balance.

Although it sounds simple and gives you a good ballpark number, the actual net number is more complicated. Some of your assets might be unavailable for reinvestment. For example, if your retirement program does not have a loan program attached, those assets are tied up until you reach age 59? Withdrawing retirement savings prematurely subjects the taxpayer to a 10-percent penalty and the withdrawal amount is included in ordinary income for tax purposes. It would take a rather large rate of return to make the alternative investment worth the withdrawal. So to determine exactly what you have available for investment purposes, subtract those restricted retirement savings. What's left is your capacity for acquiring investment real estate.

The resulting numbers here don't have to be great for you to get into the investment real estate game. With as little as $12,000 to $15,000, you can control a modest yet potentially lucrative investment or vacation property in Mexico. It may not be your absolute dream home, but it can get you in the door somewhere south of the border. Once you acquire the property, the actual cash flow cost to you should be relatively low. Rental income will help offset the monthly costs (including mortgage payment).

The second method to determine your capacity to buy Mexican real estate is the income method. This uses cash flow, rather than net worth, as the deciding variable. Once again, it requires offsetting positives and negatives. Calculate all your monthly obligations—mortgage and other loan payments, credit card debt, tuition payments, etc.—and subtract them from your monthly income. We'll call this discretionary net income, and it is the amount that is available to handle the cost of carrying the property. As mentioned, rental income will cover a good part (hopefully all) of the negative cash flow. The ability of your discretionary net income to support an investment property is substantial because of the initial unknowns about the amount of the time the property will be rented. To prove this to yourself, try a little exercise. Look on the Internet or contact a Realtor specializing in Mexican property (see Appendix), and research prices in your targeted area. Now calculate the gross cost of owning that property. This will include the mortgage (pick your own downpayment), perhaps a property management fee (10 to 15 percent of the monthly rent) and some amount for replacing house components like plumbing, electricity, roofing, siding and other depreciable items.

When you've calculated this figure, ask Realtors and present owners what you could expect to receive in monthly rent—especially if you are going to rely on rental income to make your plan work. If it's strictly for investment, it's critical to determine how often and for how long you intend to rent it. Decrease this number by 10 percent to account for likely vacancies. Compare the estimated rental income with the gross cost of owning, and the balance will either be the net cash flow to you or the amount you need to supply to carry the property. Remember that this is a cash flow number and ignores the tax benefits of owning investment real estate.

If you are thinking of eventually living in the house full-time, consider both your and the renter's preferences. What do renters really want? In a capsule, they typically value convenience to water, transportation and entertainment more than space and landscaping. Choose a property that will appeal to the renter, not to you, if the rental use will absolutely come first in your master plan. Decorate the property to accommodate common tastes, not necessarily yours. Furniture will rub against walls, so use heavy paint that really covers. Appliances will get more than usual wear, so buy those that are reliable.

If you choose a location, you also probably have envisioned your target renter. The next question is what type of property you will look for or build. This is a decision similar to location but focuses more on the configuration of the actual dwelling rather than the neighborhood in which it is located. The number and types of bedrooms, the size of the lot and other amenities all will factor into your decision as to the specific property to buy.

Besides looking at the location of the property relative to water, shopping and entertainment, your target renter will be more attracted to a home that suits his or her needs. If you seek families, then a quieter, more spacious property convenient to the pool or beach will be best. Where you are renting to groups of unrelated adults, think about family reunions—multiple bathrooms and larger bedrooms are a must.

With this background, you will be able to choose a property that will be in high demand by potential tenants.

Two suggestions:

- Ask other investors and real estate professionals about the demographics of the rental market. Who will make up the next great wave?

- Talk to resort and vacation community managers about the types of renters who enjoy that community.

Time to drill down on finances

Unless you bring a good business sense and a sharp pencil to your Mexican investment, you'll spend many sleepless hours wondering why you ever did this and feeling worse because your getaway is not exactly around the corner! Before you make your investment in Mexico, you need to be honest with yourself. It's time to roll the dice and discover whether this potential financial move will end up benefiting your wealth or whether you would be better off holding the cash in a certificate of deposit. If you can't afford to be in the deal for personal use only, follow these steps:

Calculate the total cost of the investment. This cost consists of the downpayment on the property, the settlement costs of the transaction and the interest foregone because you chose to buy this property rather than invest in something else. The two most common omissions here are to forget the settlement costs and to ignore the opportunities that might have been seized if you had not chosen to invest in real estate. Settlement costs can be more than expected, so get a real figure early in the negotiations. The proper measure of the opportunity cost is the rate of return on some low-risk security like a Treasury Bond.

Figure an estimate of the monthly cost of owning and maintaining the property. This includes the monthly mortgage payment—including the payment on your home equity line of credit if this is how you are financing the downpayment and monthly maintenance, such as utilities and repairs. If you make any major alterations or repairs on the property, you can spread the costs over a number of years, but you should include some monthly charge to your costs of ownership.

Determine the rent that you can reasonably expect to charge in your market. This can be determined by reference to other properties being rented in the area. The help of a real estate agent will be valuable here. As mentioned, the rent you charge should at least cover the cost of owning and maintaining the house. But you're not going to get this rent every single month. There will be gaps between tenants, and some tenants will miss a month or pay late. Because the house will go through periods of vacancy, you need to adjust your rental income estimates to reflect these gaps. Doing so allows you to more accurately project your cash flow. After all, you are not buying the house to lose money.

Estimate the price at which you will sell the property. This is tricky because real estate markets boom and slump with regularity. You have no way of knowing what the condition of the market will be when you plan to sell. The key here is flexibility—you can usually wait and continue renting the place out until the market rebounds before selling.

Factor in the tax consequences of your investment. The tax laws favor investment in real estate. Interest paid to finance the purchase of real estate is deductible against income, and major repairs or renovations that enhance the attractiveness of the property to potential renters can be amortized over a number of years and deducted from income as an expense.

All of these positives and negatives will net out to the expected return on your investment in Mexico. Remember, your numbers need to be adjusted for the time value of money—a dollar given away today is worth less than a dollar returned tomorrow. Inflation reduces the buying power of money because you forego the use of that money. If you don't adjust for the time value of money, your estimates of the return from your investment will be biased upward. Check with an accounting professional to find the right way to factor in the time value of money.

A tool to help compare properties

There are two keys to finding an investment property that will at least track the market. First, after you choose an investment area using the criteria listed in Chapter 6, find a property for sale whose price is lower than the average price for the entire neighborhood. These properties have the greatest potential for appreciation. In most housing markets, all the units in a given area will eventually move toward the average, so the lower-priced comparable units will be the ones most likely to appreciate the most. Granted, these houses might be underpriced because they need some work, but ultimately, they will pay off. Problem developments and condominium buildings/associations can also skew the norm.

Professor Edward Leamer at UCLA developed a creative gauge that can help you evaluate different properties for their appreciation potential. It is a variation on how stocks are evaluated. When analysts look at stocks, they often focus on the price-earnings ratio as a measure of whether the stock is overvalued or undervalued. The higher the number (especially relative to either the market as a whole or to historical averages), the more likely the stock is to decline in price over time. For example, when technology stocks were the place to be in the 1990s, most of them not only had high price-earnings ratios relative to more traditional stocks but also were trading at extraordinarily high price-earnings ratios. Consequently, the "tech wreck" really came as no surprise.

What Leamer proposed was to view real estate in a similar light. In this case, though, the ratio is the price of the investment property to the annual rental it will earn. This calculation will give you a standard by which you can judge the relative potential for appreciation of different properties in different neighborhoods and even in different cities. In other words, it helps to make sound investment decisions by giving you a tool to measure alternative investments against each other. Here's how it works:

Plan A: Suppose you're looking at a $255,000 property that will rent for $1,500 per month, or $18,000 per year. (We can assume there is no vacancy period, but you can figure in whatever you deem to be a reasonable.) You are also looking at a $120,000 property that will rent for $850 per month, or

$10,200 per year. The price-earning ratio for the first property is approximately 14 (255 divided by 18), and the second is approximately 12 (120 divided by 10.2). The second property appears to be a better candidate for appreciation since it has the lower price-earnings ratio.

Plan B: For a truly effective comparison of the two properties, you need to make a second calculation. You need to look at the price-earning ratio average for both properties relative to those properties in the same neighborhood. If the ratio for the neighborhood of the first house is 20 while the ratio for the second house is 10, then the first property might be the better buy. It is underpriced relative to its surroundings, while the second property is overpriced.

Although all this might appear complex, it's really quite simple. After all, you already know the prices being asked for the properties you are evaluating, and you should know what rent you can charge once you own them. All that's needed is to find out the averages for prices and rents in the immediate neighborhood, and you're done. Any local real estate agent or property manager should be able to help you out with these two numbers. This is a helpful process to go through if you want to choose a property that will propel you to financial success.

The second strategy for finding the most promising investment property is to look for the next hot vacation spot. Some savvy investors simply have followed in the path of large, proven developers who have been extremely successful in other areas. How do you find them? There are several ways to determine the next booming area:

Ask the professionals. As we've stated many times, the people who best understand the housing market are those who are in it every day and who depend on it for their livelihood. If you are interested in where prices will rise the most or where the best rental property buys are in your area, seek out Realtors, developers, builders and city planners. They have a feel for the market and will be able to point you in the direction of the bargains. Try this. Interview a number of the top people in each of these fields and ask them about the future of the community. Try to understand who is now living in the community and whom they think will be living in the community in the near future. Find out which neighborhoods they think are the best values and which neighborhoods will be boosted by the development going on in the community. From their answers, you should be able to form a clear picture of where the opportunities for investment are in your area.

Opportunity can come from destruction. What is being torn down in the area that will soon rise anew? Can you buy in this area and perform your own work with the help of local laborers? Often, you can recruit workers from a big contractor's project to work overtime on your project.

Read the local brochures. Not all information is in Spanish. Promotional material, news circulars and community associations have newsletters and bulletins that contain real estate information and potential projects that could affect the value of housing.

Visit the building department. English-speaking officials often are found in local jurisdictions because so many American and Canadian developers are now active in Mexico. Ask what major employment, transportation or development projects are on the drawing board. Is the municipality using federal money to place new facilities? When will these come on line and begin to change the location of jobs and residences?

The bottom line is a delicate balance

Harmonizing what you want with what you can afford can be a delicate, sticky balance. It's human nature for our wants to exceed our capabilities, so you will probably never get all you desire. The key to integrating needs and wants is to organize your goal in two different time frames. The first time frame is your best future prediction. Will the place you want buy now be the same place 20 years from now? Will you seek a different beach or neighborhood? What does your Mexican getaway look like down the road? This involves envisioning in great detail the retreat where you will spend your leisure time when you retire from the conventional nine-to-five world. (Is there anybody who *really* still works nine to five?) The more detail you can gather about this place, the greater will be the chance that you will attain your dream—or something in the neighborhood.

The second time frame is the present. For many consumers, the first investment/vacation home they purchase will be the one they keep down the road. No stepping-stone moves to see if the grass is greener—or the ocean warmer. If you have not purchased in Mexico, the starting point is right here. Ask yourself, which area—at least at this time—do you believe would be best for you? Will the place hold mostly renters in the first five years? What assets would you use to get you there? What can you do now to begin to move toward that goal? If you are currently an investor, in Mexico or elsewhere, the solution may be how can I leverage/sell property to move closer to my Mexican vision of the future? The answers will be in terms of a particular property, a plan for the property and a strategy to acquire and hold it. You should keep asking yourself that question on a regular basis. Asking will keep you on the path toward your goal.

In Chapter 8, we suggest some questions to help flush out where you really want to be.

CHAPTER EIGHT

Critical Choice: Tips on Selecting a Location

Common, specific ideas for family, renters, retirement

The best way to choose a community in which to purchase a Mexican getaway is to begin with yourself and your family. You need to know what you want before you can determine where to look. Where do you see yourself ultimately spending the majority of your leisure time? Right now, what would be your best guess even though you cannot be absolutely certain? Work your way through the following process:

How much do we intend to use this home? You have several options with Mexican property: Use it in peak season to maximize personal enjoyment or use it in the off-season to maximize financial gain. If your intent is to use the property for only specific weeks of the year, travel time becomes a significant factor.

What do you do to unwind? No vacation home will be enjoyable if members of the family cannot do what they find enjoyable. Dad's desire to sit on a remote beach and fish may not suit the adult children's desire for nightlife. Before you make any exploration of Mexican home possibilities, come to a clear understanding of what type of atmosphere, amenities and facilities the whole group wants.

Don't bank on a nostalgia trip. If you spent many happy hours on vacation with your family in a particular spot, you might want to return there and buy a home in the same location. This is a legitimate wish but you should consider how important this is to you. Sometimes, you can't go home again. Prices have risen, congestion increased and many of the things you fondly remember have disappeared. More importantly, your memories are not necessarily shared by those around you. If the vacation home is to provide satisfaction, it must meet the needs of the whole household. Even a seemingly familiar place requires investigation before you seek to relive old memories. Don't let nostalgia for the past come before the more important considerations of the present, where you live.

How long will you own this home? Plan ahead. If you want to hold this place for the long-term, think about how the preferences and needs of family members will change over time. Kids grow up, and the desire for play space evolves into the need to be with their peers. The young and vigorous will age and slow down. Things that you could once do, may now become difficult. Any successful vacation home choice will reflect a desired holding period. One that stays in the family for generations is of necessity flexible both in terms of its physical capacity and its access to recreational activities. A vacation home that will be sold in a few years must satisfy the investment criteria defined above.

The next step is to look at some specific communities and some specific properties. There are three important considerations in this process.

Go where you've been. Think about places you've visited, either on vacation or for other reasons, and that you think fit your vacation needs. This gives you a leg up because you have a working knowledge of the area, have some information to use in compiling its merits and demerits, and can get a good fix on costs (including travel time and expense) in having a vacation home there.

Visit again. This time, look at the whole community through the eyes of someone who will be part of it and not just a short-term visitor. It's important to visit during all the times you intend to be there. The lively winter, beachfront community might turn into a boring, deserted, dead summer town. The seasonal mood should match your needs, and you should visit often enough to be able to gauge those moods accurately.

Build a team. Mexico is not located just over the next hill. You will be buying a great distance from your principal residence. There are two good ways to identify a real estate agent to use. First, ask a Realtor in your own community or an acquaintance who has purchased in a Mexican locale for a referral. This avoids the shot-in-the-dark approach of simply looking up a real estate professional in the phone book. Alternatively, if you don't have a real estate professional that you can ask, use the

Internet. If you search on the areas of interest, you will find a number of real estate Web sites. You can then e-mail a series of questions that will constitute an interview to screen potential agents:

- How long have you been in business?

- How long have you been doing business in this market? (Obviously, experience is a big plus.)

- Have you had experience with buyers looking at vacation homes from a distance? (Specific familiarity with your type of need is important.)

- Can you give me the names of some of your past customers that I can call? (The agent should be more than willing to share this information with you.)

- Are you a member of a professional organization, like the National Association of Realtors or AMPI?

- What information will you require from me? (You might also want to ask how often your physical presence will be required.)

- What services do you offer? (You will be dealing at a distance, so an agent who offers all the services needed in the transaction will be more useful to you.)

- What is your usual pricing for an engagement like this? (Price is always the tiebreaker but should never be the prime consideration in a transaction of this magnitude.)

You can, of course, add to this list, but it does represent the basics of what you need to know before proceeding. Going through this process with a number of agents (three to five is usually the most efficient number) will help you find the best fit for your individual needs.

Put yourself in a renter's shoes

Even if you use a terrific real estate professional, and even if you think you know everything about the area, there are some very specific factors that you need to consider in choosing a location. Each of them can be resolved by answering a series of questions. Next, let's consider the factors, presented in order of importance from the viewpoint of the renter.

Access. The most attractive properties will be those that offer the best access to the things that renters value. For example, renters tend to want to be close to the beach, pool, golf course, recreation center or the famous amenity that brings the local area its reputation. So in evaluating a location for investment, ask (and answer) the following questions. You can score each answer on a scale of 1 to 5, and then compare total scores for each alternative property.

- How close is it to major recreational sites (beach, mountains, golf, etc.)?

- Is the property convenient to major transportation corridors? Consider both roads and public transportation.

- How convenient are shopping, amusements and recreation? Renters often use public space.

- Where is this property located in reference to employment and education centers? The closer the better.

Safety. In this environment, safety is a high priority for everyone. For renters, this is even truer than for owners. In part, this is because owners have more direct control over the security of their properties. Renters will rate alternative properties in part on the safety of the areas in which these properties are situated. So ask yourself the following questions that will rate the neighborhoods in which you seek to invest:

- What is the crime rate in your target location as opposed to the area as a whole?

- What security precautions have been taken at the property? As a related consideration, think about what you are willing to spend to increase the safety of the property after you acquire it.

- If the property is a condominium, is the community gated or the entrance tended?

Neighborhood quality. When there is pride in a community, the homes are well kept and inviting. Typically, where the community is strong, house values are high, and demand for living in the community is high, as well. Most people, renters included, want to live in vibrant, congenial place. If you are considering an investment property, the quality of the development is a very important factor. It will go far in helping you maintain strong cash flow and high appreciation on the property. The important factors are listed below.

If you are considering a single-family detached house, what percentage of the population owns in that neighborhood? Traditionally, high percentages of ownership are associated with better neighborhood quality.

- How strong are the neighborhood organizations? When a community is progressive, the residents will participate.

- Do the adjacent commercial areas in the community attract a large volume of street traffic? Busy areas are more vibrant, exciting and attractive; besides, they tend to be safer.

A peek at your retirement needs

According to the National Association of Realtors, approximately one-fifth of all second homeowners see the home as a potential retirement residence. If you are considering buying a home in Mexico that could turn into a retirement option, there are three considerations you should put on your list as you assess your options.

What is the quality of medical and social services in the area? As you age, you will come to rely more and more on the helping professions and your own mobility will diminish. Being close to good community hospitals, elder centers and recreational opportunities suitable to age becomes more important as time goes by.

Will the home age with you? Steps become a barrier as you get older, regular door openings are too narrow, regular countertops are too high for wheelchairs and regular wall studs are often too weak to hold grab bars. Before you decide on a house, inspect its construction carefully not just for now, but also for 20 or 30 years from now. We live longer these days, and you're likely to spend more time in that house than you think you will.

Can your friends and relatives or medical professionals reach you easily? The visits might be friendly and enjoyable, or they might be necessitated by a crisis, but they will come. Whether you want them to, as a break from the routine of the retirement community, or whether they have to, your friends and relatives will come more frequently if you live near a major airport or train station or bus station. When you select the home, evaluate it for convenience of access.

Many people might not be able to simply become second homeowners and slide down to their Mexican *hacienda* at the drop of a hat. For the first few years of ownership, it might be imperative to have renters help you with mortgage payments and maintenance fees. In the next chapter, we explore some methods of locating—and retaining—good renters.

CHAPTER NINE

Strategies to Find (and Keep) Good Renters

Start with relatives and friends, then fill in the blanks

Y ou have a wonderful, romantic, exotic product that consumers want. Your job is to inform the general public of the benefits this product offers to them. The basic objective is to match the needs of the renter to the features of your property in such a way that the property stays rented as long as you want it to be. In this chapter, we present marketing ideas that will help you achieve this goal. Just remember, you simply *cannot* attract rental business to your investment property unless that property is in the best condition it can be and shows as well as it can.

The best way to ensure your sanity, and your Mexican home's safety, is to first considering renting only to family, friends and neighbors. In a capsule, you *usually* get the renter you know and hopefully trust, who will give you less hassle and who is most likely to leave your getaway in the condition they found it. And they quickly become your best—and least expensive—marketing source.

Think about it: How many weeks do you realistically have available? Wouldn't you want to fill your available weeks with somebody that you know? Why rent to a stranger who has contacted you off the Internet when the Jacksons from the parish church, known for their altar-boy kids, would die to have the two weeks before Labor Day? Second home owners often underestimate the large pool of potential renters created by the number of neighbors and friends near their primary residence and second home. These two separate and independent areas often can produce more than enough folks to fill your rental calendar. And it's a huge advantage to have personally witnessed how potential renters keep their own home. You'll rest easier knowing they probably will keep your place in much the same condition that they keep their own home. Conversely, your visit to their home may be the primary reason *not* to rent to them!

Remember, friends know the going rate and usually *expect* to pay—so charge them. If your place clearly is on a resort's 50-yard line, has the best beach, kitchen area and beds, your friends and neighbors will be prepared to pay top dollar for your top spot. (Family sometimes can be a totally different matter, but....) If the getaway is in the middle of nowhere with no obvious amenities (besides serenity) and you have never rented it out, at least consider charging a price low enough to cover your utility and cleaning costs. If you are renting to someone you already know, one of the most important things to do is try and set/review some ground rules before they move in. Discuss any issues (periodic drinking water, best place to park the boat trailer, no lifeguard at the pool) that you think could arise while they occupy your place. Preparation always helps prevent some awkward situations down the road.

Marketing in your own backyard

You can reach plenty of potential renters by using local marketing techniques. The power of these is that they can be focused to have the greatest chance of reaching those whom you wish to attract. When you do advertise locally, be sure to list a phone number or e-mail address that you can use as a message drop, particularly if the rental market is tight. You might be deluged with unnecessary communications if you use your main numbers or addresses.

Consider the following local marketing techniques:

Bulletin boards. These are everywhere and they are very effective. To use them, create an attractive ad for your property. The ad should emphasize the advantages of location as well as the amenities of the property and should contain a color picture. All of this is quite inexpensive. Your cost consists of the time it takes you to compose the ad, the paper it is printed on and the time you need to post it. It helps if you have access to a digital camera, but given the power of the word-processing software that is standard on most personal computers, this is a relatively easy process (and you probably know a 10-year-old who can do it for you in minutes). Common locations:

Supermarkets. Everyone shops for groceries, so the audience here is composed of locals. This is a good place for ads about your vacation home because the family traffic here is strong. Given the volume of ads on supermarket bulletin boards, you might want to take care that your flyer stands out.

Coffee shops. These are today's town squares, and they serve the same gathering function. The crowd that loiters here tends to be younger, somewhere between college graduation and first-time home buyer, so the demographics are good for someone offering a place to rent.

Local government offices. You might want to investigate the possibility of using the bulletin board in your local housing office to advertise your rental property.

Merchandising circulars. The Penny Saver–type merchandising newspaper is everywhere. It reaches a geographically targeted audience and generally is read by people who are motivated to find something they need—a car, a boat or a Mexican rental. Unlike bulletin board ads, merchandising paper ads will cost you something, with the cost varying with the size of the ad and the length of time the paper carries the ad. Yet given the readership of these merchandising papers—interested in buying and local—this might be a very cost-efficient strategy. Finally, find out if the specialty real estate books that feature homes for sale and rent are open to advertising by individual property owners. These books are used primarily by large property owners and real estate professionals, so it might not happen, but it's worth a try.

Local newspapers. While readership is interested in nearby areas, ads for Mexican properties are very popular—especially in colder environs where residents constantly seek sunshine in winter.

Church bulletins. This is an old standby, and one glance will tell you about the concentration of real estate advertising in church bulletins. Marketing your property in the church bulletin gives you an automatic bona fide status with the readers. If you are advertising there, you must be like them, you must be honest and you must be good-hearted. Who wouldn't want you for a landlord? The bottom line here is that local advertising offers the opportunity of reaching high-probability prospects for very little cost. It's well worth thinking about.

The Internet. The Internet is particularly useful for vacation properties where the owner and customer are usually widely separated. It also gives your unit exposure all over the globe. Property owners like Christine Karpinski, author, teacher and vacation homeowner who wrote the bestselling book *How to Rent Vacation Properties by Owner*, swear by the Internet and say they would not be handling properties by themselves without it. "People new to Internet marketing are always concerned with problem renters," Karpinski says. "In my experience, I've learned that most people spending money for a nice place usually are not going to trash it. There are a lot more good people out there than bad, and you can take steps to eliminate the bad ones before they rent."

Internet advertising should be as painless as possible. You can easily create a website for your property. If you have the computer training (or know someone who does), it is a fairly simple proposition to craft the property page and then place it with any number of popular vacation sites. The "Big Four" vacation rental sites are VRBO (*www.vrbo.com)*, Great Rentals (*www.greatrentals.com*), A1Vacations (*www.a1vaactions.com*) and CyberRentals (*www.cyberRentals.com*). Each has its own major plusses. For example, CyberRentals will be happy to share all comments about a specific home.

Older snowbirds always seem to pitch in

Karpinski has been a consultant to owners of vacation rental properties for the past five years. Her helpful website, *www.HowtoRentbyOwner.com*, offers tips for renters as well. Some of her favorite clients are older homeowners who head south for the winter "snowbirds." Karpinski said a few of her clients are on set incomes and have set up monthly payment plans. They simply pay a little each month toward their next rental. That way, they can earmark an exact amount each month and don't have to pay one lump sum every year. Typically, the owner would require a reservation deposit, then the balance to be paid in one or two payments. (Most owners require full rent plus a deposit paid prior to the rental period. Payment methods vary, but most will take personal checks.)

"I love my snowbirds because many of them are so willing to help when little things go wrong," Karpinski said. "If they see something that needs attention, like a leaky faucet, they just do it. Unlike a family that's renting for a week at prime time, snowbirds are more flexible on their days of arriving and departing."

Satisfied renters will call back and tell their friends

No news here: The key to a successful, moneymaking second home is satisfied renters who want to return because of the special experience they enjoyed at your place. And if they were impressed with their time and accommodation, they are going to tell their friends and acquaintances. Although you often can't be there to place a rose in every room every time a new visitor arrives, make sure you, or your representative, take the time between cleanings to scoot back to your property and make certain your people are getting the kind of dwelling they will enjoy.

The goal is to provide a relaxing environment. Help ensure that goal is reached by investing in great bedding—especially in the largest, or parents', bedroom. Kids are resilient and can curl up in a sleeping bag in the most curious of places. But go out of your way to pamper, and even indirectly coddle, the people most likely to write the check. A great night's sleep brings people back. If they don't receive it, it's often downhill from there. They'll find fault with the inefficient corkscrew, comment on the poor water pressure or complain about getting a splinter while walking on the deck.

At least once or twice a year, put yourself in the renter's shoes. What would you expect to have in a vacation home at the rental price you are charging? When compared to your competition, are your rates fair and in line with the rest of the pack? When it pours rain for three straight days, is there enough to do to keep your renters from harming themselves? While cable television is the scourge of many vacation-bound parents, some owners have found cable has really made a difference for some of their customers. What could be done right away—perhaps deeper cleaning than you are getting from your service—that would make your stay more enjoyable? During the high season, what could you accomplish with $20, one helper (your loving husband?) and four hours dedicated to intense elbow grease? Be sensitive to smell, aware of color.

A couple of times a year, substitute the throw rugs in the kitchen with inexpensive, colorful new ones. Not only do they help give the home a clean and fresh look, but such moves show renters that you care about the condition of your home—and that you expect the same from them.

Top 10 tips to keep renters

Here's a quick honey-do list you can complete with that 20 bucks, one helper and four hours. Never underestimate the renter's first up-close look. Remember, these people are on vacation! Make it memorable from the start.

- Buy a welcome mat if you don't have one. This will save you time and effort cleaning interior rugs and also gives a good impression.

- Clean the front door and make sure the doorknob and lock work and look sharp. It's a pain to wrestle with a difficult lock in the dark.

- If the street numbers are dirty, paint or clean them. If you have a screen door, repair any holes in the screen and wipe the metal frame. Clean all cobwebs from the light fixtures and fingerprints from the entry.

- Don't make any side or backyard area the dumping ground just because most people probably will come and go from the front of the house.

- Make sure your shrubs don't look like grubs.
- Make sure your deck surface and is not slippery, sending a visitor for a surprise slide ride.
- Clean all kitchen appliances, and don't let the refrigerator resemble a bulletin board. Save the kid photos for home. Replace Teflon pans if the scratches resemble golf divots. Make sure drinking glasses shine.
- There should be no mold—anywhere—especially in the bathrooms. If necessary, replace the toilet seat.
- Find an easy, safe place to put keys while out of the house.
- Never apologize for the condition of your home. Offer a clean, comfortable home for rent and hope for the best.

Be clear on the terms of the rental

At the time of occupancy, tell the tenant in writing what your responsibilities and theirs are. You will be grateful later on if the tenant does something you forbade or doesn't do something you specified and a disagreement ensues. Unless you are clear at the outset who will do what, you open yourself up for a lot of headaches.

Use a printed lease, even if you're leasing your waterfront condo to a cousin. This might sound like a burden for you, but it will minimize the hassle of disputes that can resolve themselves into a "he said, she said" type of argument. Spell out all the terms that are important to you, such as:

- How much of a deposit is expected on the property? Usually, the landlord requires the first and last month's rent as well as some amount for damage.

- When and under what conditions will that deposit be returned or kept? Increasingly, the law requires landlords to hold the deposit in escrow and to return it with some form of interest accrual attached.

- When, where and how will the rent be paid? The last day or the first day of the month is traditional, but you need to specify whether that day is for postmark or for receipt. You might specify a grace period, but be specific as to how long and any penalties that will be incurred if the grace period is exceeded.

- Who will be responsible for utility hookups and payment? This can be either you or the tenant. Putting the account in your name ensures continuity of service when a tenant leaves. Because utilities are requiring large payments to reestablish service, continuity is a considerable benefit. Even though you will put some estimate of utility costs in the rent, having the account in your name puts you on the hook for more outlays, whether your tenant pays the rent or not.

- Can the tenant sublet the property? Subletting can reduce the gaps you might experience in tenancy, but it will also decrease your control over who is in the property.

- Will the property be furnished or unfurnished? This also includes the appliances that might be part of the lease and should specify the condition of the furnishings as agreed to by both owner and tenant.

- What restrictions will you impose on the use of the property? This will cover things like the number of adults who can live in the house, any pets that are allowed or banned or any age restrictions on occupancy. It can also cover whether the premises can be used for other than residential purposes.

There are three potential sources for a lease document. First, you can simply draw one up yourself or get a generic form on the Internet or at a stationary store. For most property owners who have a single investment property or whose needs are simple, this is the most cost-effective and efficient way of creating a lease document.

If you have a number of rental properties or if there are some complications attached, you might want to consult an attorney who will draw up the lease for you. In general, it is a good idea to talk with a real estate attorney before you launch into the investment just in case there are local ordinances that will affect your ability to rent your property or your flexibility in its use. For example, Florida imposes a tax on any rental of less than six months in duration, treating such rentals as the state treats hotel rooms. Using annual (or semiannual) leases will avoid that extra cost.

The third source of lease documents is the management company if you own an investment or vacation unit. In many cases, condos are built with the expectation that owners are investors and will seek to lease their property. Generally, the management company will use standard documents that cover all local death knell requirements.

If you have your mind made up to take on all management responsibilities, here are some steps to consider before making that commitment:

- Are you a people person? Do you have the time and patience to field inquiries and calls from potential applicants? Check the costs of hiring a local rental manager, who often arrives with solid, reliable leads. Good managers can be worth an entire season's commission by quickly handling an emergency.

- Don't sell in public. More people know about you and your home than you realize. Save conversations about your—and your renters'—comings and goings for the friendly confines of your home.

- Friends come first. They're usually good renters. Rent to friends (or friends of friends) you know. They'll usually treat your place with care—and often leave it in better condition than strangers.

- Off-limits space. Don't forget to keep a locked closet or storage area for your supplies and favorite possessions—like a prized water ski you want no one else using. It's also a good idea to load up on cozy comforts like large televisions with DVD and VCR, a top-of-the-line gas grill and all kitchen essentials. You want renters to return and nothing's a bigger turnoff than having only three plates and two forks.

- Bulk is best. Rent by the month or season. It will lessen cleaning and maintenance—and extend the life of your favorite throw rugs.

- Know the territory. Your group of luxury homes or condos may limit—or prohibit—renters. Research any association restrictions before you rent.

Owning Mexican real estate, or any investment real estate, is different from other investments in one very large way—it requires interaction with people. When you own a share of stock and its price falls, you don't need to confront your broker. You just dump the stock. With investment real estate, it's a different ballgame. We get to know the tenants, albeit sometimes only electronically. It's harder to simply cut and run because it requires that we confront a real human being. Hard decisions and difficult conversations are often necessary in the rental business, and property managers do this for a living. Remember, though, this service comes at a cost and you will need to factor that into the rent you charge.

Property managers: The *adiós* option

Perhaps you don't want to be in the marketing business. You bought your investment property as a source of income and capital appreciation, and you'd rather do the things you really enjoy. On your scale of pleasure, dealing with renters is not even on the radar. It is possible to hire someone to manage your property, market it, collect rents and arrange for necessary repairs.

Property managers are pretty easy to find. If you've purchased a Mexican home in a development, the management of that property will probably come along with the purchase. Either the developer will have an onsite manager, whose job it is to represent the owners in all these matters, or a local real estate firm will have the franchise on marketing and rental management for the development. In many cases, except for specific rentals that you would like to carve out (say for friends or relatives) and the time you will be using the property, you will be required to use the onsite property management.

For your individual full-time rental unit, you might want to hire your own manager. Realtors will be a good source for developing a list, or they may even handle the chores themselves. Be clear on the services that the property manager offers and the cost to you for these services. You should expect that the property manager will send the rents to your specified location (lock box, bank account, etc.) within a certain number of days of the rent due date and ensure the enforcement of any late penalties for unpaid rent. The manager should be available to tenants and responsive to their requests within a (short) specified time period. The manager should also maintain a reference file of reliable tradesmen who can be used to fix anything that goes wrong with the house. Check on references not only to assure yourself that this property manager is a reliable and effective one, but also that the property manager has the experience in managing your type of property—single-family house, high-rise or garden apartment, condo, high rent, low rent, etc.

This might not seem like marketing, but it actually is. Using a property manager can ensure that you have as few gaps as possible in the rental period for your house. For this peace of mind, you can expect to pay about 10 percent of the rent for the property management service, yet some larger firms demand a 50-50 split of all rental income.

CHAPTER TEN

Checking Out the Parcel for Purchase

The proper way to succeed is all about research

$\int$ everal years ago, there was an article in Arizona newspapers entitled "Bad Day at Rocky Point." It was a story detailing why U.S. citizens were unhappy that they had to pay significant sums of money to the Sonoran government and the Mexican developer of a well-known Rocky Point (Puerto Peñasco) subdivision in order to have legal "title" to their residences. In essence, they were being required to purchase the single-family lots they had leased in years past as part of the local governments attempt to bring the residential subdivision into mandated development law compliance. Potential homeowners simply could not understand why they had to buy the lots and establish Mexican bank trusts (*fideicomisos*) when they had been allowed to lease the lots and build their houses in years past.

In a nutshell, the Mexican developer had not complied with the established state government procedures for subdivision development, and as a result, foreign purchasers could not acquire legally recorded beneficiary interest on their residential properties. Unfortunately, this same issue has affected many other Arizona purchasers in other Sonoran projects and the problem continues today. Many Americans think our neighbors to the south just throw lots on the ground and start selling because "that's the way it's done in Mexico." Although that has been the case in some residential projects, it is not the fault of the Mexican system but of the developers and gullible, uninformed American purchasers. The "margarita syndrome"—or "trust me, everything will get done but it takes time in Mexico"—should not be used as a prudent basis of acquisition by foreign buyers. Mexico is not unlike the United States (or Arizona for that matter) when it comes to the development of real estate. There is formality in law, approval of intended development and requirements of compliance with authorization by local municipalities and the state government. In order to be more informed, and to avoid future acquisition nightmares, it is critical to know and understand in particular what the specific state government of Mexico mandates for the development of residential subdivisions.

Types of property and how to divide them

Under Article 27 of the Mexican Constitution, there are three recognized property types in the country: private, social and public property. In 1976, the government of Mexico established the Human Settlement Law for the regularization of land development and, in essence, to eliminate property development chaos. Each state in Mexico has its own development law and subsequent requirements. In the case of Sonora, there is the Law of Urban Development for the State of Sonora (*La Ley de Desarrollo Urbano Para el Estado de Sonora*). It is commonly referred to as Urban Development Law 101. The procedure to authorize the development of a subdivision (*fraccionamiento*) is specified by the Office of Urban Administration, Secretary of Urban Infrastructure and Ecology for the State Government of Sonora (*Direccion de Administracion Urbana, Secretaria de Infraestructura Urbana y Ecologia*, [SIUE], *Gobierno del Estado de Sonora*). Typically, the process to receive approval for an intended residential subdivision is as follows.

Initially, the developer must take the necessary steps to obtain a land use license from the city council (*ayuntamiento*) or local municipal authority. This process includes (1) submission of an environmental impact study on the land to be developed, (2) deeds of ownership on the property (*escrituras*), (3) a land plan of the tract, and (4) a location map of the overall property. The developer must also submit a draft or blueprint (*anteproyecto*) of the proposed development.

The city council will then present the draft of the proposed project along with the land use certificate, deeds, location map and land use plan, including a layout of the lots and blocks of the subdivision to SIUE. At the same time, the city council or municipality will facilitate and obtain the feasibility of potable water service, drainage and electrical service for the proposed subdivision from the appropriate municipal agencies by presenting the land use license and the land plan of lots and blocks to the respective authorities. The developer will then receive initial approval for the intended subdivision from the city council or municipality.

Once initial authorization is granted, the developer must submit a formal executive development plan and all required documents to the city council or municipality according to Article 129 of Urban Development Law 101 of Sonora. The local authorities will present the project again to SIUE with the calculations of water and sewer use for review, revision and approval. Additionally, the municipality will submit the calculations for electrical usage and street lighting to Mexico's Federal Electricity Commission (*Comision Federal de Electricidad*) for their possible revision and subsequent approval.

After a satisfactory review of the general project plan by the authorities, the developer will be authorized by way of formal agreement with the municipal president or mayor that will establish the obligations and the time period required to complete the proposed subdivision. After the developer donates 15 percent of the overall land as required to the local municipality (which is generally utilized for common areas, green belts and/or schools) and pays the development fees as mandated, they must publish the subdivision approval in the *boletín oficial* (official bulletin). The *boletín* gives the public notification and government approval of the intended development. Finally, the developer must record the agreement in the Public Registry of Property along with the unilateral declarations of intention to develop the property with copies going to the local tax assessor office, the treasury department and SIUE.

Residential development in most of Mexico has made a significant change for the better. No longer are most developers starting subdivisions without first obtaining the necessary approvals. Some have even gone to the point of having complete authorization and publication of the intended project prior to beginning their lot sale process (lots cannot be conveyed to foreign purchasers until bank trusts can be obtained). And although development considerations continue to improve in Mexico, a prudent and informed buyer knows what to look for in residential acquisitions. There should never be any reason why a buyer does not ask certain basic questions that can provide more comfort and security when contemplating a residential purchase.

In short, ask the developer if the subdivision in question is approved and ask for a copy of the published authorization. Also ask if the property (lot or residence) will be conveyed to a *fideicomiso* at the time of sale. If not, inquire as to why and try to better understand the outstanding development issues that may exist on the subdivision. In the end, you'll appreciate the peace of mind that comes with knowing you bought a "legal" piece of Mexican real estate and not being in the uneasy situation of wondering when you'll acquire good and enforceable title. Insure your Mexican property with a title policy just like you would in the United States and always consult competent legal counsel on any real estate acquisition.

Speaking of subdivisions, the folks around Rocky Point for years had been dreaming of a first-ever golf course in the nearby sand dunes. Not just any golf course, but a Jack Nicklaus *signature* golf course. Rumor had it that the course would be developed and irrigated with brackish water, a design concept utilizing grass that grows when salt water is combined with fresh water. Visitors agreed that golf would be a real boon to Rocky Point, but no one banked on it happening. Well, it's no longer a developer's hope and dream; a Nicklaus signature golf course has become a reality.

Nine of the 18 holes on this championship layout are surrounded by a beautifully iridescent green water lagoon, a virtual island. The golf course is part of the Laguna del Mar gated master-planned residential community. The development, offering condominiums and single-family lots, is an amazing design achievement with its location adjacent to the estuary, giving Laguna del Mar a natural and stunning ambiance of interconnected lagunas, palm trees, tropical vegetation and flowers. The Phoenix developers have been successful in "raising the bar" for new planned communities in Rocky Point. They have defied the naysayers who said that a golf course could never be built because "grass won't grow in the sand." Laguna del Mar has come to Peñasco; it has real grass and it's actually green—unlike some other courses south of the border.

Other residential projects are also doing well—just check the building activity on Sandy Beach. Condominium sales continue to break records with five major projects having been started in the last few years. The Princesa, Sonoran Spa, Sonoran Sea, Las Palmas, Casa Blanca Golf Villas and Bella Sirena have gone from the drawing board to the beach in a hurry in an attempt to capture the pent-up demand for second homes and weekend rentals. The present success has sparked the interest of more developers and new condo projects are in the planning stages. Costa Diamante, the residential subdivision on Sandy Beach, has enjoyed active lot sales for several years and its developers are looking for new parcels to consider. Commercial land sold for retail development has also had a significant impact on the Sandy Beach area.

What is most encouraging about the Puerto Peñasco market are the recent settlements in longstanding land disputes and court battles involving protracted litigation. Other Rocky Point developments have also ended their conflicts between U.S. buyers and the developers. The market still is not perfect (and there are still legal issues to be resolved), but the overall landscape has improved dramatically over the past three years and gets better each day. Case in point would be the Las Conchas subdivision that is finally being properly entitled to many Arizona purchasers. With the litigation resolved, many buyers can now get their *fideicomisos* (bank trusts) established after waiting for more than 10 years. Likewise, an agreement has been reached for the benefit of the Playa Dorada homeowners involving the Playa Norte (North Beach) development where the purchasers also will receive their bank trusts. The Miramar subdivision, which has been entitled as an *ejido*, has now been privatized and the title is vested in a master bank trust.

Homeowners and lot purchasers in Miramar will finally be able to receive their *fideicomisos* as well. Unfortunately, it has taken well over five years to get to a point of resolution. Even the condominiums at El Pinacate, next to the Plaza Las Glorias Hotel, are in the process of entitlement to establish a protocolized beneficiary interest for each of the foreign buyers, the majority being from Arizona. Each deed or *escritura publica* will be recorded in Puerto Peñasco's Public Registry of Property and Commerce.

But what happens to buyers when the developers don't adhere to mandated development law in the State of Sonora, or in any Mexican state for that matter, where purchasers cannot establish Mexican bank trusts for residential properties in the restricted zone? The answer is very simple: Purchasers pay money for real estate they don't get title to at the time of payment or closing. It has happened for years in Rocky Point. The good news is that this situation is changing rapidly. Why? Because foreigners are better informed, better educated and have a greater knowledge of Mexico's real estate conveyance issues. They are no longer willing to accept that tired adage of "Mexico's different, that's the way we do business here, trust us."

Puerto Peñasco now publishes a list of subdivisions and condominium projects that are completely approved, those in process of approval and those that have no approvals at all. Couple this information with the work of the Real Estate Task Force on Mexico, the creation of an MultiList Service system as well as a AMPI chapter for Rocky Point, and it adds to a combined effort to raise the level of professionalism, disclosure, awareness and ethics in the real estate market. Companies like Coldwell Banker, First Mexican Investments, Twin Dolphins Real Estate and Sandy Beach Resorts have made significant strides in how they transact sales with a greater level of disclosure. Overall, the market continues to improve and it should. Everyone has a right to buy real estate that is a safe and secure investment they can enjoy and feel confident in owning.

CHAPTER ELEVEN

Third-Party Escrow Is a Wise, Efficient Option

Steering the deal away from the seller and his or her agent

Money, and the possession or deposit of it into "broker escrow accounts," has historically been the downfall of many alleged competent real estate professionals. Real estate agents and companies have literally been run out of town for abusing funds in broker escrow accounts. To help curtail this type of abuse, real estate practitioners in the United States now must complete state-mandated educational requirements and testing competency to obtain a real estate salesman license. At the forefront of any real estate school's education curriculum is the emphatic and stringent requirement that agents cannot and should not "co-mingle" purchasers' earnest money deposits in broker accounts. If there has ever been one real estate concept that can have catastrophic consequences to all parties involved, it is not handling a purchaser's deposit in a safe, secure and accountable manner with the implicit understanding that there is a "fiduciary" obligation to safeguard the buyer's money...always.

It has long been preached about Mexico that if a purchaser is willing to give money to the seller or the agent in a real estate acquisition, be prepared not to get it back. Unfortunately, it is a sad reality that has reared its ugly head in more than one place south of the border. Purchasers in a particular Mexico market deposited funds in good faith and entrusted the cash to the agent's broker trust account. (One would think that the term "trust" would imply some sort of confidence and security in the deposit vehicle, yet in this case, it was an oxymoron.) The stark reality is that the money, more than a tidy sum, is gone. The agent is gone as well, having fled Mexico and leaving these unprotected "good faith" buyers to ponder what now. Their sole remedy and recourse was to file complaints with Mexico's consumer protection agency, PROFECO (*Procuraduría Federal de Consumidor*). However, the likelihood that any of them will recover any of their money is slim to none—and Slim already left Mexico!

The alternative to broker escrows or giving money to the seller is to utilize third-party escrow accounts. Some Mexican banks will handle deposits for real estate transactions, charging an escrow fee of approximately $450 to $500. There are, however, several drawbacks to Mexican bank escrow accounts. First and foremost is that Mexican banks do not utilize formalized escrow agreements that have been negotiated and executed per mutual agreement between the seller and the buyer and additionally signed with acknowledgement by the bank as agent. Mexican banks simply hold the money until notification to release it. They traditionally do not invest the money into interest-bearing accounts for the benefit of the depositor. It has also been the practice of the banks to use the funds internally. The end result is that the subsequent refund or transfer of the deposited amount is not readily available nor is it handled in a timely and expeditious manner.

As discussed previously, the best and most favorable manner to handle earnest money and escrow deposits involving Mexican real property transactions is with a U.S. title insurance company that has a fiduciary obligation and responsibility as the escrow agent. Some agents and developers in Mexico do not like to utilize escrow accounts in the United States for one simple reason—the agents and developers do not control the money. Understanding that there is a total lack of construction financing in Mexico, an overall level of illiquidity in lending of any type and the subsequent upfront deposits required by many developers to begin construction notwithstanding, there is still no reason why third-party escrows should not be used to protect the foreign buying public. The prevailing concept of "passing the money" when the seller and buyer enter into a promissory agreement is antiquated, self-serving and at best a huge risk for purchasers. As in the United States, consideration of the purchase price due—less any earnest money deposit— should be paid when a buyer is able to receive a protocolized deed by the *notario publico* and at the transfer of the real property interest. It should not be when the buyer can get the keys to the condo or "possession" of it.

The ultimate benefit of third-party escrow is the basic fact that an escrow agreement exists, fully negotiated and mutually agreed upon between the seller and the buyer. It is a "stand-alone" document that instructs the escrow agent precisely in the manner in which the escrowed funds are to be deposited, handled and ultimately disbursed. The escrow agent is bound to the stated terms of the agreement and has a fiduciary obligation to follow the letter of the agreement. It is not subject to interpretation or conjecture, nor is the escrow agent required to interpret how money will be handled per a purchase contract. Moreover, the escrow deposit can be put in a federally insured depository with the establishment of a money market interest-bearing account. The subsequent accrued interest can be designated for the benefit of the seller or the buyer. But at all times, the parties know where the money is. It is verifiable once the account has been opened and it is always referenced directly to a guaranty file as maintained by the escrow agent with full disclosure of all salient facts and account numbers. If a dispute arises between the parties concerning the disposition of the escrowed funds, the escrow agent may "interplead" the funds with a court of competent jurisdiction. But at no time will the money be released to anyone without the written mutual consent of the parties.

Tips, terms and common practices

Licensing laws. At this time, there are no government license laws regulating real estate brokerage and sales in Mexico. Just about anybody can offer properties for sale. However, the states of Sonora, Sinaloa and Guanajuato require the registration of real estate practitioners. Agents working with clients in those states should verify local requirements for specifics. In addition, the Mexican Association of Real Estate Professionals

(AMPI) has developed a Code of Ethics that must be observed by all members of that organization. Violation of the provisions may result in (1) a warning, (2) an admonition, (3) the temporary suspension of rights, or (4) expulsion from the association. An Honor and Justice Commission oversees compliance. Non-Mexicans must obtain an immigration status permitting them to work in the field. This status could be a business visa for single transactions or the FM-3 (nonresident) or FM-2 (resident) status. Mexican consulates in the United States and Canada can provide further information about the requirements for each different status.

No minimum educational requirements are in place, although AMPI has signed agreements with the Normalization and Certification Board of Labor Competency (CONOCER), which establishes criteria and tests basic proficiency in the subject matter. This is a new program that is being tested in Monterrey, Mexico, and may be extended to the rest of the country. Research and then ask questions of other professionals to find an established and reputable real estate company. A potential buyer may want to check with local chambers of commerce or prominent law firms regarding the reputation of a potential agent.

Typical broker activity. Most real estate transactions are "opened" after a written purchase offer is accepted by the seller and when a purchase-sale agreement (promissory contract) is signed by both parties. In most cases, a deposit is required by the broker in order to transmit the offer to the seller. If the transaction is being conducted directly with the seller, it is highly recommended that a real estate broker or a lawyer be consulted before signing any papers or handing over any money. In some areas it is common practice to deliver to the seller, as an advance payment, the equivalent of 20 to 50 percent (including the initial deposit) of the total price upon signing the purchase-sale agreement that should contain a penalty clause applicable in case there is a breach of contract by any of the parties. Normally, when signing the *escritura,* or official deed, which needs to be certified by a *notario publico,* or notary public, the balance is paid and the property is delivered. This should not take more than 45 days.

In certain resort areas the custom of using escrows is being implemented. According to AMPI, brokerage activity typically involves showing the property, loan origination activities, advertising property, preparation of legal contracts, negotiating the sale, income analysis where appropriate, selling title insurance and ancillary activities. A major difference from the United States process is the significant role of the notary, who plays a major role in the transaction.

Notary. The notary public is a government-appointed lawyer who processes and certifies all real estate transactions, including the drawing and review of all real estate closing documents, thus insuring their proper transfer. All powers of attorney, the formation of corporations, wills, official witnessing, etc., are handled and duly registered through the offices of the notary public, who is also responsible to the government for the collection of all taxes involved. In connection to real estate transactions, the notary public, upon request, receives the following official documents, which by law are required for any transfer:

- A nonlien certificate from the Public Property Registry based on a complete title search.

- A statement from the treasury or municipality regarding property assessments, water bills and other pertinent taxes that might be due.

- An appraisal of the property for tax purposes.

MultiList Service. A few electronic similar to the multiple listing services in the U.S. (MLSs) are now operating in Mexico. This service will soon be widely offered with state-of-the-art technology measuring up to the highest standards found in the United States.

National Association of Realtors (NAR) affiliate. The only national professional real estate organization in Mexico is AMPI, with 24 chapters in 398 cities. The organization is somewhat similar in organization to the NAR in the United States, and in fact, has a reciprocal cooperating agreement with NAR.

How they differ: Mexico–U.S. transactions

Closing costs. It is common practice that the buyer pays the transfer or acquisition tax as well as all other closing costs including the notary fees and expenses, and the seller pays capital gains tax and the broker's commission. Since January 1, 1996, the federal law regarding the real estate transfer tax, which was 2 percent for the entire Republic of Mexico, was modified to allow each of the Mexican states to determine its own tax. The range may be from 1 to 4 percent of the tax appraisal value, generally less than the sales value. The rest of the closing costs, which exclude the transfer cost mentioned above, may vary from 3 percent to 5 percent of the appraised tax value or more, depending on the particular state. These percentages are applied to the highest value of the following: the amount for which the property is sold, the value of the official tax appraisal or the value designated by the property assessment authorities.

Cost of the real estate trusts. Based on the present tariff, the bank charges the person desiring to set up a real estate trust, or *fideicomiso*, an initial fee of approximately $500 for drawing up the original trust agreement and establishing a trust, plus a percentage according to the value of the property. In addition, the bank charges an annual fee, depending on the value of the property, to cover its services as a trustee.

Escrow, title insurance and home insurance. It is the notary public who, in effect, acts as a "holding agent" for the involved parties, and for this reason, there are few escrow companies in Mexico. At present there is no general use of title insurance in Mexico, although some American companies are providing coverage in some resort areas of the country. But insurance companies do provide full home coverage throughout Mexico.

Real estate broker's commission. Most real estate companies in Mexico charge a commission of 5 to 7 percent based on the actual sales price of the property. However, different area broker rates reflecting higher broker expenses may be found, such as in resort areas. Some franchises such as Century 21, Realty World and ReMax encourage transnational referrals but success is limited since many Mexican practitioners are not yet accustomed to representing different parties and sharing commissions.

Capital gains taxes. In Mexico the concept of capital gains tax does not apply in the sense in which it is understood in the United States. The gain from the sale of property is considered as normal income at a tax rate of up to 35 percent. In order to determine the gain, the following costs and expenses are deducted from the amount for which the property is officially sold:

- Original land cost and depreciated construction cost, based on the number of years the property was held and adjusted for inflation according to the official consumer price indexes.

- Additions, modifications and improvements, but not maintenance, made on the property (construction), adjusted as described for inflation.

- Commissions paid to real estate brokers by the seller.

- Closing costs, including all expenses, taxes and fees paid by the seller.

The notary retains the calculated gain after making appropriate deductions and forwards it to the Mexican tax authorities. The seller then deducts this amount from his annual tax return, which becomes an adjustable tax credit in the case of persons filing U.S. tax returns. On the other hand, there is no capital gains tax in Mexico if there is conclusive proof the seller has had the property as his or her primary residence for the previous two years.

CHAPTER TWELVE

The Strongest Link
to a Peaceful Mind

U.S. title companies bring new coverage and assurance

The real property conveyance process in Mexico, like any other civil code system in South and Central America and many other countries in the world, is reliant upon individuals to transfer ownership rights. These highly educated and "hand-picked" public notaries have the obligation, right and privilege to consummate all real estate transactions within their given territorial jurisdiction. Their acknowledgment and certification procedure provides "judicial certainty" to the authenticity of the process. With this process in place, Mexico can be said to have a good land conveyance system. However, one must never lose sight of the fact that it is a system reliant on the performance of various people, not just the public notary. Sellers, buyers, agents, surveyors, property recorders and municipal employees all come into the mix. And as we have all learned throughout the annals of time, human beings, though not intending to do so, do make mistakes. Errors are made; individuals are not infallible.

In real estate matters, though, mistakes can be costly and create significant losses. For that reason alone, reliance upon a monetary indemnification that guarantees remuneration in the event of loss because of a title defect or error is a must. Suing the seller to recover property or money, whether in the United States or in a foreign jurisdiction, is a difficult, expensive, anxious and time-consuming alternative to the viability of title insurance.

Title insurance on Mexican real estate is more than just a title insurance policy. It is an in-depth examination concerning title documents and the real estate closing process. In order to issue an Owner's Policy of Title Insurance and assume the inherent monetary liability that comes with the policy issuance, the insuring company must be as certain as possible regarding all of the various elements in the property transfer.

The service and function of the title insurance company is to eliminate risk by examining all of the relevant issues available. When a policy is purchased, a title insurance company's job is to help inform both buyer and seller of the relevant concerns that may be outstanding or in process prior to the consummation of the property conveyance.

This type of investigation coupled with financial indemnification gives the non-Mexican purchaser of real estate comfort and security knowing that a U.S. company with credibility and decades of expertise has examined all of the title matters and issues a title policy. When compared to the other closing costs associated with real property conveyances in Mexico, i.e., transfer taxes and notary fees, an Owner's Policy of Title Insurance will be one of the least expensive and most important.

What about the *notario publico*?

It is often said that it is the responsibility of the *notarios* to provide title assurance and that they have the same requirement of certification as a title insurance company. That is true. However, it is not often understood that, in Mexico, a title policy not only protects against liens, encumbrances and tax issues, but also against fraud, misrepresentation, impersonation, secret marriages, incapacity of parties, undisclosed heirs and other hidden risk as provided by the policy. Even the best of *notarios* or attorneys may be unable to discover these title problems. Since title policies are fully negotiable contracts of indemnity, a title company can consider and insure a variety of title matters for the benefit of the proposed insured. For example, a title insurance policy has the ability to provide affirmative coverage and endorsements that protect purchasers against risks that may be discovered in the title search process. A *notario publico* often does not offer the same type of assurances. No matter who tells you that title insurance isn't necessary, just remember that it is the only monetary indemnification that you will receive protecting your ownership rights.

Historically, *notarios* have been the main conduit for the real estate closing process in Mexico. They provide a "cradle-to-the grave" service for the establishment of real property rights in this nation. Not unlike other civil code jurisdictions throughout the world, these highly specialized Mexican attorneys create judicial certainty in the conveyance of realty and they will not be replaced. In essence, public notaries in Mexico are the equivalent of the title company (or attorney) we utilize in the United States to close property transactions.

Notarios, however, do not control the development of real estate nor what a developer does in its legal entitlement process to insure good title to the property. Mexico's public notaries are neutral and work for the benefit of the parties in any property conveyance. Development law is normally mandated by the respective state, along with compliance at the city or municipal level. It is incumbent upon the developer to adhere to procedures and requirements as prescribed by law. It is not the responsibility of the *notario* to enforce or "police" the development process in any given state.

As mentioned, foreign purchasers may establish beneficiary trust rights (a *fideicomiso*) for residential real estate located in Mexico's restricted zone. As is often the case in the Mexican Republic, developers pre-sell properties under a promissory agreement with the provision that the *fideicomiso* (Mexican bank trust) will be provided once the residential lot subdivision is legally authorized or the condominium regime is filed of record. Too often, this can take months after a purchaser has paid the full purchase price for the real estate. Foreign buyers are given the right to "possess" or occupy the property but do not have title to it. Once the required documentation is finally in place, the developer must begin the process to convey the realty and establish the bank trust for each non-Mexican purchaser. This can be a daunting task for even the most sophisticated development company. There are many logistical matters, procedures and documentation issues that must be satisfied to establish the *fideicomiso*.

In order to acquire beneficiary trust rights at the time of closing, among other requirements, a foreign purchaser is required to obtain a bank trust permit issued by Mexico's Ministry of Foreign Relations. There is also a requirement for payment of the annual trust fee, a letter of trust acceptance fee and a fee for the trust letter to be filed of record with the bank acting as trustee, as well as other requirements related to the specific transaction. In addition, the foreign buyer must pay the applicable transfer tax to the federal government of Mexico at closing (approximately 2 percent of the declared value of the operation), a notary fee, a fee for an appraisal required by the trust bank on the subject property, a lien certificate fee, a tax debt certificate fee, recordation fees and other closing costs.

Some documents must be "apostilled" in order for them to be accepted by the *notario publico*—including verification of citizenship, a process that provides certification by the respective buyer's Secretary of State. Obviously, these closing matters and required documents can create a paper process that is logistically difficult for most Mexican developers, especially when dealing with customers from the United States or Canada.

Currently, an ancillary turnkey closing service from a U.S. title insurance company is available and is being rolled out in Mexico to help facilitate the real estate closing process. This centralized service can be provided for any type of Mexican development, property or project. The heart of the process is that it is coordinated from the United States with a U.S. title insurance company acting in a fiduciary capacity as escrow agent. That company will provide escrow and funding services, closing package origination to the respective buyers and wire transfer capabilities to anywhere in Mexico—basically applying a U.S. standard of closing assurance on Mexican real estate.

Purchasers using this service will have the comfort and security of knowing that their funds are being held in the United States and ultimately disbursed by a title company. Those funds will be tied to a fully executed escrow agreement with disbursement instructions as agreed by the parties to the transaction. The company will send a letter of instruction in the closing package, setting out the requirements and procedures, in addition to a settlement statement for the release and payment of the various fees, permits, closing costs and appraisal. Additionally, it will include the necessary forms required by the trust bank that need to be executed by the respective buyer to initiate the *fideicomiso* process. Once the package and required information is complete—along with receipt of the needed funds into the escrow account—it is forwarded to the developer for processing, deed preparation and ultimately funding to the various entities.

Investment of any type is a choice. Purchasing real estate in Mexico can be one such alternative that provides enjoyment and hopefully monetary appreciation and terrific family experiences. A Mexican real estate acquisition should be a safe and secure process and U.S. companies now provide an attractive alternative to the *notarios*. A turnkey closing service provided by a U.S. title insurance company is one more creative step in an evolutionary process that provides greater certainty and protection for buyers of real estate in Mexico.

The genesis of title insurance

Since purchasers first began claiming and acquiring ownership of land, there has never been a time when they have not needed some form of title assurance. The very nature of land induces a need for title assurance because its characteristics differ from other forms of property. Land titles are symbolic because the title is what a purchaser receives when he purchases real estate rather than actual delivery of the property. For this reason, it is important that a purchaser have the best assurance possible that his or her title is valid, unencumbered and free of flaws, or that the purchaser have an indemnity against loss because of a title defect.

Historically, a purchaser's lack of knowledge of the complexities of land titles has caused him or her to discount the importance of land title assurance. Knowing little or nothing about titles, real estate buyers have consistently relied on the advice of others. They have been led to believe that it is not necessary to look back into a title beyond a couple of previous ownerships, that the public records contain information with respect to every possible title hazard and that an attorney's opinion gives positive assurance of a safe title. Conditioned as the public has become through traditions and practices, it is inconceivable that a title could be completely lost irrespective of the customary assurances available. Prior to the inception of title insurance, it became obvious in the late 1800s that the U.S. needed a more secure form of title assurance—a form based upon indemnity dollars instead of word-of-mouth reliability. And today, more than 100 years later, foreign purchasers of real estate in Mexico face the same dilemma.

The land conveyance process in Mexico has become efficient. However, any title defect that can occur in the United States can also occur in Mexico, with other potential hazards looming on the horizon uncommon in U.S. property conveyances. *Ejido* claims or expansions, labor liens, *fideicomiso* (Mexican bank trust entitlements), property regularization and permitted use issues can pose significantly detrimental problems to unknowing purchasers of Mexican real estate. Moreover, little if no legal recourse is afforded potential purchasers against the public notary who closes all real estate transactions in Mexico or against Mexico's public registry of property concerning title or lien defects, omissions, gaps in ownership or recording errors. A title insurance policy issued on Mexican property provides a comfort and security benefit to foreign purchasers and is the only safeguard against title pitfalls resulting in eventual Mexican lawsuits and monetary losses.

CHAPTER THIRTEEN

Working North-South Models

Arizona-Sonora and others have impressive history of bilateral cooperation

Today's communication and cooperation between Arizona and Sonora—specifically in the real estate sector—is the result of more than a decade of hard work by governments, agents, title companies, appraisers and buyers. It did not come easily and was honed by confusion and experience, as mentioned in other sections in this book. However, the relationship is now the foundation for other U.S. and Mexican states—for example, Colima and Minnesota—that now enjoy thriving real estate and cultural connections.

In this chapter we examine why the Arizona-Sonora affiliation has become a good example of why U.S. second home buyers are flowing into all of Mexico. The bond between those two states helped clarify purchase and sale procedures and eliminated the casual "go with the flow" reputation attached to buying a getaway south of the border. A session of the Arizona-Mexico Commission (AMC) and the Sonora-Arizona Commission recently concluded in Phoenix with a number of action items being presented for inauguration. The central theme of the AMC's Real Estate Task Force initiatives was establishing greater public awareness about real estate subdivisions in Sonora and the registration of all real estate agents as mandated by Sonora's agent registry law, especially in Puerto Peñasco. Both governors Janet Napolitano of Arizona and Eduardo Bours of Sonora acknowledged the importance of these bilateral action items. Four members of the Task Force then traveled to Hermosillo, Mexico, to meet with representatives of the Sonoran government to begin a dialogue between the border states examining the issues most critical to real estate investment in Sonora. The Secretary of Economic Development (a state government cabinet member), along with representatives from the Office of Urban Infrastructure and Ecology (SIUE), the Sonoran Economic Development Council and the office of ICRESON (the public registry and tax assessor office for Sonora), were present for the discussion. Conversation between the delegates centered on two primary matters: registering agents who work in the Sonoran real estate market and setting the process for Sonoran residential subdivisions and condominium projects to get a public report from the Arizona Department of Real Estate (ADRE).

WORKING NORTH-SOUTH MODELS

Also discussed was making Sonora's Agent Registry Law a more mandatory requirement—not voluntary—for Sonoran agents, as well as how to expedite the public report process in Arizona. The Sonoran representatives were enthusiastic about gaining a better understanding of Arizona's public report process and learning more about the licensing and continuing education requirements for Arizona real estate professionals, and participated in meetings with the ADRE and the Task Force.

The most vivid result is that the real estate market in Puerto Peñasco, or Rocky Point, is not only flourishing, but it also has become one of the hottest and most active venues in all of Mexico. As one of only two "drive-in" beach destinations, real estate sales continue to escalate and new residential developments abound. In recent years, more than $700 million in land acquisition and infrastructure improvements have been invested in Rocky Point. That number grows larger each month. Clearly, both governors have a keen awareness for the level of activity in Sonora's real estate sector and both recognize the monetary and socioeconomic benefit that each state receives in this cross border relationship. For these and other reasons, the governors have pledged their support of and participation in enhancing the growth, perception, viability and security in Sonoran real property investment. "Bilateral cooperation" is no longer just a buzz phrase. There has been a greater sense of urgency to implement initiatives for one simple reason: to promote and enhance the relationship that each state shares with the other.

In 1959, the late Arizona Governor Paul J. Fannin said of the Arizona-Sonora affiliation, "God made us neighbors, let us be

193

good neighbors." In the years since he created this creed, both states have expanded their efforts to enhance bilateral cooperation and enrich economic prosperity for the region. This could not be more apparent than in the real estate sector. Both Arizona and Sonora should not only be proud of their continued commitment to one another and their citizens but in knowing that other regions are following in their footsteps.

Consumer education creates public awareness. This is certainly not a new concept or axiom. It has become, however, a very important initiative in the past several years when it comes to protecting non-Mexican national buyers of Mexican real estate.

Governor Fannin's intentions were followed up in November 2001, when then Arizona Governor Jane D. Hull and Sonora Governor Armando Lopez Nogales signed the first-ever bilateral declaration for the resolution of existing land disputes in the state of Sonora. With this agreement, both governors committed their states to the promotion of consumer education to enhance the confidence and security of real property acquisitions in the Sonoran market. Under the recommendation and auspices of the Arizona-Mexico Commission, Governor Hull then created the Task Force on Real Estate Practices, Investment and Development. Comprising U.S. and Mexican attorneys, developers, real estate agents, an appraiser, an accountant and a title company executive, this diverse group of real estate experts also includes members from Arizona's Department of Real Estate and Office of Tourism as well as the Arizona Association of Realtors. In 2003, Governor Janet Napolitano, as chairman of the Arizona-Mexico Commission, re-established the Task Force on Mexico for two simple reasons: (1) to protect Arizona consumers interested in buying real estate in Mexico, and (2) to promote economic development throughout the region. Governor Napolitano's vision for Arizona-Mexico relations is to enhance the educational tools developed by the task force and to support regulatory reform within each state.

The task force produced the most comprehensive body of educational information that to date has ever been created on Mexican real estate. Divided into three main categories of information, its work includes a 16-point buyer's checklist, a detailed buyer's advisory to be used as a guide on purchasing property in Sonora and Mexico in general, consumer protection information with a listing of the PROFECO office locations in Sonora, a seller's checklist, a seller's disclosure for improved and unimproved property and a developer's addendum disclosure. There is also information about how to procure an Arizona public report for any Sonoran residential development that advertises in Arizona as well as information about real estate professionals. Many of the available advisories, checklists, disclosures and general data are available in the Appendix of this book, or they can be downloaded at *www.azmc.org/realestate*.

It is important that buyers of Mexican realty have access to current information at all stages of the real estate transaction process. It is equally critical that local lawmakers, whether in Arizona or Sonora, provide a regulatory framework designed to protect foreign investment and foster sound economic growth. In May 2002, the state of Sonora passed a law for the inception of a real estate agent registry. The registry, as it exists today, is the first to be created among the Mexican states requiring that all individuals engaged in the sale of real property in Sonora be registered. As part of the registry's requirements, all agents must obtain a permit of authorization to conduct real estate sales and earn commissions. Although the registry is in fact a federal entity, Sonoran law mandates that the registry be obligated to obtain background information on the agents; that it has the right to inspect the agent's sales office and verify compliance as established in the permit; and that it must require a continuing education platform over a two-year period.

The establishment of this regulatory entity represents the first significant governmental attempt anywhere in Mexico to improve the educational integrity of agents and initiate a higher standard of ethics and professional behavior in the real estate community. It should be noted, however, that to date there is no determination of how compliance with this new law will be upheld or how the registry will enforce registration and within what timeframe.

When you think about it, the Arizona-Sonora alignment was a natural. Americans have traditionally enjoyed going to the beach to vacation or simply to have days of "fun in the sun." West Coast, East Coast or the Gulf Coast—it is just a matter of driving to your favorite spot along America's coastlines. Some vacationers cross state borders to do so but the closest beach for Arizonans is south across the international border. (Half of Phoenix goes to San Diego during the summer months because Mexico can cook in July!) Being a "land-locked" state creates the necessity for the populace of Arizona to explore their beach property desires in a foreign jurisdiction unless they go to the West Coast. Who, really, can afford to buy a getaway on the West Coast? The Mexican state of Sonora has long provided an attractive venue for weekend outlets of sand and sea pleasure. With only a four-hour drive from Phoenix or Tucson to Puerto Peñasco, the lure of owning a beach house or condo has stirred many a Southwesterner to take a certain leap of faith and acquire real estate in this Sea of Cortés municipality. And these folks are being welcomed with open arms.

Tourism is Mexico's third largest generator of gross domestic product. Especially with the investment in real estate along the country's coastlines, tourism produces jobs, infrastructure development, tax revenue and ultimately a huge income for local markets. Its dependency on American and Canadian dollars cannot be understated. When the U.S. economy gets a cold, Mexico suffers from pneumonia. Rocky Point, like Los Cabos, Puerto Vallarta, Cancun, Cozumel, Mazatlán and others, is no different. Mexico's real estate development laws are not unlike those of the United States. Inherent within the laws are state and municipal regulations, procedure, formality of process and governmental approval. This is particularly true with the state of Sonora. But who safeguards and protects a foreign buying public if the developers, sales agents and homeowners don't comply with government regulations and procedure?

Buyers are left to educate themselves and to seek competent legal advice to understand the intricacies of purchasing property anywhere in Mexico. Remember, not getting good title to real estate in Mexico is not the fault of the government, nor is it the lack of legal structure and protocol within Mexico. The laws to protect purchasers do exist. More times than not, it is a question of whether sellers and/or agents comply with what is mandated to protect consumers. In the past few years, significant strides have been made to create a heightened awareness of consumer protection, coupled with buyer education on Mexican real estate matters. The non-Mexican buying public is certainly a more enlightened purchaser. Disposable income and discretionary spending concerns have given way to a "wait and see" attitude on buying a vacation or investment property. The dynamics of a U.S. recession and the ensuing consequences of September 11 have completely changed today's real estate climate, both in the United States and Mexico. U.S. buyers no longer accept the "that's the way we do business here, trust me" caveat. They simply can't afford the risk—nor should they have to.

Sonora and Puerto Peñasco, although aggressive and proactive with the changes they have mandated, are not unique in their efforts to implement real estate reforms. Other prominent beach markets, such as Los Cabos and Puerto Vallarta, have also made significant changes to the manner in which they disclose information, how they handle money and escrow account considerations and how they disclose closing and income tax issues. Even real estate agent ethics and professionalism have been addressed. Los Cabos, has already solicited agent participation in a code of ethics and is requiring local professionals to adhere to standards as established by the local AMPI chapter. Additionally, AMPI has stringently requested that agents utilize neutral third-party escrow accounts for buyer deposits and earnest money, rather than broker accounts. Local MLS chapters meet regularly in Cabo, Vallarta, Cancun and Nayarit to discuss the general state of the market, to share ideas and to increase the professionalism of local agents.

It's a new world of real estate in Mexico. If real estate developers, sellers and agents don't protect the foreign investment available to any given market, that money will seek another opportunity. That's just the way it is...in any market.

PART THREE

The Money Picture: Exploring Mortgages and Tax Ramifications

CHAPTER FOURTEEN

The Status of Residential Financing in Mexico

U.S. lenders finally come to the fiesta

How have second homes been financed in Mexico? Traditionally, it's been "get out your line-of-credit checkbook, add any savings you could muster and then pray that the seller would carry the paper" until you found another way to refinance the balance. Now, with changes in the appraisal and foreclosure process, U.S. lenders have begin to offer a better selection of loan programs aimed at second home buyers and retirees.

In early 2007, GMAC International Mortgage (www.gmacinternationalmortgage.com) was the first lender to roll out a 30-year, fixed-rate mortgage for Americans buying property in

Mexico in addition to a "stated income" or limited documentation option for a slightly higher interest rate. Both components also are available to borrowers for "cash-back" refinances, allowing customers to pull out up to 70 percent of the cash value of their primary residence or second home in Mexico, according to Dan Bryant, director of GMAC International Mortgage. Other North American lenders—including Collateral International, GE Money, Wachovia, M & I, Textron, IMI, Johnson Capital and CS Mortgage—probably will follow GMAC's lead and tweak their long-term loan products.

Twenty-year, fixed-rate loan programs historically were the loan of choice, requiring a 20 percent downpayment and an origination fee of 2 percent of the loan amount. Interest rates average 1.5 percentage points higher than the going rate in the United States, depending upon downpayment and credit score. Under NAFTA and other reforms, the Mexican government cannot discriminate against foreigners in terms of property ownership.

In this chapter, we explore the relatively new presence of United States lenders in Mexico while explaining why it took so long for them to get there. We'll discuss some of the offerings now available plus the possibilities for financing that are down the road. In Chapter 15, we offer a few new roads, perhaps avenues you have not considered, to help you get in the door of a second home in Mexico.

For the average citizen in Mexico, real estate transactions are generally cash deals with limited owner financing available. The high cost of money (interest rates) within the Republic has historically made financing properties unattractive; however, the recent appearance of mortgage company services from the United States now makes financing an option.

In the United States, owning a home has long been an ideal that we all strive to realize. Since World War II, home ownership has become a fundamental goal in our quest to achieve the "American Dream." And yet we, as a buying public, often take this wonderful opportunity for granted and we do not realize that it doesn't exist in most other countries in the world. Certainly not to the extent we have become accustomed to in the United States. For every 10 U.S. residences, approximately nine have mortgages on them. We have created a system that affords longer terms of debt repayment at low interest rates coupled with interest deduction on the note against our personal tax liability. But what is most important is the fact that through our mortgage system, we have established the basis for creating "personal net worth" through home ownership. For the most part, this incredible financing vehicle simply is not available in other countries and, particularly, not in Mexico for Mexican citizens. By contrast, for every 10 residences in Mexico, only one has a mortgage. This unfortunate fact has finally begun to change, thanks to political elections and a greater awareness of housing as an important industry.

In order for the mortgage market to emerge and have the ability to sustain itself, there are many primary requirements that must be in place. The U.S. mortgage system has become the benchmark model for other loan origination programs in the world. In the United States, the mortgage market can be explained as a "360-degree" process and any buying public, U.S. or otherwise, should understand its basic components. First, financial institutions that originate loans must qualify prospective borrowers relative to their assets, debts and the requested loan amount. Subject to this assessment is the loan to value ratio and the required downpayment. In essence, lenders arrive at a profile of the borrower's overall credit worthiness and determine the acceptable parameters for a given mortgage.

Once the mortgage has been originated, the loan is pooled with other mortgages and the loan portfolio will be rated according to the specific lender, borrower, financing terms, the asset itself and the "age" of the mortgage. The rating that is placed on the loan pool will determine the "discount rate" for selling the portfolio. Selling the loan portfolio in the secondary mortgage market and offering mortgage-backed securities to investors on Wall Street completes the cycle of liquidity in order to re-capitalize primary mortgage lenders across the country.

Although this explanation is extremely simplistic, it is the basis for how the U.S. mortgage system thrives. In order for the system to thrive and moreover, to survive, certain assurances and guarantees must be in place. Investors in mortgage-backed securities don't know local market conditions where the mortgages originate, but they do know they will receive a certain yield on their investment and that the investment is guaranteed and secure. These assurances include private mortgage insurance, title insurance, FHA and VA guarantees, as well as a nonjudicial foreclosure process, deeds of trust and other standardized mortgage instruments. Unlike the United States, Mexico has no primary mortgage market nor a secondary market. The peso devaluation in 1994 further compounded the matter, leading to a banking crisis of major proportion that has reduced the liquidity of Mexican banks. Resources for new lines of credit have largely disappeared. As a result, there is an estimated pent-up demand for 6 million dwelling units in the country today because the country's inability to finance housing.

U.S. buyers of Mexican residential real estate, however, don't face this same situation. There is an ever-growing awareness among U.S. purchasers that financing is available on Mexican properties. Financing residences in Mexico has inherent advantages for lenders when weighed against the additional costs associated with mortgages—origination fees, discount points, bank appraisals and processing fees. All residential transactions in Mexico (regardless of the purchaser's country of residence) require payment of a transfer tax on the declared value of the operation (which should be the purchase price and not what the seller or developer declares to minimize the capital gains tax), notary fees, and recording costs. These expenditures are the norm in any Mexican property transfer, and they are not inexpensive by U.S. standards. Foreign buyers must also pay for the permit from the Ministry of Foreign Affairs, a bank appraisal fee and an annual bank trust fee to administer the *fideicomiso*. These expenditures are also customary and required. At the end of the day, the comparative expense of a cash transaction should run between 5 and 7 percent, whereas, financing will average about 8 to 10 percent of the purchase price, the difference being the cost of the mortgage origination as previously mentioned. U.S., Canadian and other foreign buyers need to realize that real estate deals in Mexico are just more expensive than what we are accustomed to in the United States.

There is a distinct and protective benefit that purchasers receive in financed operations that should be noted and understood by foreign buyers. First and foremost, in order to finance Mexican residential properties within the restricted zone, there must be a transfer and conveyance to a Mexican bank trust authorized by the *notario publico* that establishes a recorded and renewable beneficiary interest for 50 years for the non-Mexican buyer. This is a legal concept mandated by Mexico's foreign investment law on property within the restricted zone.

The bank trust, or *fideicomiso,* does not apply to property in the interior of Mexico being acquired by non-Mexicans. In a seller-financed deal or, as is sometimes referred to as a seller "carrying the paper," there is no conveyance to the buyer. Since the seller is financing the residence, he or she will retain the title to the property until the debt obligation has been paid off, then transfer title. One can easily see the risk associated in these transactions over several years of repayment; they are unlike what we are accustomed to in the United States through a deed of trust conveyance. Also, the interest rate commonly charged by Mexican developers will normally exceed U.S. interest rates on Mexican property.

Second, U.S. financial institutions, like those mentioned above, require a more detailed process to originate loans in Mexico. Possession of the property is not tantamount to ownership. Lenders must be assured, through a competent title search of the property and issuance of a Commitment for Title Insurance, that there is a complete chain of title for the respective residence. They want to know how the title is vested and that it is valid.

Lenders rely on the company investigating the title to confirm that a subdivision has been approved and published or that a condominium development has a condominium regime filed of record. Escrow considerations and escrow agreements are common with U.S. lenders on Mexican transactions as well. Certified surveys should be provided so that ultimately the lender can receive a Loan Policy of Title Insurance protecting its priority of lien interest as filed of record by the *notario* in the public registry of property. All of these elements work toward the protection of the borrower as well as the lender. As has been said previously, Mexico is not the "Wild West" as many perceive. Lenders want a higher standard of assurance that the loans they originate are secure, and that the public deeds vesting the bank's lien interest are in fact valid and enforceable. Again, this works to the benefit of the borrower.

Former president Vicente Fox of Mexico vowed to make mortgage financing available to Mexican citizens. He indicated that it is of prime importance to start reforms on a securitization process and has said *Fondo de Operacion y Financimiento Bancario a la Vivienda* (FOVI), Mexico's governmental guarantor of loans, needs to make funds available to Mexico's financial loan institutions (SOFOLES) for affordable housing loans. Mexico can only realize its goal of providing affordable housing through secured lending transactions once legislative changes are initiated at the local and state levels and a viable secondary mortgage market is created. U.S. buyers don't have to wait. Anyone acquiring residential real estate can at least have the opportunity to check with U.S.-based mortgage lenders on the availability of a Mexican home mortgage. Loan transactions for Mexico are now originated and processed every month. Hopefully it will become an even more common concept with U.S. purchasers. Many foreigners are still paying a premium to finance their deals, either through loans at Mexican banks that can charge interest rates greater than 13 percent or through short-term builder financing. The peso-denominated loan from a Mexican bank, which offers shorter term financing at a variable rate, can cost the borrower big-time during periods of higher inflation.

For U.S. borrowers, there are several advantages in working with a U.S. lender:

- The minimum downpayment is typically 20 percent of the purchase price. Although rates will be more favorable with a larger "down," developers usually require a 30 percent downpayment.

- The loan is in dollars, not pesos.

- 20-30 year programs. Developer financing on average runs 10 years.

Why have 20-year term mortgages, and not the conventional 30-year fixed-rate loans, been more popular in Mexico? When U.S. lenders first began offering loans in Mexico, a majority of the borrowers were older retirees who saw no merit in 30-year loan terms. They also had not grown up with ARMs and were simply more comfortable with reliable, fixed-rate payments. Most of these folks were members of the so-called "greatest generation," the pay-it-off segment who saw debt as an evil that needed to be eliminated as soon as possible. Today's baby boomers—the children of the "greatest generation"—are quite the opposite and don't flinch at negative amortization or rising credit-credit balances. The 20-year mortgage catered to the needs of the borrowers at the time—providing consistent payments, lower interest rates than 30-year fixed, yet a term that could be paid off in their lifetime.

The Mexican market has grown from a narrow, unserviced gap of U.S. retirees to a huge international niche featuring ready, willing and able buyers from all over the world. American buyers remain the largest potential home-buying group, but Canadians also are flying south for the winter. U.S. lenders have competed to corral bilingual mortgage specialists who understand the challenges and culture and who have begun to jockey for position in some of the more attractive markets.

Among the Mexico-bound lenders are Phoenix-based M&I Bank and IMI Group; Minneapolis-based GMAC-RFC, Collateral International and Boone, North Carolina–based GS Mortgage Securities. Birmingham, Alabama–based Collateral International (www.collateralinternational.com) now offers fixed-rate and adjustable-rate mortgage programs for primary and second home buyers under its "Mexico—My Dream" campaign. The going has not been that easy. Building the lending business involved the creation of strategic alliances with Mexican attorneys, notary publics and title agencies to bring down closing costs for buyers.

According to Aida Pantoja Maynard, vice-president of resort finance for Lakewood, Colorado-based Textron Financial, one of the key elements that has been missing for lenders is an exit strategy. As mentioned, there is no secondary market (like Fannie Mae and Freddie Mac) to which lenders can sell loans made in Mexico. Lenders are now playing an active role in developing those conduits, which should make pricing more appealing for consumers.

Two other factors have been critical challenges for U.S. lenders interested in tapping the Mexico market. The first has been the enormous amount of red tape lenders face when a borrower defaults and the lender attempts to foreclose. American banks simply have been skittish to lend cash for deals with an unreliable road to getting the property back in the event of default. The second is the traditional Mexican appraisal. Most appraisals in Mexico are geared to determining replacement costs. Lenders want to ascertain market value through comparable sales. Their concern is knowing that they are extending funds to a property that is truly worth the amount of the purchase price. "There have been improvements on both fronts," Maynard says. "In 2003, the Mexican legislature provided some clarity to the foreclosure provision. These measures have been abbreviated and stipulate a nonjudicial foreclosure when the property is held in the Mexican trust. There has also been more scrutiny and security with appraisals on the national front. The compensation to the appraiser has been based on the cost of the property, and that is changing as well. Developers are now seeking certified individuals and utilizing comparable sales."

Why lenders had balked at the Mexican market

Bruce Greenberg, a Tucson, Arizona–based appraiser, also has an office in Mexico City and has made more than 500 professional appraisals in Mexico in the past decade. He has seen U.S. lenders come and go, mainly because of unreliable sales data but also because some lenders believe the market is too small. "My lender/clients have been from Italy, Germany, Spain, England, Canada and the United States," Greenberg says. "The lenders have shared one major concern with me. The common issue is that there is a lack of reliable data in the confirmation of comparable sales. The Public Registry in Mexico is a nonreliable source!" In a 12-month period from 2003–2004, Greenberg estimated that *gringos* acquired both new construction and resales units worth approximately $650 million in the four corridors of Cancun, Los Cabos, Puerto Vallarta and Puerto Peñasco. Less than 1 percent of those acquisitions were with the assistance of U.S. lenders. He then pointed out if qualified buyers could acquire real estate with a

20 to 30 percent downpayment and interest rates in the 7 to 8 percent range that the volume of $650 million per year example would quickly expand.

Greenberg also estimated that there were a total of 50,000 *gringo*-owned properties in the Cancun, Los Cabos, Puerto Vallarta and Puerto Peñasco areas. According to Greenberg's study, those 50,000 properties are worth $100,000 each, or about a $5 billion market for U.S. lenders in the four areas alone. His study also showed that less than 1 percent of the properties owned by *gringos* had gone into foreclosure or default. He concluded there was too much cash equity for properties owned by *gringos* to go into default. Furthermore, under the auspices of the new guaranteed bank trusts (*fideicomiso* Guarantee), there now is a faster remedy for repossession. The process that once took five to 10 years to get a property back now takes four to eight weeks.

(There are no official totals on the number of U.S. citizens owning property in Mexico. The National Association of Realtors "guestimates" 100,000, while others believe that figure is too high. The number of retirees who receive Social Security checks outside the country—anywhere in the world—rose from 188,000 in 1992 to 242,000 in 2002. Thousands more ex-patriates have their checks sent to U.S. addresses. However, according to the Association of Americans Resident Overseas, about 4.1 million Americans reside in other countries with about 1 million living in Mexico and 688,000 living in Canada. If all of these residents living abroad were placed in one U.S. state, it would be the 25th most populous state in the country, the association reported. The statistics don't include travelers who are visiting briefly and who don't secure visas, and don't include members of the U.S. military.)

Arizona Governor Janet Napolitano appointed Greenberg to serve on the Committee on Real Estate Practices, Investment and Development for the Arizona-Mexico Commission. He is a member of AMPI and MultiList of Cabo San Lucas as well as being a member of MultiList in Puerto Vallarta and Puerto Peñasco. He shared his thoughts on where Mexican appraisals have been and where they are heading: "In the world of appraising, there is a principle called the principle of change," Greenberg said. "The appraisal and lending professions in Mexico stand at the threshold of that principle of change and, if Mexican appraisers can deliver user-friendly, stronger appraisal reports to lenders, the opportunity exists for the development of more mortgage financing and increased housing development."

Changes underway

Recently, the government of Mexico has implemented new appraisal standards including an updated manual on valuation methodology, the requirement of Errors and Omissions Insurance coverage, and the retention of records for their registered appraisers, Greenberg noted. The new appraisal law in Mexico also lays out the penalties for noncompliance. International lenders are applauding these provisions and changes. Historically, the Mexican public registry system has been of limited value as a source of reliable information. Lenders do not consider *Catastro*, Mexico's National Registry System, to be a viable alternative because it is not truly a registry open to the public, and it is specifically not appraiser friendly. Access to public records is often not readily available. The sales prices reported in the public registry, in many cases, do not represent the true selling price. Currently, lenders are unsure whether such data is accessible and/or reliable from the public registry. Because investors, lenders, bankers and financial institutions want accurate, verifiable primary sales data, it becomes clear that legal and administrative reforms are needed to increase the accessibility and accuracy of the public registry. The increased quality of appraisals will fuel more lenders to enter the Mexican mortgage marketplace, also contributing to the growth of the housing sector. The higher the quality of appraisal product, the lower the risk to the lenders and to the secondary market, according to Greenberg.

The appraisal topic is a major issue because American mortgage bankers have been burned before, and some of them never fully recovered. Some financial analysts even blame faulty appraisals for the downfall of U.S. savings and loans more than two decades ago. In the late 1970s, when U.S. property was appreciating almost overnight, many lenders made out-of-state investments without ever seeing the property for which they were lending money. Inflation can cover a lot of mistakes. And if a home was appraised too high, it didn't matter so much because it would quickly reach the appraised value. The recession and higher interest rates in the early 1980s began uncovering errors. Property values in some areas had plunged, and there was a building glut in many markets, especially in the Sun Belt. Consumers and mortgage insurance companies lost money. Some lenders lost respect after peddling loans in the secondary mortgage market. Lenders also were staggered with inflated appraisals. Newcomers to the Mexican market do not want to make the same mistake.

What area is bringing the most interest? Lenders are seeing a lot of building in the Yucatan Peninsula because it is so easily accessed by people in the eastern United States. The off-the-charts interest in Cancun and the Yucatan has pushed development south, almost to the Belize border. There are so many units going up south of Cancun on the blue Caribbean shore that lenders say a bulk of their new business could come from that area in the next several years.

In reality, U.S. lenders in Mexico will be competing against the home-equity loan markets back home. A U.S. borrower is not going to pay a 12 percent interest rate for a Mexican home to a bank or individual seller when he or she can take out a home equity loan in the states for 7.5 percent. Or if the home equity loan is not a viable option, consumers will simply find another way—like margining a stock portfolio or pleading to wealthy Uncle Wally, the jolly soul who has played sugar daddy to others in the past. The mindset of "finding a way" to borrow to get in the door, an unheard of stretch for older folks, has evolved into an attractive, luring challenge. Borrowing money against a primary residence—the dreaded "second mortgage" once reserved only for desperation situations—is now part of everyday life. Homeowners write a check from their home equity line of credit for tuitions, boats, furniture, weddings and funerals. With most of those now behind them (except funerals), why not tap the house for this affordable, golden place they always wanted in the sun?

As we explore in the next chapter, home equity loans still provide a terrific way to help finance a second home in Mexico. But there are other logical, underused avenues as well that might just fit your situation. Just remember, dreams have a way of clouding a family's financial reality. Clear sky and blue water have a way of taking funds that should clearly go elsewhere. Don't come home from Mexico with the same feeling you experienced when you were coaxed to sign on the dotted line for that gorgeous timeshare offered by that wonderful man dispensing margaritas in the hotel lobby. Make sure you understand and can handle the responsibilities of being a second home owner—then take as much time as you can to enjoy it!

CHAPTER FIFTEEN

Six Solutions to Funding a Second Home in Mexico

Creative options that could provide the keys to your comfy retreat

The "greatest generation" took pride in being debt free. Owning the roof over their heads was a lifelong goal, and it took a lot of persuading to get Mom and Dad to even consider the concept of tapping into the equity of a home they already had paid off. Members of this group often were reluctant to spend money on themselves in order to make their lives more comfortable.

Conversely, their children, the bouncing baby boomers, never met a loan they didn't like. They borrow for toys, schools and especially for second homes they see as piggybanks where they can also spend time. The boomers' borrowing philosophy can get extremely creative when conventional financing no longer is in the picture. And financing for Mexican properties has been anything but conventional. Today's second home buyer in Mexico often knows what he or she wants—and the possible alternative solutions on how to finance it.

Here are six creative options that might not have entered your big picture when pondering a second home purchase south of the border. There may even be one that is palatable for Mom and Dad.

Mexican real estate IRAs: Great for investors, but no personal use

Suppose your best friend from college has pestered you for more than a decade about the financial advantages of investing in real estate in Mexico. This person, Lucky Lenny, has struck gold with recreational properties in a variety of locations and has renters clamoring to rent his units every month. Occupancy has been so good that Lucky Lenny could have rented his places during the winter months "three times over" and now doesn't want to give up the rent money by using the units himself. Larry has evolved from user to user/investor to investor only. Larry appears at the college reunion and he shares with you a lead on the next undiscovered Mexican paradise that snowbirds will fall over themselves trying to reach. According to Larry, not only will the place be worth a ton down the road, but it also will produce an immediate annual cash flow because of the premiums renters will be more than willing to pay for the winter months.

If you think Mexico is an absolute bargain yet you have no money to purchase a property there, do your research and then consider the funds in your Individual Retirement Account. Perhaps you've been seeking an alternative to some lackluster mutual funds that have only been treading water for years. Like foreign stocks, foreign real estate qualifies for an IRA— but you can't use it yourself until you retire. And like Lucky Lenny, you would have to be an investor only, but the move would give you the opportunity of gathering appreciation and equity with the only funds you have available.

In this chapter, we explore how Individual Retirement Accounts—plus some other unfamiliar alternatives—can help you on your way to your goal of an investment home in Mexico. These roads could take some extra labor to pave (like finding a trustee or administrator who will establish a real estate IRA), but the effort could provide you with the seed money for a retirement weekend getaway and other financial rewards.

You cannot use IRA money to buy your own residence or any other property in which you live. It has to be investment property. But when you retire, you can direct your IRA to turn it over to you as a distribution at the current market value.

Self-directed real estate IRAs are not only relatively easy, they are also not subject to some of the guidelines that apply to employee-sponsored qualified plans enforced by the Department of Labor. The trustee, as directed by the individual, has complete and total control over the investment. In addition, the trustee, as account holder, has an obligation of investigating each investment to be considered. This personal due diligence is a substitute for the rules that govern some employee-sponsored qualified plans. You can invest self-directed IRA money in a wide range of investments, including stocks, bonds, mutual funds, money market funds, saving certificates, U.S. Treasury securities, promissory notes secured by mortgages or deeds of trust, limited partnerships and...real estate. This includes single-family homes, timber parcels, terrific getaway condos and office properties.

To prepare for your real estate IRA, designate the amount of your retirement funds that you wish to use in the property deal and open a new IRA account with an independent administrator. The best place to start is an independent community bank—then get set for the possibility of a long afternoon of shopping. Many banks will not service real estate IRAs (some will say "never heard of it") because it must act as owner—pay the taxes, collect servicing fees—which involves paperwork many lenders don't want or need. Community banks, however, often will offer this trust account service for existing customers, especially if the bank can easily see that there's value in the purchase and a great potential for appreciation. And remember, because there are no limits on the number of IRA accounts a taxpayer may have, you will not be restricted to just one purchase.

The guidelines covering real estate IRAs are stringent. If you break one of these rules, you could jeopardize your tax-free status on your account.

- The land or house must be treated like any other investment.
- All rental profits must be returned to the trustee.
- You cannot manage the property. But your trustee can hire a third party—a real estate broker or local manager—to collect rents and maintain or improve the property.

- The house or property (or proceeds from its sale) must remain in the trust until distribution at retirement. If a trustee is instructed to sell the property, funds can be transferred to another account for reinvestment.

"It's a simple case of people selling IRAs not dealing in real estate," says investment advisor Jeff Moormeier, president of Quantum Advisors (*www.quantum-advisors.com*). "What is needed is people who specialize in real estate and deal in it everyday, our local Realtors, to understand the self-direct IRA process. It's a huge market that is just starting to emerge."

The challenge with real estate IRAs has been lack of funds to make a meaningful purchase. Historically, real estate IRAs had been purchased with cash and the trust then held the property free and clear. One way to crack a huge financial nut was to get several investors to buy shares in one property. Now some banks are discovering the real estate IRA niche and granting a "non-recourse loan" to the trustee for specific properties. Non-recourse means if the loan goes into default and the lender needs to foreclose, the property would be the only asset the lender could claim. It's similar to a nonjudicial foreclosure where the property becomes the lender's only focus.

The problem with IRAs involving Mexican real estate is a bit more complex. Cash talks—there is no problem finding an administrator to facilitate a Mexican property purchase with your IRA funds. But as we learned in Chapter 14, most U.S. lenders now active in Mexico stipulate that their funds secure "second homes," not investment properties. Hence, most consumers wishing to purchase Mexican property with their IRAs will probably have to pay cash, unless they have an unusual relationship with a local banker who would be willing to grant a "non-recourse" loan.

John Fairchild, president of Pacific Crest Savings Bank in the Pacific Northwest, says his bank was now making U.S. IRA-leveraged loans to customers with good credit scores and large downpayments. "We really like to see about 50 percent equity in the property plus more coming in monthly in rents than going out in mortgage payments," Fairchild explains. "The loan would not work in all IRA real estate deals—for example, vacant land." Fairchild said the loan would carry slightly higher fees and rates than a conventional mortgage, but he feels the package will be attractive to investors, especially if a property has the potential for rapid appreciation. "Once the Realtors really understand it, the concept will catch on much faster," Fairchild notes. It's a loan nobody has spent a lot of time thinking about until recently." Would Fairchild consider making IRA mortgages on property in Mexico? "We're pretty new on the product here in the U.S. Let me get this right first, and then we'll see."

For companies specializing in real estate IRAs, visit PENSCO Trust Company—*www.pensco.com*; Sterling Trust Company—*www.sxterling-trust.com*, Lincoln Trust—*www.lincolntrust.com*; Entrust Administration—*www.entrustadmin.com*; Mid Ohio Securities—*www.midoh.com* or Oarlock Investment Services—*www.oarlock.com*.

The buddy system

Remember when you went to camp and you had to have a partner for swimming, hiking and clean up? Take that buddy system concept and apply it to purchasing a casita with people you trust and enjoy. Having two or more families, couples or individuals combine their assets and purchase the property as partners makes sense, especially for couples who enjoy being together yet know they will never be able to afford a getaway of their own.

The often overestimated factor in a second home purchase is time. People who buy a second home and retain a primary residence often do not spend as much time in the second home as they had hoped—especially if it's in another country. And when a block of time surprisingly surfaces, owners often find themselves traveling to a place they have never been or using the time for a family reunion. But with the buddy system, multiple owners can share the time as well as the costs.

Here's how the buddy system works. Let's say the Waterses and the Carrs are sailing buddies. Nancy Waters would love a place in La Paz—an escape from Midwest winters—but she and her husband Steve do not have the cash to buy a place outright and can't handle the monthly drag of an extra mortgage payment. But Nancy does have some cash she inherited from her grandmother. One day, while playing golf with David and Pat Carr, Pat discloses that her father is selling a small home near La Paz that he has used as a second home for more than 30 years. Since his wife passed away three years ago, the place has been rarely used. Not only does it have great access to a boat launch for both couples' Hobie Cats, but it also has a secure, fenced yard for trailer storage. The couple could get a bargain price from the father, but they do not have the cash for a downpayment. David's new job, however, gives them a comfortable monthly cash flow.

Nancy shares that she is longing for a place in La Paz, but even though she has a small inheritance to invest, she and Steve can't swing another mortgage payment. Bingo! A deal is struck whereby the Waterses would make the downpayment and the Carrs would make the monthly payments plus pay for all fees for three years. After three years, they agree to the option to refinance or sell the place—a realistic timeframe to reassess the wants and needs of both couples. At that time, the Waters would get their downpayment back with a minimal interest allowance, and the two couples would split any appreciation upon sale. If one couple wishes to sell and the other wants to remain, the couple staying has the option to buyout the seller at a price submitted by a mutually approved appraiser. Another possibility is substituting a mutually agreeable new partner for the couple that wants out of the deal.

Seller financing…with a plain vanilla home equity starter

Sure, there have been all-cash buyers for gorgeous places in the sun. We've all heard rumors of a dusty Texas oilman, New England attorney or Northwest software executive sauntering out of a Mexican taxi and writing a check for a massive hacienda high on a hill overlooking the Pacific. But how many average folks have all cash for a second home in Mexico? Maybe years ago they did, but not today.

Historically, the most common method of financing property in Mexico has been to scrape up a downpayment then pray that a seller, or Mexican bank, would help with the rest. Until recently, U.S. and Canadian banks did not lend money on real estate in Mexico, and the rates charged by some Mexico lenders resembled the sky-high times of the U.S. in mortgage markets of the 1980s. Although Mexico remains behind the times in mortgage banking, remember that not all sellers in Mexico—especially in regions close to the coast—are Mexican nationals. Sellers are Americans and Canadians who might have to dispose of an investment for reasons beyond their control—loss of spouse, divorce, loss of job. These people know that conventional bank financing still is in its infant stage, and they could very well be open to creative options that they have exercised—or heard about—back home. Never underestimate the possibility of an owner accepting a "seller financing" or "carry-the-paper" proposal, especially if it comes from a person, couple or family the owner enjoys or trusts. And seller financing can benefit both sides. It can provide reliable income to the seller (especially to a budget-conscious, single senior) while allowing the buyer to bypass the significant fees and the often higher-than-imagined interest rates brought by conventional financing.

Buyer and seller are free to negotiate terms, including downpayment amount and the interest rate on the loan. Often, if the downpayment (secured by a home equity loan against the buyer's primary residence) is minimal, the rate on the loan could be higher than the conventional market, and vice versa. Any type of equally agreeable arrangement can get things rolling. The deal-maker might be a three- or five-year cash-out clause that gives the seller confidence his or her cash is not too far down the road while allowing the buyer time to peruse the new mortgage offerings by U.S. lenders. It's a new era for mortgages in Mexico, and there's no harm in sitting on a seller-financed deal for a few years until all the early wrinkles are ironed out of the brand new loans from the United States. Who knows? You might even get a developer/builder to carry the paper for a few years.

Lease option

It is often difficult to find the right property in a short period of time—especially for an out-of-country buyer. Although you hear about people buying "the first house we saw," potential buyers can also spend months researching house size and style, beach break, water availability, neighborhoods, and transportation before finalizing any deal. For those who do not want to be forced to act within a tight timeframe, renting or leasing with an option to buy can be a sensible alternative. As mentioned above, there are more and more Americans now selling homes in Mexico that are familiar with financing options other than a flat-out sale. Many real estate agents know of available properties, and renting for a year to 18 months is quite common among newcomers from the United States or Canada.

Sometimes, this rental or leased spot can turn into the permanent second home for the renters, which is why a lease with option to buy is sometimes preferable to a straight lease. A "lease option" allows the renters (potential owners) to buy time to research the area while getting a portion of the monthly rent credited toward the downpayment if they decide to pursue the option. The lease agreement includes an option allowing the vacation tenant to buy the property within the lease period. Here's how a typical lease option works.

The owner and tenant agree on a purchase price, often a figure based on today's market value plus an estimate of the average rate of inflation (let's use 3 percent) in the next 12 months. Let's say the agreed upon amount is $165,000 and represents the home's value 12 months down the road.

The owner charges the tenant a nonrefundable fee for the option to buy. The amount can vary, depending on how eager the seller is to move, the size and quality of the home, etc. Typically, the higher the fee, the better the tenant maintains the property. The one-time fee—let's say it is $1,500—is in addition to the monthly payments, and it gives the tenant the right to purchase the property for $165,000 at any time within the 12-month lease period.

The monthly rent is typically greater than market rates because no downpayment has been made, but a portion of it will apply toward the downpayment. The owner and tenant decide what portion will be credited. For example, if the monthly rent is $1,000, $500 of each month's rent could be credited to the downpayment. The owner and tenant must be sure to specify both lease and sale terms in the agreement. For example, it's a good idea to set an interest rate ceiling in the agreement, or agree that the owner will finance the sale if conventional interest rates are at a certain level. This guards against the tenant being unable to qualify for a loan because interest rates are too high when it's time to exercise the option to buy. Lease option forms are available at some stationery stores that carry professional forms. If you are concerned about the language of the agreement, consult an attorney or escrow officer.

Buy an option

The purchase of an option is the clearest and strongest right that can be granted that gives a potential buyer flexibility in the future. Under this plan, the buyer, or option grantee, is given the right to rent or buy a specified property during a specific period of time. However, the buyer, usually having paid a fee to obtain the option, is under no obligation to perform. To be enforceable, the option should set forth the price, dates and terms on which the option is exercisable.

First right of refusal

Have you ever stayed in a terrific place that provided you special times and memories and then told the seller: "Let me know if you ever want to sell this place"? You would be surprised how many properties are acquired this way—especially if the renter has gone out of his or her way to take care of the property.

Unlike an option, a right of first refusal does not entitle the holder of the right to force the other party to sell or lease the property. Instead, if and when the seller decides to sell the property, the holder of the right of first refusal can acquire the property for the same price and terms that the seller is willing to accept from a third party. A right of first refusal is not as strong for the potential buyer as the option. That's because it does not set the price for the property in advance, and it allows the seller to decide whether and when to sell or lease. A property owner generally will resist granting a right of first refusal because it can negatively impact the marketing of the home. (What outside buyer is going to get excited when he or she knows an inside buyer holds the first right of refusal?) In reality, many owners deal to favorite renters or friends.

Ready to retire? Reverse your way to Mexico

It's true...the primary purpose of a reverse mortgage is to help seniors stay in their homes and live more comfortably in their later years. But let's look beyond the basic box and explore how a reverse can purchase a second home in Mexico.

The versatility of reverse mortgages has come a long way since the instrument was first established in 1989. Once perceived only as a last-ditch effort to keep the family home, reverse mortgages are now used to purchase cars, make needed home repairs and improvements, finance education, pay for in-home care, provide supplemental income and buy second homes in other countries. The funds can be used for any purpose.

Here's how the reverse mortgage, which must be attached to a primary U.S. residence, can also be used to acquire a second home south of the border. Let's say June and Ward Cleaver own a home valued at $235,000. Ward is 72 years old and June is 68. They execute a reverse mortgage on their residence based on June's age and an expected interest rate of 7 percent via a HUD Home Equity Conversion Mortgage (HECM), which is one of the more popular reverse options available today. The HECM loan limit, which often follows the increases in the Fannie Mae/Freddie Mac loan limit, varies by geographic area.

The Cleavers net a lump sum of approximately $106,000 on the closing of the reverse mortgage. Shortly thereafter, they purchase a vacation condo in Huatulco, where June loves to snorkel and swim, for $125,000. They use the $106,000 from the reverse mortgage and an additional $19,000 from Ward's retirement funds to own the Huatulco condo free and clear.

After a decade of wonderful vacations and no loan payments, the couple chooses to downsize. They sell their primary residence, pay off the underlying debt from the reverse mortgage, and move to the Huatulco condo. Using an average appreciation rate of 4 percent on the primary residence and a 7 percent interest rate on the loan, the balance on the reverse mortgage would have increased to $253,198 from $106,000 while the value of their primary home increased to $347,857 from $235,000. Assuming the home nets that amount upon sale, June and Ward Cleaver would put $95,659 in their pocket. Also, remember that they have made no mortgage payments for the past 10 years and have no debt on the Huatulco condo.

When did reverse mortgages become an option?

In 1989, HUD tried to help "home-rich, cash-poor" seniors by establishing a program that would enable them to take cash payments out of the home's equity. These reverse mortgages carry a variety of payment options. And repayment of the loan is not required during the homeowner's lifetime unless the property is no longer occupied as a primary residence. The reverse mortgages, however, are still expensive, with fees of 4 percent of the loan amount and more depending upon the program. Financial Freedom Senior Funding has a "jumbo" reverse mortgage that is better suited to owners of more expensive homes. The jumbo reverse mortgage is not based on geographic location.

The homeowner cannot be displaced and forced to sell the home to pay off the mortgage, even if the principal balance grows to exceed the value of the property. If the value of the house exceeds what is owed at the time of death, the balance goes to the estate.

The loan is aimed at individuals 62 years or older who own their homes—either debt-free or close to it—and who have a need for additional cash. According to HUD, approximately

70 percent of America's elderly own their own homes and 80 percent of these homeowners do not have mortgage debt. The potential reverse mortgage market continues to be absolutely huge. Reverse mortgage loan amounts to homeowners are based on age, interest rate, type of plan selected and value of the property.

All HECM loans are guaranteed by the Federal Housing Administration, the agency established by the National Housing Act of 1934 to stabilize a depressed housing market and provide insurance on loans to home buyers who otherwise could not find loans. In 1983, the government ceased to control the interest rates on mortgages insured by the FHA and started allowing the rates to "float" with the rest of the market.

FAQs on reverse mortgages

What's the difference between a home equity loan and a reverse mortgage?

A reverse mortgage is a home equity loan without a payment. You do not repay the loan as long as the home remains your principal residence. Your income and credit rating are not considered when qualifying for the loan. There is no requirement that you requalify each year.

With a home equity loan, you must make regular payments to repay the loan. These payments begin as soon as the loan is originated. To qualify for such a loan, you must earn a monthly income great enough to make those payments. If you fail to make the monthly payments, the lender can foreclose, and you could be forced to sell your home. In addition, you may be required to requalify for a home equity loan each year. If you do not requalify, the lender may require you to pay the loan in full immediately. Although both the reverse mortgage and the home equity loan enable you to turn the equity in your home into spendable dollars, there are some important differences between the two types of mortgages.

Who helps clarify the reverse process?

All potential borrowers must first meet with an independent reverse mortgage counselor before filling out an application. The counselor's job is to educate and inform consumers about the various reverse programs and the alternative options available. This required counseling session is at no cost to the borrower and can be done in person or over the telephone.

How much money can be borrowed?

The reverse mortgage loan amount is based on the home value, the number and age of the homeowner(s) and the current interest rate. The maximum allowable home value varies depending on the program selected. The FHA program has limits depending upon the county.

Will my heirs owe anything if I die?

You, or your heirs, will never owe more than your property is worth. Upon your death, the loan balance consisting of principal paid to you or on your behalf, plus any accrued interest, becomes due and payable. Your estate/heirs may choose to repay the loan by selling the property or they may want to pay it off by other means so they can keep the home. If the loan should exceed the value of your property, your estate will owe no more than the value of the property; the mortgage insurance will cover any balance due to the lender. No additional financial claims may be made against your heirs or estate.

Can I be forced to sell if property values decline?

As long as you continue to occupy the property as your principal residence, you cannot be forced to sell or vacate the property. That's still true even if the total amount you owe on this loan exceeds the value of the property or if the fixed term over which you received monthly payments has expired. No deficiency judgment may result from your loan. Mortgage insurance covers any further obligation to the lender.

What if I decide to sell my home?

If you choose to sell your home, the outstanding balance becomes due and payable to the mortgage lender. Any proceeds left over once the loan is paid belong to you.

Can I sell my home to my children and continue to live in it?

If you sell your home to your children or any other individual (or simply give them title), the loan will become due and payable. After the loan is repaid, any arrangement for your continued occupancy of the property must be made with the new owners.

Must I pay off any loans or liens that are against the property?

Reverse mortgages require that all prior loans and liens must be paid off so that the reverse mortgage loan is in "first place," or in first lien position. Many times, the proceeds from the reverse mortgage can pay off the underlying loans. A senior does not have to own the home "free and clear" to obtain a reverse mortgage.

If my home appreciates in value during the mortgage term, who will be entitled to that appreciation?

Today's reverse mortgages do not provide the lender with an equity share in the appreciation of your home. Any money remaining after the mortgage is paid belongs to you, or upon your death, to your estate. You, or your estate, are legally required to pay back to the lender only the outstanding balance due.

National reverse mortgage sources

Reverse Mortgages of America
seattlemortgage.com/revmort.html

Financial Freedom Senior Funding
www.financialfreedom.com

Wells Fargo Home Mortgage
www.reversemortgages.net

National Center for Home Equity Conversion
www.reverse.org

U.S. Department of Housing and Urban Development
www.hud.gov

National Reverse Mortgage Lenders Association
www.reversemortgage.org

CHAPTER SIXTEEN

Mexico Offers an Investment Alternative

Property outside the United States
provides diversification, potential rewards

A few short years ago, many of us watched our investment income and net worth diminish significantly because of the woes of the U.S. stock market. Historically, Wall Street has been a pretty good long-term investment vehicle. The "Tech Wreck" that began in the spring of 2000 taught us to be more cautious. It also made us look to investments outside the conventional financial markets and investing in real property also has been a reliable, consistent investment option. Throughout history, great personal wealth has been attained through real estate ownership, but for most of us, it has been limited to investment in a primary residence. Although Mexico real estate also can be a viable investment venue, Americans have had a great deal more trepidation considering properties south of the border because of the highly publicized problems with some acquisitions.

Given today's investment climate, however, Mexico provides an alternative, attractive arena for potential investment. It is less expensive than most U.S. destinations, and unlike Hawaii, close enough for some people to actually reach via automobile. Real estate in Mexico should have a similar appreciation "upside" as does real estate in a U.S. development—coupled with the advantage of use and enjoyment of the property as a second residence. In fact, some Mexican projects have significantly higher internal rates of return with greater near-term value escalation, because of higher demands and less supply considerations given within a respective market or locale. Nonetheless, interested buyers must be savvy and educated because acquiring real estate in Mexico is not like buying property in the United States.

Never before has there been more information available to the buying public concerning real estate in Mexico. Web sites have become more plentiful, with real estate agents displaying more pertinent information and available property listings. In some beach markets, a local multi-listing service (MLS) is available, and more agents participate in the Mexican Association of Real Estate Professionals (AMPI) at the municipal, state and national levels. The state of Sonora has created the first-ever real estate agent registry, and now requires that all who endeavor and earn commissions in the sale of real property be registered and comply with specified guidelines on education and professional ethics. There is greater awareness of property conveyance, tax and legal matters, and greater attention is being placed on safeguarding foreign investment through the use of neutral third-party escrow agreements.

In addition, agents are now recommending that buyers obtain a commitment for title insurance, acquire coverage at the time of closing and follow through with the subsequent title insurance policy once the deed (*escritura publica*) is recorded. Snell Real Estate in Los Cabos and Coldwell Banker La Costa Realty in Puerto Vallarta are two of the real estate companies at the forefront of this important initiative.

It would appear that no one's "crystal ball" has been too clear nor has anyone predicted big time run-ups in stock market investments since the dot.com shakeout that began in 2000. It seems more people are content to have cash in certificates of deposit that guarantee a fixed rate of return. However, real estate still represents a strong investment opportunity in many areas of the world. For this reason, if you have an interest in Mexican real estate—perhaps you have thought long and hard about the lure of a residence on the beach or a colonial villa in Mexico's interior—now just might be the time.

Mexico after September 11, 2001

Like the United States, Mexico was very quiet in the fourth quarter of 2001. It had already been a difficult year because of U.S. economic woes and recessionary concerns pervading the U.S. economy. Being heavily dependent on trade with its biggest neighbor and business partner to the north, Mexico suffered additional financial loss and national anxiety with the turmoil created by the events of September 11.

Americans quit traveling, deciding to stay within the secure confines of U.S. soil. With the border *maquila* market already down, employee layoffs in plants increasing and reductions in product output resulting in diminished trade revenues, Mexico got hit with the brunt of America's "staying home" attitude. (A *maquila* is a plant in Mexico that retains a Maquiladora Permit from the Mexican government to import raw materials duty free into Mexico for manufacturing, assembly, repair or other processing. The foreign company must agree to re-export a majority of its production.) The tourism industry, the lifeblood and a vital part of Mexico's gross domestic product, began to suffer. Mexico's beautiful and popular beaches, adjacent hotels, stores and shops dependent upon U.S. occupancy and money were nearly empty. Real estate companies and their agents wondered, then worried about the state of things to come during the latter part of 2001 and in the future. They asked whether Americans, given all the circumstances and financial uncertainty, would return to Mexico? Would the tremendous real estate investment potential that this great country presents to a foreign buying public continue to lure Canadian and American capital?

The events of 9/11 made the world stop, gaze horrifically at the senseless tragedy, reflect on the fragility of life and question its everyday uncertainty. As human beings living together on this planet, we became globally united in a common spirit and one unwavering belief. Terrorism is not acceptable, it will not be tolerated and people cannot live in fear. We will go on with our lives, though a little more skeptical and certainly more cautiously.

By early 2002, the prognosis for Mexico again became positive and encouraging. Conditions in the United States improved, not only with travel and our willingness to venture outside the country, but the overall economy and outlook had strengthened. The stock market rebounded to pre-September 11 levels and investor confidence was a little less pensive, less guarded. Investor 401(k) accounts that took a serious whack during September began a gradual rebound during the fourth quarter, signaling a strong rally that U.S. recovery was on its way. With 11 interest rate cuts by the Federal Reserve during 2001, the U.S. government attempted to jumpstart our sagging economy out of its year-long doldrums.

During the months of November and December 2001, it was business as usual concerning Mexico properties. Phones rang, inquiries and requests for information were steady, and new orders for title insurance policies were placed. As in prior years, many transactions had to be closed before the public registries of Mexico ended their operations for the Christmas holidays.

The residue of 9/11 has made our eyes clearer and our ears keener. We ask more questions and seek more explanations—not just concerning safety and travel but also about major issues and challenges we face everyday. The aftermath of 9/11 is one of the reasons potential buyers better understand the issues concerning ownership of land in Mexico. They are more willing to learn and to be armed with the right questions. These buyers are simply more savvy and know if their questions cannot be answered by an individual, they will turn to information provided on the Internet. In addition, Mexico's real estate developers and agents have increasingly become more aware that purchasers do understand the issues. Buyers are concerned with title matters, use of an escrow agreement, subdivision authorizations, recorded deeds and condominium regimes, capital gains tax implications and property conveyance procedures, to name a few. No longer is this buying public willing to just accept that old adage of "trust me, that's how we do business here in Mexico." The margarita syndrome has lost a considerable amount of its swagger, and 9/11 contributed to the new focused attitude and approach.

Also since 9/11, title companies have gained approval and official authorization from Mexico's National Commission of Bonds and Insurance. For example, Stewart Title Guaranty de Mexico, S.A. de C.V. (STGM), not only has corporate offices in Mexico City, but also can issue a title policy governed under Mexican law to any acquirer of real estate in Mexico. What does this mean? Mexican banks, financial institutions, developers and Mexican individuals can now get the comfort and security that a property ownership policy can provide with official government certification directly on the policy from the *Comision Nacional de Segurosy Financias.* This policy should also enhance the prospects of a formalized mortgage lending system with lower interest rates and longer terms of repayment, leading to the creation of a securitization process on Mexican mortgages. This same Mexican policy will be issued to U.S. buyers of real estate in Mexico, as well. Any foreign purchaser—Canadian, French, American, etc.—can obtain the benefit and protection from a contract of indemnity that will protect his/her ownership rights as vested in the public deed and recorded in the public registry of property. U.S. buyers can seek restitution under the STGM policy in Mexico or in the United States. STGM will have the ability to enhance the title search function, escrow procedures, closing by the *notario publico* and the recording of the public deed in the registry.

MEXICO OFFER∫ AN INVE∫TMENT ALTERNATIVE

Although taxes can be a huge benefit in the acquisition of real estate, they also can be a burden. In the next chapter, we examine what to expect when considering tax consequences on both sides of the border.

CHAPTER SEVENTEEN

Understanding Taxes: What to Expect From Uncle Sam

Residency requirements,
capital gain exemptions, tax-deferred exchanges

I n the United States, American citizens may exclude the capital gain they realize when they sell their principal residence after occupying it for a period of not less then two years during the five years preceding the sale and meeting other specific IRS requirements. There is no federal income tax liability on up to $250,000 gain in U.S. dollars ($500,000 gain for joint filers) on the sale of a primary residence.

Mexico has a similar provision in its tax code for primary residences—even for U.S. citizens. The Mexico Tax Revenue

Code (*Código Fiscal de La Federación*) states that Mexican nationals and foreign owners of a home in Mexico may be entitled to certain tax exemptions on the capital gain realized if the home is a primary residence. In fact, Mexico has no ceiling on the gain rendered by the sale of a primary residence, but U.S. citizens must stay within the $250,000–$500,000 limits, regardless of where their primary home is located.

The issue of capital gains tax has long been a troubling problem for many foreign purchasers of residential property in Mexico whether it is used as a residence or investment. Many sellers, whether Mexican or foreign, have tried to reduce their tax liability on the sale of a residence by using a lower "declared value" in the transaction rather than using the actual sales price. As a result, unknowing buyers can inherit additional tax consequences when they ultimately sell the home in question because their "basis" in the property is less than what they actually paid. For several years now, some real estate agents in Mexico have advised their non-Mexican clients not to worry about capital gains taxes because they would qualify for an exemption. They often advised the prospective buyer that he or she would be able to demonstrate to the local public notary (*notario publico*), who is responsible for the collection and payment of the capital gains tax, that the residence was their primary residence and therefore they qualify for the exemption. At the very least, this was misleading and poor advice to receive from a seller or real estate agent. At its worst, it could be considered tax fraud.

According to recent amendments of the Mexico Tax Revenue Code, a foreign national who is a "homeowner" may qualify as a "resident" of Mexico for Mexican tax purposes and may qualify for a capital gains tax exemption on the sale of residential property in Mexico. The following are some points to consider to determine whether you qualify as a Mexican resident:

- Is your primary residence in Mexico?

- Is more than 50 percent of your total income generated or earned in Mexico?

- Is your main business operation or your main professional center for business income purposes located in Mexican Territory?

If you have answered "yes" to these questions, you may be considered a Mexican resident and may be entitled to some residency benefits such as the capital gains tax exemption. You should always contact a local *notario publico* to discuss the specific requirements and benefits of Mexican residency. You should also consult with other Mexican legal counsel and tax advisors to explore these and other possible benefits. American and other foreign buyers of Mexican residential property must be aware of Mexico's capital gains tax liability when they sell. If the original seller did not declare the total purchase price when selling the property, the buyer could face increased capital gains tax liability when the buyer sells the property because of the artificially reduced basis, as discussed earlier. It is not uncommon for this consequence to be a "deal killer" when the buyer seeks to sell the property and discovers that he or she must write a check just to cover the income tax due at the pending sale. This is a clear chapter in the famous case of *caveat emptor:* Let the buyer beware. Obviously, the simple solution to this problem is to declare the actual purchase price in the sale of all real estate. Always consult with legal counsel and a tax advisor to make sure you understand the property's basis and tax ramifications.

Underestimated financial options of the Tax Relief Act of 1997

With one stroke of his pen, President Bill Clinton changed the financial status of not only the average American home but also the primary residences of U.S. citizens held abroad. When the Taxpayer Relief Act of 1997 went into law on August 5, 1997, it changed not only the $125,000, one-time home sale exclusion for persons over 55 years of age, but also the "rollover replacement rule." In essence, the home began to move from the "shelter" column into the "financial portfolio" column. Under the old law, a taxpayer could defer any gain on the sale of a principal residence by buying or building a home of equal or greater value within 24 months of the sale of the first home. Tax on the gain was not eliminated, but merely "rolled over" into the new residence, reducing the tax basis of the new home. If you sold a primary residence and failed to meet the requirements for deferral, the taxpayer faced a tax on current and previously deferred gain. The old law also contained an once-in-a-lifetime $125,000 exclusion ($62,500 if single, or married and filing a separated return) of gain from the sale of the primary residence.

The intent of the new tax code, which replaces the "rollover" provision and $125,000 over-55 exclusion, is to allow most homeowners to sell their primary residence without tax. It also dramatically simplifies record-keeping for many people. Although it's still wise to retain proof of the original cost of the home and significant improvements, tedious collection and retention of invoices and other records to substantiate the cost of home improvements probably won't be necessary. Many taxpayers, including retirees who have already used the one-time over-55 $125,000 exclusion, do not realize they are eligible to sell their primary home again—and do it every two years—under the Taxpayer Relief Act of 1997. The 1997 law repealed all former tax laws on primary residences and significantly changed the role of the home in regard to financial planning. Here are the keys to one of the best ways the average home-owner can now accumulate more wealth for retirement, per-haps buying a smaller home in the states and a primary home in Mexico, and an explanation of why the home has become the largest piece in the average taxpayer's financial puzzle:

In order to qualify for the $500,000 capital gains exclusion ($250,000 for single persons), a taxpayer must have owned and used the property as his or her principal residence for two out of five years prior to the date of sale. Second, a taxpayer must not have used this same exclusion in the two-year period prior to the sale. The only limit on the number of times a taxpayer can claim this exclusion is once in any two-year period. What is often mis-understood is that both the earlier one-time exclusion of up to $125,000 in gain for persons over 55 and the deferral of all or part of a gain by purchasing a qualifying replacement residence are gone. You no longer can utilize parts of either portion and you absolutely do not have to buy a replacement home. Persons who used the $125,000 exclusion can make use of the new exclusion if they meet the two-year residency test. The law enables seniors to "buy down" to less expensive homes without tax penalties. For gains greater than the exemption amounts, a 15 percent capital gains tax usually will apply. Homeowners with potential gains larger than the excludable amounts should keep accurate records in an attempt to reduce their gains by the amount of all eligible improvements.

To qualify for the full exclusion, either married spouse can meet the ownership requirement, but both must meet the use requirement. Although exclusion can be used only once in each two-year period, a partial exclusion may be available if the sale results from a change in place of employment or health, or from unforeseen circumstances. If you have owned the house fewer than two years, you would receive a proportional amount of the maximum exclusion under special situations. For example, if you owned a home for one year and made a $55,000 profit, the entire $55,000 would be tax free because your total exclusion was chopped in half to $125,000 from $250,000 (and from $500,000 to $250,000 for married couples) because of the one-year time frame. Consumers can turn Mexican homes (plus yachts and recreational vehicles) into principal residences simply by meeting the residency requirements. Divorced or separated spouses also are not out in the cold. If an "ex" lived in the home for two of the five years before the sale, that person is able to use the exclusion. However, nothing changes on the loss side of the primary home sale ledger—losses on the sale of the primary home still are not deductible in the United States, Mexico or elsewhere. If a nondeductible loss seems unavoidable, it might be a good idea to convert the house to a rental property (where losses are deductible), but you would have to be able to prove the move was not just to avoid taxes. If depreciation were claimed on a property, the maximum capital gains tax liability would be 25 percent to the extent depreciation was claimed.

Two key guidelines:
Use and residency requirements

For married taxpayers who file a joint return, only one spouse need meet the two out of five-year ownership requirement, but both spouses must meet the two out of five-year use requirement. That is, if the husband has owned and used the house as his principal residence for two of the past five years, but his wife did not use the house as her principal residence for the required two years, then the capital gains exclusion is only $250,000.

For those who leave their home because of a disability, a special rule makes it easier to meet the two-year requirement—especially if you were hospitalized or had to spend a significant period in a similar facility. In such cases, if you owned and used the home as a principal residence for at least one of the five years preceding the sale, then you are treated as having used it as your principal residence while you are in a facility that is licensed to care for people in your condition. This rule enables the family to sell the home to raise cash for the expenses without incurring a large tax bite.

The tax-deferred exchange from U.S. to Mexican property is not "like kind"

In the United States, a tax-deferred exchange (commonly known as IRS Section 1031 Exchange) proceeds just as a "sale" for you, your real estate agent and parties associated with the deal. Provided you closely follow the exchange rules, however, the IRS will "sanction" the transaction and allow you to characterize it as an exchange rather than as a sale. Thus, you are permitted to defer paying the capital gain tax. Section 1031 specifically requires that an exchange take place. That means that one property must be exchanged for another property, rather than sold for cash. The exchange is what distinguishes a

Section 1031 tax deferred transaction from a sale and purchase. The exchange is created by using an intermediary (or exchange facilitator) and the required exchange documentation. Here are the typical steps:

- You (taxpayer) receive an acceptable offer for your property.
- You assign your seller's rights in the relinquished property purchase and sale contract to the buyer. The buyer gives "your" cash to the intermediary. This is the first leg of the exchange.
- You make an acceptable offer to acquire the replacement property.
- You assign your purchaser's obligations in the contract to the intermediary.
- The intermediary acquires the relinquished property and instructs the seller to deed it directly to you to complete the trade.

In an exchange, you must trade an interest in real estate (sole ownership, joint tenancy, tenancy in common) that you have held for trade, business, or investment purposes for another "like-kind" interest in real estate. The like-kind definition is very broad. You can dispose of and acquire any interest in real property other than a primary home or a second residence. For example, you can trade raw land for income property, a rental house for a multiplex or a rental house for a retail property. However, the definition does not include trading a U.S. property for another property outside the country. You cannot trade a home in Tampa for a condo in Ixtapa—it's not like-kind. However, the IRS does permit a trade of a foreign property for another foreign property on a tax-deferred exchange. For example, if you had a ski condo in Whistler, British Columbia, and became tired of the snow, you could trade it for a cozy place on the beach in Los Cabos. You could defer the gain by identifying a place of equal or greater value in Los Cabos within 45 days of the sale of the Whistler ski condo and then close the deal within 180 days of the sale of the Whistler property. While you would owe no U.S. tax on the deal, you would still face significant tax liability in both Canada and Mexico because those countries would charge tax on the respective sales.

The "no-touch" rule

If the taxpayer actually receives the proceeds from the disposition of the relinquished property, the transaction will be treated as a sale and not as an exchange. Even if the taxpayer does not *actually* receive the proceeds from the disposition of the property, the exchange will be disallowed if the taxpayer is considered to have "constructively" received them. The code regulations provide that income, even though it is not actually in the taxpayer's hands, is "constructively" received by the taxpayer if it is credited to his or her account, set apart for him or her, or otherwise made available so that he or she may draw upon it at any time. In a nutshell: "If you touch it (or even get too close), the IRS will come."

Vacation becomes property search

There have been numerous times when people from the frozen north have traveled south for the winter (just like any smart bird) to avoid shoveling snow, icy roads and pent-up office anger. Let's say you left Lincoln, Nebraska (Go, Big Red!), after the bowl games in January and followed your longtime friends to Zihuatanejo, the lovely seaside village where Tim Robbins and Morgan Freeman charted to meet in the movie *The Shawshank Redemption*. Your friends had been after you for years to visit and you finally blocked time to go. After a couple of days of secluded rest, delicious meals and warm water, you begin the think that this stress-free life more than makes sense. Before you know it, you begin checking real estate prices and even cruise into a brokerage office to gauge values and areas. More interest quickly surfaces when you begin to ascertain the low cost of living, inexpensive labor and acceptable phone and Internet access. Why not consider buying a vacation home? What about an investment property ("half of Lincoln would love it here") that you could rent out to friends, use yourself in January and then consider moving into it as a primary residence when you retire? How would your purchase go over with your accountant, and more importantly, with the IRS?

If you use your Mexican getaway solely as a vacation home, real estate taxes and mortgage interest can be deducted on your federal return as itemized deductions. If you find that in order to afford the house, you need to rent the property out when not using it, other tax rules apply. Depreciation, maintenance expenses, operating expenses, mortgage interest, property taxes and insurance during the rental period become itemized deductions. If you actively participate in the management of the property, you may be able to use up to $25,000 of your real estate losses to offset other income on your U.S. tax return. To actively participate, you need to be involved in the management of the property and own at least 10 percent of the investment property. You can have a property manager do most of the work, but you will have to make all major management decisions such as choosing tenants, rental rates, capital expenditures and repairs.

After years of renting out your Zihuatanejo hideaway, you cash in your chips and try living in "Z-Town" full-time. You now have a primary residence in Mexico and rent your Lincoln home to an assistant football coach from the University of Nebraska. You would qualify for the usual deductions that would apply to a principal residence in the U.S. You may deduct foreign property taxes and any remaining mortgage interest expense on your tax return. Down the road, you may decide to sell the Zihuatanejo home. Upon sale, you may pocket realized gains up to $250,000 for single taxpayers and up to $500,000 for married couples. In order to exclude up to $500,000 in gains you will need to have owned and used the Z-Town house as your principal residence for at least two of the last five years.

Gift and estate taxes are other U.S. taxes to consider. Under current U.S. law, if you are a citizen or resident of the United States, your Mexican real estate will be included in your gross estate for tax purposes if you hold title to the property or if title is held through a Mexican trust. If you give your property away, say to a family member, or allow them to live there rent free, these are considered gifts. If the value of the gifts is greater than $11,000 per year, you will be subject to gift taxes. Mexico does not have either an estate tax or an inheritance tax.

Considering taxes in different countries

Confusing tax issues can surface when you own property in more than one country. Various taxes related to real estate transactions are calculated differently in Mexico and the United States. The key is to determine in which country you deem your primary residence. Both Mexico and the U.S. consider you a tax resident of the country in which you keep your principal residence. For example, you may have been living in Mexico on a tourist visa the last five years, but for tax purposes you would more than likely be considered a tax resident of Mexico. U.S. citizens and residents are required to report and pay tax on income made anywhere in the world, regardless of where you live. In addition, both Mexico and the U.S. reserve the right to tax property within their boundaries.

Mexico property taxes are known as *predial*. Compared to property taxes in many U.S. cities, the cost of the *predial* is a bargain. It is a local tax, usually posted in the mail that can typically be paid at local banks three times a year. Some owners request the bill be sent directly to the bank where it is deducted from the account when the bill becomes due and payable. It's best to keep an accurate paper trail of the paid tax bills. You will need to show the paid receipts when the property in question is sold, mortgaged or traded.

According to the Mexico–U.S. Income Tax Treaty and the Mexican Income Tax Law, rental income generated in Mexico is subject to Mexican income taxes. If you are a resident in Mexico, rental income outside of Mexico should also be reported on your Mexican tax return. If you are renting out property for nonbusiness use, you will not be required to collect a Value Added Tax (*Impuesto al Valor Agregado* [IVA]) on the rental income, as long as the property is unfurnished. Furnished homes and other property rented for business use are subject to IVA. If you own a business-related property, you will need to add the IVA tax on top of any rent that you may be collecting. No IVA is due when buying or selling a home.

There is a tax on certain gifts in Mexico involving real estate, which is payable by the recipient. However, gifts between spouses and direct family members are not taxable. Therefore, you could gift a home to your children, and they would not need to pay taxes on the gift in Mexico. When acquiring property by purchase, gift, inheritance or otherwise, there are several taxes and fees that you should be aware of. Principal among these is the acquisition tax, which runs about 2 percent of the property value. Other fees include a certificate of nonencumbrance, *notario* and other attorney fees and appraisal fees. The parties to the real estate transaction usually negotiate who will pay the fees for the certificate on nonencumbrance and the appraisal. *Notario* fees are generally split equally between the parties. The acquiring party pays for the acquisition tax and the seller bears the burden of the capital gains taxes.

When property changes hands and capital gains taxes are due, the *notario* withholds a certain percentage of the gains according to a formula, on behalf of the seller. The seller pays the remaining portion of the capital gains when he or she files their annual tax return in Mexico. How capital gains are calculated on the sale of property in Mexico involves a complicated, confusing method. Two of the main factors are that the cost basis of the property in Mexico is adjusted for inflation, and, as mentioned above, the price used to calculate the tax is not necessarily the sale price. Let us assume that you bought a condo two years ago at $100,000 and then sold it at the end of the second year. Inflation during that period was 15 percent for the first year and 10 percent for the second year. The price of the home would be adjusted to $115,000 the first year and then $126,500 for the second year. A second difference of note is that the price used to figure out the sale of the property is not necessarily what the property was sold for, as in the United States. Remember, unlike the States, many people in Mexico use the appraised value or the municipal assessed value as the sales price, even though the property may have been sold for a different amount. Obviously, you may want to use the lower figure, depending upon your buy-sell circumstances, but be certain your *notario* understands your request. In the end, however, Mexican capital gains tax on investment real estate is not as expensive as in the United States. In any case, the net result is that in Mexico the seller will pay substantially less capital gains on real estate transactions.

More discussion on second residence... or rental property

A home and a primary residence have different meanings, benefits and drawbacks to tax persons. For example, do you want the depreciation and maintenance benefits of a rental home or the mortgage-interest deduction of a second residence? A personal residence cannot be depreciated. An individual can have several homes yet only one primary residence. A home refers to where a person is physically living, as long as his or her stay is more than a temporary one. Primary residence involves both physical presence in a place and intention to make that place one's home. Residence without "the intention to remain indefinitely" generally will not constitute primary residence. An individual's motive for changing primary residences—even for tax reasons—does not raise red tax flags. However, consumers must show at least some sort of intent to establish a primary residence.

If you are considering making your Mexican home your permanent residence, now or in the future, you should begin planning for a change in primary residence. If you have been using your Mexican home as a rental, consider converting it to personal-use for a period of at least two years. That way, if you have to sell unexpectedly, you can keep up to $500,000 in gains tax-free. However, use caution and keep a paper trail. Some people who retain homes and remain active in business or community affairs in their original states are finding that state tax officials are challenging their change of personal residence. The states say that these folks are still residents for income or estate tax purposes because they have not abandoned their original personal residences. However, when intent conflicts with facts and circumstances, determining which residence is actually an individual's primary residence can be confusing. The determination is usually based on the individual's objective and facts, such as:

- Payment of local taxes
- Time spent in state of residency
- Continuous car registration and driver's license
- Furnishing and appointing primary residence more extensively

You will also want to consider the potential of U.S. state income tax consequences of a change of residence. If you have bonuses coming, stocks options or other deferred compensation (as is the case, for example, with many corporate executives), plan carefully how you receive these funds relative to your move to avoid excessive state income taxes. Many states have become more aggressive in enforcing their sales and use tax laws. They have gone to great lengths—examining U.S. Customs reports, auditing tax gallery sales, personal checkbooks and credit card statements and sharing that information with other states. Some states have enacted strict filing responsibilities and record retention statutes with respect to individuals who flip-flop principal residences.

A home does not have to actually be used to qualify as a residence. If there is no rental or personal use of a residence for an entire year, it can be designated as a "qualified residence" and mortgage interest can be fully deducted. If it is rented a majority of the year and used just two weekends by the owner, no interest can be deducted under the personal-residence rule. The rule is that personal days must exceed the greater of 14 days or 10 percent of rental days. The personal-use requirement must be met before a property can be designated a qualified residence. If the home is rented more than 140 days, there will have to be 15 days of personal use before the interest can be deducted fully under the residence rule. Since the 1986 Tax Reform Act left mortgage interest on first and second homes intact, accountants and tax advisers have asked clients to weigh renting versus personal use very carefully. The deductibility of rental expenses and mortgage interest enters a gray area when you alter the cut-and-dried, 14-day or 10-percent guideline. If you have the ability to rent winter and summer, you can also get in more personal-use days under the 10 percent rule. A Mexican resort might have the potential for 250 rental days a year, allowing the owner to use it for 25 days without forfeiting its rental status.

Another way to pick up a day or two on the beach without eating into your 14-day or 10-percent limit is to clean the house yourself between renters, perhaps monthly snow birds from the Midwest. Days spent maintaining the house do not count toward your personal use limit. You can even deduct travel costs to get to the house and expenses such as paint and cleaning supplies. The house also must be rented at fair-market value. If you rent to relatives at discount rates, the IRS may rule that the house is not a business and disallow many of your deductions.

It's a good idea to consider a second home—for rental or personal use—simply because houses will continue to appreciate in many areas of Mexico for some time. The boom is likely to continue especially in the most popular areas. If you want that getaway all to yourself but find you can't afford the mortgage payments after you buy it, go ahead and rent it. You can juggle rental and personal use status from year to year. The getaway that was once viewed only as a luxury is now not a bad place to stick your savings. And in a few years, you may even be able to retire into what has become the best investment you ever made.

Use may matter to your lender

The personal residence or rental question also will surface when dealing with a lender. In Chapter 15, we offer some creative ways you may not have considered to help you get in the door of a second home. However, the conventional method typically entails making a downpayment (from savings, liquidating other assets) or taking out a home equity loan on your primary residence for the "down." The remaining balance then can be financed over a term similar to the loan on your primary home—30 years, 15 years or a variety of adjustable-rate mortgage periods. If the home is a second residence, the rates probably will be more favorable than if the home is a rental unit, commonly referred to as a "nonowner occupied" dwelling. In fact, some U.S. lenders will not finance investment properties in Mexico, only second homes. If you plan to rent out your home, a lender willing to make an investor loan will want to see proof that you're actually going to generate a cash flow that will help pay the monthly mortgage plus taxes and insurance. In many cases, the lender will ask for a cash flow statement for a property showing its rental history. And don't count on your bank to take all of a home's estimated rental income into consideration. Even for a property with a long rental history, most lenders will only consider 75 to 80 percent of the total take. If possible, make purchase offers contingent upon your loan being approved—some lenders will not extend funds in condominium developments where there are renters other than owner occupants. Also, make sure you know all insurance costs for your new property.

A second home in Mexico can also be a long-term tax shelter for future retirement. For example, if you are 45 years old and plan to slow down at 60, you can buy a rental home disguised as a vacation home, furnish it, enjoy some personal use time and have renters pay for it. When you have carved off every bit of tax depreciation advantage out of it, you can move in and convert it to a full-time private residence while still renting it out a couple of weeks a year. And because most mortgages "front-load" interest, you will have used up most of your tax deductions from the mortgage in the 15 years you were working and renting the home. In the later years of the mortgage, when interest deductions are relatively low, you probably will be less concerned because your income will have fallen off. Although future tax proposals undoubtedly will change the current tax landscape, second homes in any environment should be spared the big axe when compared to other proposed restrictions on real-estate investments. You can sell your primary residence, pocket the gain and retire to your second home in Mexico. If you no longer like the Mexican getaway you purchased years ago, make sure you have lived in it two years as your primary residence, sell it, pocket the gain and move on down the beach to another home.

Congress really helped the potential for second homes

Unknowingly, when members of Congress approved the Taxpayer Relief Act of 1997, they completely overhauled and multiplied the possibilities for second home purchase, use and sale. Ironically, the reason why taxpayers are able to reap the advantages of having two homes in the first place can be directly traced to our members of the U.S. House of Representatives and Senate. Why are we able to deduct the mortgage interest on two homes rather than just one? It's because Congressional members "needed" two homes—one in their home state and another in the nation's capital. (Some accountants even refer to the curious guideline as the "Congressmen's Rule.") When you couple the ability to own two (or more) personal residences simultaneously, then toss in the capacity to convert a rental property into a personal residence, you will be overwhelmed to discover the windfall profits brought by simple combinations of appreciation and tax savings. Let's examine several examples that are applicable to traditional age brackets and investment phases. But never forget—you can always move in to your rental and you can sell your primary residence every two years and pay no tax.

More than one home— in the United States or Mexico

As most taxpayers know by now, the 1997 tax legislation added a generous exclusion for sales of primary residences. If you own one or more residences, there are some tax-saving strategies to be considered chess moves to be made, all legal and proper, but preparation and timing are always important. The basic gain exclusion qualification rule is simple: You must have owned and used the home as your main residence for at least two years out of the five-year period ending on the date of sale. To repeat, if you are married, the full $500,000 capital gains break ($250,000 for singles) is available as long one or both of you satisfies the residency and ownership guidelines (explored thoroughly in Chapter 3).

Let's say Houston Spade and his wife, Sparky, are married and own three homes. First there's their current main home, not far from the landscape and garden center they started in Dallas, which qualifies for the $500,000 capital gains exclusion. They paid $550,000 for the place, sell it for a net of $850,000 and put $300,000 of gain in their pocket because it is less than the $500,000 maximum exclusion. Houston and Sparky then move to their Cancun vacation home where Houston likes to scuba dive. After living in Cancun for two years, Houston and Sparky sell the home, pocket $475,000 (their net again was less than the maximum $500,000) of tax-free gain and move to Loreto, where Houston has been hired to oversee the landscape design of a new housing development. After living in Loreto for two years, Houston and Sparky can sell, pocket up to $500,000 in gain tax free, move again...the tax-free windmill continues and the gain goes in their pockets. Living in Mexico gives you the same capital-gain benefit on the sale of your primary residence as you would enjoy north of the border.

It's true—few people want the hassle of moving to a new primary residence every two years. But you could, and the buying prospects probably are more attractive now in Mexico than they will be 10 years down the road. All investments you own now could be involved later, tax-free. If you permanently convert, or temporarily flip-flop, the status of rental properties to personal residences, more moneymaking possibilities quickly surface. Here is an example of a useful strategy:

Schoolteacher bought years ago— and it paid off

For example, Susie, 40, a single woman and schoolteacher, has a principal residence in New Jersey and a condo in La Paz that she bought years ago after a two-week vacation to her aunt's beach home. Both properties have significantly appreciated in value over the past decade. Sally sells her principal residence, takes her capital gain exclusion of up to $250,000 on that residence and decides to retire to the La Paz condo and help a friend who opened a restaurant there. The condo now becomes her principal residence. Sally lives in the condo for two years and thereby satisfies the use and occupancy tests. Sally then sells the property and realizes another big-time gain of which $250,000 can be excluded. It makes no difference that most of the appreciation on the second property was realized years before she moved in. Sally has prepared and has met all of the requirements to exclude the gain. She's simply avoided significant capital gains tax while building a considerable nest egg by understanding the tax laws and carrying out a simple plan. And she'll do it again. She has used the accrued appreciation to buy another condominium in Mazatlan across the Sea of Cortés. Susie will use one as a primary residence and the other as a second home, renting it periodically to friends until she eventually occupies it full time.

If you work your residences, recruit great renters and make logical upgrades, will you eventually be able to sell your wonderful Mexican getaway for a satisfactory price? If you have done all the right things in the right place, can you come out whole? In the final chapter, we discuss what you can expect when you're ready to exit your south-of-the-border retreat.

Pondering the Exit: If You Buy, Will You Be Able to Sell?

The boomers' appetite is huge for exotic, personal experiences

As amazing as the housing market was in the United States between 2000 and 2005, the second-home market in Mexico was even more prolific for U.S. and Canadian buyers seeking appreciation for their vacation or retirement residences. In some Mexico markets, it was not been uncommon for foreign purchasers to realize at least a 30 percent increase in home values over a two-year period. It really isn't hard to understand. Owning a residence has long been the way in which Americans create personal net worth. Houses have historically accounted for the largest and single most important acquisition one makes. If our disposability of income reaches a threshold where we can make prudent investments, real estate has long been a lucrative avenue.

If you roll the dice and buy in Mexico, who will be *your* likely buyer? With the number of people looking to real estate to acquire wealth and leisure time, the resale prospects for well-situated home in Mexico appear to be extremely bright. And for at least the next 20 years, the numbers are overwhelming. According to the U.S. Bureau of the Census and the National Center for Health Statistics, the number of Americans aged 45 to 64 increased 34 percent from 1990 to 2000 and now sits at approximately 71 million. Every day, the 50-plus population is growing by 10,000 people, and this trend is expected to continue for the next 20 years. Right now, an American turns 50 every seven seconds.

Why is this important to the outlook for Mexican real estate? This is the largest, healthiest and wealthiest group ever appearing on the U. S. growth landscape and it is just beginning to grasp the concept of *fideicomiso*, the trust creating a 50-year beneficiary right for any foreign buyer purchasing a residence in Mexico's restricted zone. Much like the boomers' parents—members of the greatest generation—targeted Florida, the boomers will target Mexico because of the different experience, the attraction to perceived risk and the thrill of the exotic. In many cases, it's simply the lure of the beach and a step outside the predictable second home box. Remember the popular advertising line "this is not your father's Oldsmobile"? Mexico, except for some longtime retirees who saw the light early, "is not your father's second home spot." That was Florida, now too expensive and a touch too common for the boomers' taste. Some may say they will buy in Florida or Arizona, but you can never rely on what this group collectively says it will do.

"Baby boomers are famous for believing one thing and then behaving totally different from what they think they do," says Eric Snider, who has a doctorate in social psychology and serves as Shea Homes' marketing director for Trilogy, the homebuilding company's upscale active adult communities. "They are after exclusivity, amenities and personal experiences. Boomers are all about personal experiences."

In a 2004 economic study prepared by the Urban Institute for AARP, authors Barbara Butrica and Cori Uccello contend that boomers will amass more wealth in real terms at retirement than will the two previous generations. Median household wealth at age 67 will grow from $448,000 among 2004 retirees to $600,000 among boomers. Income at retirement is consistent with trends in wealth at retirement, the study shows. Projected household income at age 67 will increase from $44,000 among current retirees to $65,000 among boomers.

As we mentioned in Chapter 15, baby boomers never met a loan they didn't like. The bottom line is that they will continue to drive the second home stampede to Mexico because they like to be creative with financing, and they love having the status—and the actual experience—of a second home. Owning a property in a place as mysterious as Mexico will further push their fun and romance buttons.

And they will introduce Mexico to their children. If you think the baby boomer group was immense and steered the housing market plus every element of the retail industry, get ready for a throng that contains many of their consumer-crazy children—the proud members of generation Y. These youngsters, born in 1979 or later, will have 74 million members (an estimated three million more than the boomers) and make up 34 percent of the population by 2015. They will prefer homes that will be useful rather than prestigious, and they will be willing to trade size for lifestyle and convenience factors. Doesn't that sound like a small bungalow close to the beach or a casita with a view of the mountains?

Although Mexico is just beginning to see a prolific and energetic home-buying market, the great equalizer is the basic law of supply and demand. Mexico is not making more land on the beach, and the popularity of its vast other regions is rapidly growing. Supply continues to be a diminishing commodity and the members of generation Y haven't even shown up yet with their checkbooks. Will they also be buying memories of great family times under the Mexican sun? Absolutely. And the numbers will be overwhelming, driving prices higher and probably investment returns as well.

If you ever sell, you can probably hand-pick your buyers and awe them with stories of the days when the beaches were vacant and fishermen simply arrived in *panga* boats every morning without even a phone call.

PART FOUR

Helpful Sources

Realtors from Both Sides of the Border

Members of the National Association of Realtors Specializing in Mexico— Residing in the United States

Arizona

William Powers
Realty Executives International, Inc.
2398 East Camelback Rd., Ste. 900
Phoenix, AZ 85016
Phone: 800.252.3366 **Fax:** 602.224.5542
Email: *billpowers@realtyexecutives.com*
Member Type: Designee

Diane Jackson
Buyer Brokers Realty of Sedona
Old Market Pl., Ste. 1, 1370 Hwy 89A
Sedona, AZ 86336
Phone: 928.821.2237 **Fax:** 928.203.4677
Email: *diane@arizonabuyers.com*
Member Type: Candidate

California

Armida Martin Del Campo
Sunshine Realty
4150 Bonita Rd. • Bonita, CA 91902
Phone: 619.479.9700 Fax: 619.479.9780
Email: *armidasun@aol.com*
Member Type: Designee

E. Robert Miller
E. Robert Miller & Associates
330 Primrose Rd., Ste. 606
Burlingame, CA 94010
Phone: 650.373.0705 Fax: 650.373.0709
Email: *elymiller@hotmail.com*
Member Type: Designee

Bernardo Bicas
Prudential California Realty
678 3rd Ave., Ste. 305
Chula Vista, CA 91910
Phone: 619.476.4476 Fax: 619.422.1176
Email: *bernardo@bemaxrealestate.com*
Member Type: Candidate

Barbara Cooke
ZipRealty, Inc.
4341 Rosina Court
Concord, CA 94518
Phone: 925.408.9488 Fax: 925.265.9067
Email: *barbarac@ziprealty.com*
Member Type: Designee

Bob Bishop
Century 21 King REALTORS®
161 McKinley
Corona, CA 92879
Phone: 909.318.1952 Fax: 909.734.5534
Email: *bobishop@deltanet.com*
Member Type: Candidate

Danielle Carlson
CDC Real Estate & Financial Services
PO Box 4104
Garden Grove, CA 92842
Phone: 714.537.3595 Fax: 714.537.8370
Email: *danielle@cdcre.com*
Member Type: Designee

Susan Laxson
Prudential California Realty
1299 Prospect St.
La Jolla, CA 92037
Phone: 858.459.0501 Fax: 858.459.3275
Email: *SDHOL@aol.com*
Member Type: Designee

Theodore Deuel
Deuel International Group, Inc.
24022 Calle De La Plata, Ste. 400
Laguna Hills, CA 92653
Phone: 949.707.4999 Fax: 949.859.0617
Email: *Tdeuel@deuelinternational.com*
Member Type: Designee

Peggy Little
California Real Estate
PO Box 46
Los Angeles, CA 90078
Phone: 323.512.2053 Fax: 323.882.8180
Email: *homebuyercare@msn.com*
Member Type: Designee

Sabine Birkenfeld
Homestead Realty
350 N. Sepulveda Blvd, Ste. 10
Manhattan Beach, CA 90266
Phone: 310.376.9464 Fax: 310.376.9466
Email: *sabine@sabinebirkenfeld.com*
Member Type: Designee

Steve Goddard
RE/MAX Beach Cities Realty
400 S. Sepulveda Blvd, Ste. 100
Manhattan Beach, CA 90266
Phone: 800.861.3333 Fax: 310.376.6522
Email: *steve@stevegoddard.com*
Member Type: Designee

Jason Buck
Coldwell Banker
68 Malaga Cove Plaza
Palos Verdes Estates, CA 90274
Phone: 310.265.4268 Fax: 310.373.2340
Email: *jasonbuck@dataframe.net*
Member Type: Designee

Dianne Randall
Coldwell Banker Palos Verdes Realty
600 Deep Valley Dr.
Palos Verdes Peninsula, CA 90274
Phone: 310.544.8407 Fax: 310.544.6353
Email: *dianne@diannerandall.com*
Member Type: Designee

Huesan Tran
Millennium, Inc.
225 South Lake Ave., 3rd Flr.
Pasadena, CA 91101
Phone: 626.272.7746 Fax: 626.628.3610

Email: *huesan@yahoo.com*
Member Type: Designee

Kathy Jenkins
Keller Williams Realty West
225 Ave. I, Ste. 201
Redondo Beach, CA 90277
Phone: 310.643.5267   Fax: 310.725.0266
Email: *kjenkins@kw.com*
Member Type: Designee

Margaret Wang
Coldwell Banker George Realty
19220 E. Colima Rd.
Rowland Heights, CA 91748
Phone: 626.810.6660   Fax: 626.810.7166
Email: *margaretwangsold@hotmail.com*
Member Type: Designee

Linda Dorris
Coldwell Banker, Gay Dales, Inc.,
REALTORS®
444 S. Main St.
Salinas, CA 93901
Phone: 831.424.0771   Fax: 831.424.1750
Email: *ldorris@coldwellbanker.com*
Member Type: Designee

Dianne Rath
ERA Eagle Estates Realty
9906 Carmel Mountain Rd.
San Diego, CA 92129
Phone: 858.780.1202   Fax: 858.484.5961
Email: *diannerath@aol.com*
Member Type: Designee

Robert Warburton
The Warburton Company International
Network Emerald Plaza
402 W Broadway
San Diego, CA 92101
Phone: 530.265.4973   Fax: 619.595.3150
Email: *bob-konnie@warburtoncompany.com*
Member Type: Designee

David Chien
ePacifica Real Estate
268 Bush St., #3640
San Francisco, CA 94104
Phone: 510.429.1415   Fax: 510.429.1455
Email: *info@ePacificaRE.com*
Member Type: Designee

Wanda Klor
Realty World, Wanda Klor & Associates
4990 Speak Lane, Ste. 260
San Jose, CA 95118
Phone: 408.267.8808   Fax: 408.264.8858
Email: *wanda@wandaklorandassoc.com*
Member Type: Designee

Gerardo Padilla
G. P. Real Estate, Inc.
50 Airport Pkwy.
San Jose, CA 95110
Phone: 408.437.7731   Fax: 408.528.7725
Email: *padillag@pacbell.net*
Member Type: Designee

Kevin Young
RE/MAX Santa Barbara
1715 State St.
Santa Barbara, CA 93101
Phone: 805.564.3400   Fax: 805.564.3400
Email: *kyoung@sbre.com*
Member Type: Designee

Colorado

Lana Le Chabrier
Thor Trust
PO Box 3757
Boulder, CO 80307
Phone: 805.637.3100
Email: *thor@rmi.net*
Member Type: Designee

Brian Morgan
Keller Williams Realty – Brighton
1401 E. Bridge St.
Brighton, CO 80601
Phone: 303.659.3101   Fax: 303.659.0413
Email: *morgprop@aol.com*
Member Type: Designee

Nancy Mikoda
Prestige Real Estate Group
520 Zang St., Ste. 200
Broomfield, CO 80021
Phone: 888.887.7617   Fax: 303.280.1333
Email: *nancymikoda@qwest.net*
Member Type: Designee

John Starke
RealtyPro International, Ltd.
7061 S. University Blvd, Ste. 100

Centennial, CO 80122
Phone: 303.730.4800   Fax: 303.730.4898
Email: *john@realtyprousa.com*
Member Type: Designee

Rosalinda Chaney
RE/MAX Properties, Inc.
5080 Broadmoor Bluff Dr.
Colorado Springs, CO 80906
Phone: 719.332.8800   Fax: 719.576.1746
Email: *rosalinda.chaney@wesellmore.com*
Member Type: Candidate

Paula McGowan
Paula McGowan, Real Estate Broker
3604 Galley Rd., Ste. 105
Colorado Springs, CO 80937
Phone: 520.419.0718   Fax: 719.573.1815
Email: *pamcgowan@aol.com*
Member Type: Designee

David Powell
Ensign Realty Corp. – Colorado Springs
1709 Acacia Dr.
Colorado Springs, CO 80907
Phone: 719.522.1227   Fax: 719.531.7414
Email: *powelldavid@adelphia.net*
Member Type: Candidate

Sherry Romero
Choice REALTORS®
2790 N. Academy Blvd, Ste. 344
Colorado Springs, CO 80917
Phone: 719.559.4663   Fax: 719.623.0678
Email: *sherryromero@topproducer.com*
Member Type: Designee

Liliane Rowe
ERA Shields Real Estate
5475 Tech Center Dr., Ste. 300
Colorado Springs, CO 80919
Phone: 719.535.7349   Fax: 719.548.9357
Email: *lrowe@erashields.com*
Member Type: Designee

Raymond Mallard
United Property Brokers, Inc.
3515 S. Tamarac Dr., Ste. 100
Denver, CO 80237
Phone: 303.671.9311   Fax: 303.694.2520
Email: *upbi@aol.com*
Member Type: Candidate

Joe Martinez
RE/MAX Northwest, Inc.
12000 Pecos St., Ste. 160
Denver, CO 80234
Phone: 303.255.4334   Fax: 303.255.4396
Email: *joe@denverhomesells.com*
Member Type: Candidate

Pamela Boyd
Pamela Boyd Real Estate
PO Box 320
Dillon, CO 80435
Phone: 970.389.7450   Fax: 970.513.0588
Email: *captpamela@yahoo.com*
Member Type: Designee

Lance Chayet
Hanover Realty/Hanover Commercial
13095 West Cedar Dr., Ste. 102
Lakewood, CO 80228
Phone: 303.399.9000   Fax: 303.763.5470
Email: *hanoverrealty@aol.com*
Member Type: Candidate

Kay Corken
Marx Real Estate Corp.
1295 W. Littleton Blvd.
Littleton, CO 80120
Phone: 303.761.4006   Fax: 303.761.7334
Email: *kcorken920@aol.com*
Member Type: Designee

Dena Schlutz
Estate Professionals
9767 North 89th St.
Longmont, CO 80503
Phone: 303.588.7532   Fax: 303.772.2928
Email: *schlutz@peoplepc.com*
Member Type: Designee

Hilda Schlutz-Barrientos
RE/MAX of Longmont
2350 17th Ave.
Longmont, CO 80503
Phone: 303.588.7578   Fax: 303.774.7080
Email: *hildaschlutz@remax.net*
Member Type: Designee

Judy Spear
Help U Sell Home Gallery
600 S. Airport Rd., Bldg. B, Unit B
Longmont, CO 80503
Phone: 303.786.7355   Fax: 303.417.1828

Email: *judy@spearteam.com*
Member Type: Designee

Lee Holfeltz
Coldwell Banker Massey
Real Estate Consultants
29919 U.S. Hwy 160
South Fork, CO 81154
Phone: 719.873.5131 Fax: 719.873.5380
Email: *lhol@amigo.net*
Member Type: Designee

Tracy Bossow
Prudential Gore Range Properties, Inc.
511 Lionshead Mall
Vail, CO 81657
Phone: 970.476.2482 Fax: 970.476.6499
Email: *tbossow@vail.net*
Member Type: Designee

Suzanne Dugan
Suzanne J. Dugan, Broker
PO Box 3768
Vail, CO 81658
Phone: 800.595.8955 Fax: 970.476.2564
Email: *dugan@sdugan.com*
Member Type: Designee

Robin Cunningham
RE/MAX Northwest, Inc.
12000 Pecos St., Ste. 160
Westminster, CO 80020
Phone: 303.457.4800 Fax: 303.252.8133
Email: *cobuyeragt@aol.com*
Member Type: Candidate

Jennifer McGraw
The Group, Inc.
7785 Highland Meadows Pkwy.
Windsor, CO 80528
Phone: 970.226.0700 Fax: 970.229.5727
Email: *jmcgraw@thegroupinc.com*
Member Type: Designee

Connecticut

"A.J." Bernard
Real Estate Professionals of Conn.
39 Mill Plain Rd., Ste. 3
Danbury, CO 06810
Phone: 203.743.2545 Fax: 203.790.9249
Email: *ajbrealestate@juno.com*
Member Type: Designee

Stella Montana
Prudential CT Realty
1583 Post Rd.
Fairfield, CT 06824
Phone: 203.255.2800 Fax: 203.255.1149
Email: *stelmontana@hotmail.com*
Member Type: Designee

Anne Miller
Anne Miller Real Estate
975 Main St.
Manchester, CT 06040
Phone: 800.647.8002 Fax: 860.645.3166
Email: *anne@annemillerrealestate.com*
Member Type: Candidate

Florida

Ana Ordaz
Coldwell Banker Real Estate, Inc.
20803 Biscayne Blvd., Ste. 102
Aventura, FL 33180
Phone: 305.613.6751 Fax: 954.458.0772
Email: *ana406@bellsouth.net*
Member Type: Designee

Frank Kowal
Coldwell Banker Real Estate, Inc.
575 Indian Rocks Rd. North
Belleair, FL 33770
Phone: 727.581.9411 Fax: 727.585.0482
Email: *fkowal@tampabay.rr.com*
Member Type: Designee

Maria Guevara-Gatley
RE/MAX Downtown
1902 S.E. 39th Terrace
Cape Coral, FL 33904
Phone: 239.945.8500 Fax: 239.945.8501
Email: *info@DavidGatley.com*
Member Type: Designee

Christian BonJorn
BonJorn Real Estate
516 W. Hwy 50
Clermont, FL 34711
Phone: 800.243.2114 Fax: 352.394.6907
Email: *cbonjorn@aol.com*
Member Type: Designee

Matilde Aguirre
Esslinger-Wooten-Maxwell, Inc.,
REALTORS®

1360 South Dixie Highway
Coral Gables, FL 33146
Phone: 305.667.8871 **Fax:** 305.665.8332
Email: *aguirre@matimex.com*
Member Type: Designee

Martha Pomares
New Image Realty Group
2655 Le Jeune Rd., Ste. 412
Coral Gables, FL 33134
Phone: 305.779.6888 **Fax:** 305.728.3115
Email: *pomares@mindspring.com*
Member Type: Designee

Rita Mesquita
Campbell & Rosemurgy Real Estate
1233 East Hillsboro Blvd.
Deerfield Beach, FL 33441
Phone: 954.571.3526 **Fax:** 954.427.0117
Email: *rmesquita@bellsouth.net*
Member Type: Designee

Amelia Barreto
SellState Achievers Realty Network
7431 College Pkwy.
Fort Myers, FL 33907
Phone: 239.253.9274 **Fax:** 239.947.0245
Email: *amelia@ameliabarreto.com*
Member Type: Designee

Carola Rathke
Coldwell Banker Real Estate
1127 Seminole E, Ste. 23-B
Jupiter, FL 33477
Phone: 561.745.5119 **Fax:** 561.746.3992
Email: *carola@myflproperties.com*
Member Type: Candidate

Truette Wyman, II
La Primera, Inc.
705 N. Main St.
Kissimmee, FL 34744
Phone: 407.847.817 **Fax:** 407.847.3103
Email: *laprimerainc@earthlink.net*
Member Type: Designee

Carlos Fuentes
VET Realty
23738 Peace Pipe Ct.
Lutz, FL 33559
Phone: 813.598.4224 **Fax:** 813.948.0535
Email: *cfuentes@ccim.net*
Member Type: Designee

Jorge Cantero
EWM, Inc.
671 Brickell Key Dr.
Miami, FL 33131
Phone: 305.530.1900 **Fax:** 305.530.8383
Email: *apollore@gate.net*
Member Type: Designee

Pablo Langesfeld
Fortune International Realty
2666 Brickell Ave.
Miami, FL 33129
Phone: 305.857.3613 **Fax:** 305.470.7441
Email: *propiedades@aol.com*
Member Type: Designee

Patricia Millan
Fortune House International Realty
1401 Brickell Ave., Ste. 440
Miami, FL 33131
Phone: 305.450.7118 **Fax:** 305.373.6665
Email: *pat@miamirealestateisme.com*
Member Type: Designee

Armando Montero
MGI Realty, LC
9130 S Dadeland, 1902 Datran Twr.
Miami, FL 33156
Phone: 305.670.0367 **Fax:** 305.661.5364
Email: *Amontero@mgi-realty.com*
Member Type: Designee

Oscar Resek
Keller Williams Eagle Realty
700 N.E. 90th St.
Miami, FL 33138
Phone: 305.694.5354 **Fax:** 305.759.8991
Email: *oresek@kw.com*
Member Type: Designee

Leon Weinschneider
RE/MAX Beach Properties
9511 Collins Ave., Ste. 1507
Miami Beach, FL 33154
Phone: 305.812.1090 **Fax:** 305.865.6287
Email: *Leon@Weinschneider.com*
Member Type: Designee

Kristina Tomblin
John R. Wood, Inc. REALTORS®
616 Fifth Ave. South
Naples, FL 34102
Phone: 239.820.2226 **Fax:** 239.434.0141

Email: *ktomblin@earthlink.net*
Member Type: Designee

Joan Miller
Joan S. Miller Real Estate, Inc.
3266 Lake Shore Dr.
North Hutchinson Island, FL 34949
Phone: 772.467.2646 Fax: 772.465.2791
Email: *Joan@Joan-S-Miller.com*
Member Type: Designee

Leon Srebrenik
Lumer Real Estate
16300 N.E. 19th Ave., Ste. A
North Miami Beach, FL 33162
Phone: 305.948.9480 Fax: 305.948.9755
Email: *info@leonsrebrenik.com*
Member Type: Designee

Donna Srebrenik
VIP Properties of Distinction
1983 PGA Blvd.
North Palm Beach, FL 33408
Phone: 561.317.8288 Fax: 561.694.2401
Email: *cipshawaii@juno.com*
Member Type: Designee

Robert Pulliza
Coldwell Banker Real Estate, Inc.
211 East Colonial Dr.
Orlando, FL 32801
Phone: 407.765.5331 Fax: 407.6494.353
Email: *rpfmc@hotmail.com*
Member Type: Designee

Alexander VanGrondelle
Keller Williams Realty
3980 Town Center Blvd.
Orlando, FL 32837
Phone: 407.581.3387 Fax: 321.221.2919
Email: *alex@HotPropertyStore.com*
Member Type: Designee

Margaret Begley
Prudential Network Realty
1000 Sawgrass Village Dr., Ste. 101
Ponte Vedra Beach, FL 32082
Phone: 904.285.1000 Fax: 904.285.3036
Email: *alamar1@bellsouth.net*
Member Type: Designee

Eric Matthews
Gulf Coast Realty International

4409 Sweetbay St.
Port Charlotte, FL 33948
Phone: 941.766.7091 Fax: 941.766.8102
Email: *matthewsgulfcoast@comcast.net*
Member Type: Designee

Noreen McCarthy
Burnt Store Properties, Inc.
25001 Harborside Blvd.
Punta Gorda, FL 33955
Phone: 941.637.7779 Fax: 941.637.8022
Email: *noreen@noreensells.com*
Member Type: Designee

Judith Pittman
Mapp Realty & Investment Company
3120 Southgate Circle
Sarasota, FL 34239
Phone: 941.302.1720 Fax: 941.379.5720
Email: *jspitt97@comcast.net*
Member Type: Candidate

Grissel Fernandez
RE/MAX Prestige Realty
10590 Forest Hill Blvd, Ste. 100
Wellington, FL 33414
Phone: 561.301.1945 Fax: 561.753.7927
Email: *misseyf@bellsouth.net*
Member Type: Designee

Gloria Carrero
RE/MAX Hometown, Inc.
2500 Weston Rd., Ste. 105
Weston, FL 33331
Phone: 954.675.0031 Fax: 954.385.5794
Email: *gloriacarrero@realtor.com*
Member Type: Designee

Pilar Moscoso
RE/MAX Hometown, Inc.
2500 Weston Rd., Ste. 105
Weston, FL 33331
Phone: 954.453.1665 Fax: 954.453.1668
Email: *pilarmosc@bellsouth.net*
Member Type: Designee

Richard Lawrence
Florida Property World, Inc.
446 West Plant St., Ste. 6
Winter Garden, FL 34787
Phone: 407.654.6433 Fax: 407.650.2653
Email: *rcl@flpropworld.com*
Member Type: Designee

John Lawrence
RE/MAX Town and Country Realty
1315 Tuskawilla Rd., Ste. 101
Winter Springs, FL 32708
Phone: 407.366.1934   Fax: 407.366.7265
Email: *jsylvia@att.net*
Member Type: Designee

Georgia

Judi Barrett
Atlanta Classic Real Estate, Ltd.
400 Galleria Pkwy., Ste. 1500
Atlanta, GA 30339
Phone: 404.713.0822   Fax: 770.612.8058
Email: *acreltd@bellsouth.net*
Member Type: Designee

Renee Hutchinson
Harry Norman, REALTORS®
2660 Peachtree Rd., Ste. 23-H
Atlanta, GA 30305
Phone: 404.816.5141   Fax: 404.365.0026
Email: *reneehut@bellsouth.net*
Member Type: Designee

Van Yon
RE/MAX Commercial Atlanta, LLC
5600 Roswell Rd., Ste. E-275
Atlanta, GA 30342
Phone: 404.978.2288   Fax: 404.978.2288
Email: *vanyon@remax.net*
Member Type: Designee

Wanda Stephens
Wanda G. Stephens & Associates
37 Henry Grady Hwy
Dawsonville, GA 30534
Phone: 706.265.0625   Fax: 706.216.4282
Email: *wandagstephens@remax.net*
Member Type: Designee

Oscar Melara
RE/MAX Action Realty
5387 Fairburn Rd.
Douglasville, GA 30135
Phone: 678.287.1265   Fax: 770.942.6654
Email: *oscar@oscarmelara.com*
Member Type: Designee

Raquel Lavender
Exit Advantage Realty
825 Fairways Court, Ste. 200

Stockbridge, GA 32081
Phone: 770.317.9205   Fax: 770.692.1105
Email: *raquel@homesinsouthatlanta.com*
Member Type: Designee

Iowa

Karl Reichert
Muscatine Real Estate
1424 Park Ave.
Muscatine, IA 52761
Phone: 563.263.2575   Fax: 563.263.6173
Email: *karl@iowahomenet.com*
Member Type: Designee

Illinois

Sylvia Rivera
Coldwell Banker Brokerage
321 N. Weber Rd.
Bolingbrook, IL 60490
Phone: 630.759.3100   Fax: 630.759.3354
Email: *srivera@coldwellbanker.com*
Member Type: Designee

Dana Ringewald
Coldwell Banker Brokerage
8101 S. Park Ave.
Burr Ridge, IL 60527
Phone: 630.887.8617   Fax: 630.887.9883
Email: *dringewald@adamsandmyers.com*
Member Type: Candidate

Andrea Schmidt Poling
The Prudential Landmark Real Estate
100 Trade Centre Dr., Ste. 102
Champaign, IL 61820
Phone: 217.352.1933   Fax: 217.378.1281
Email:
andreapoling@prudentiallandmark.com
Member Type: Designee

Raymond Covyeau
Troy Realty Ltd.
5420 North Harlem Ave.
Chicago, IL 60656
Phone: 773.704.0600   Fax: 773.625.1824
Email: *raycovyeau@aol.com*
Member Type: Designee

Gerardo Galan
Galan Realty
1536 West Walton
Chicago, IL 60622

Phone: 773.394.6382 Fax: 773.394.6418
Email: *mybluemarble@aol.com*
Member Type: Designee

Zelimir Stakic
Zel Realty LLC
2238 W. Foster Ave.
Chicago, IL 60625
Phone: 847.324.0155 Fax: 847.674.4772
Email: *zelrealty@aol.com*
Member Type: Designee

Sukey Holzman
Coldwell Banker
350 Linden
Wilmette, IL 60091
Phone: 847.331.2228 Fax: 847.256.8307
Email: *sukey@sukeyholzman.com*
Member Type: Candidate

Massachusetts

Fernando Illanes
Century 21 Hughes
319 Broadway
Lynn, MA 01904
Phone: 781.599.1776 Fax: 781.598.9310
Email: *fmillanes@msn.com*
Member Type: Designee

Michigan

Frank Eichelberg
Eichelberg REALTOR® LLC.
7183 Lakeridge Pl.
Kalamazoo, MI 49009
Phone: 269.375.1646 Fax: 269.375.1177
Email: *frankeichelberg@aol.com*
Member Type: Designee

Minnesota

Steven Strand
RE/MAX Results
2100 Ford Pkwy.
St. Paul, MN 55116
Phone: 651.698.8006 Fax: 651.698.7686
Email: *sstrand@minnesotahomes.com*
Member Type: Designee

Missouri

Susan Kirkpatrick
Carol Jones, REALTORS®
PO Box 2061

Branson West, MO 65737
Phone: 417.338.8746 Fax: 417.338.1115
Email: *hugandco@aol.com*
Member Type: Designee

Georgiann Casey
James Andrew GMAC Real Estate
502 So. Truman Blvd.
Festus, MO 63028
Phone: 314.609.9466 Fax: 636.931.9010
Email: *jcasey@jamesandrewre.com*
Member Type: Designee

Norma Nisbet
Vista Properties & Investments
PO Box 8642
St. Louis, MO 63128
Phone: 314.843.6048 Fax: 314.842.4810
Email: *normanisbet@realtor.com*
Member Type: Designee

Mississippi

John Dean
Landmart/Dean Land & Realty Co.
PO Drawer 272
Leland, MS 38756
Phone: 662.686.7807 Fax: 662.686.7890
Email: *jdean@deanlandmart.com*
Member Type: Designee

North Carolina

Maggie Bowers
Helen Adams Realty
15235-J John J. Delaney Dr.
Charlotte, NC 28277
Phone: 803.323.7525 Fax: 704.431.3923
Email: *mechthild@infoave.net*
Member Type: Designee

Deborah Cook
Segrest International REALTORS®
PO Box 1956
Wilmington, NC 28402
Phone: 910.470.4800 Fax: 910.762.6568
Email: *Deb@SegrestRealty.com*
Member Type: Designee

New Mexico

Susan Feil
French & French Sotheby's Realty
326 Grant Ave.

Santa Fe, MN 87501
Phone: 505.954.5540   Fax: 505.954.5519
Email: *susan@susanfeil.com*
Member Type: Designee

Christopher Webster
Webster Enterprises
54 1/2 Lincoln Ave.
Santa Fe, NM 87501
Phone: 505.954.9500   Fax: 505.954.9501
Email: *Chris@ChrisWebster.com*
Member Type: Designee

Ernest Romero
Taos Management Co., Inc.
5522 NDCBU, 829 Paseo Sur
Taos, NM 87571
Phone: 505.758.0080   Fax: 505.758.5677
Email: *eromero@c21success.com*
Member Type: Candidate

Philip Valaika
RE/MAX of Taos
723 Paseo del Pueblo Sur
Taos, NM 87571
Phone: 505.758.5400   Fax: 505.758.0925
Email: *remax@taos.newmex.com*
Member Type: Candidate

Nevada

Michael Ornelas
McCall Realty, Inc.
PO Box 11685, Zephyr Cove
Lake Tahoe, NV 89448
Phone: 775.771.6449   Fax: 775.588.2224
Email: *mikentahoe@aol.com*
Member Type: Designee

Leslie Trayer
Century 21 Aadvantage Gold
2279 North Rampart Blvd
Las Vegas, NV 89128
Phone: 702.862.8500   Fax: 702.242.0428
Email: *ltrayer@cox.net*
Member Type: Designee

New York

Farouk Ali
Fasons International Properties, Inc.
265-17 Union Turnpike
New Hyde Park, NY 11040
Phone: 718.347.0100   Fax: 7183478816

Email: *fasonsali@aol.com*
Member Type: Designee

Eugenia Foxworth
Coldwell Banker Hunt Kennedy
1200 Lexington Ave.
New York, NY 10028
Phone: 212.327.1200   Fax: 212.327.1361
Email: *eugenia.foxworth@cbhk.com*
Member Type: Designee

Ohio

Diane Eplin
RE/MAX Affiliates, REALTORS®
7239 Sawmill Rd., Ste. 210
Dublin, OH 43016
Phone: 614.766.5330   Fax: 614.766.0153
Email: *blues1_singer@yahoo.com*
Member Type: Designee

Oklahoma

A. Earnest Gilder
Interstate Properties, Inc.
218 W. Okmulgee, PO Box 2519
Muskogee, OK 74402
Phone: 918.682.1119   Fax: 918.687.7200
Email: *interstate@interstateproperties.com*
Member Type: Designee

Oregon

Susan Estes
RE/MAX Signature Properties
2717 N.E. Broadway
Portland, OR 97232
Phone: 503.282.4000   Fax: 503.282.8558
Email: *susan@susanestes.com*
Member Type: Candidate

Puerto Rico

Rolando Acosta
Universal Real Estate
Calle 519 Bloque 184, #30
Villa Carolina, Carolina 00985
Phone: 787.647.0179   Fax: 787.276.2451
Email: *rolandoacosta@centennialpr.net*
Member Type: Designee

Gianna Mendez Zamora
Home Team
PMB 417 Avenida De Diego 89, Ste. 105
San Juan 00927

Phone: 787.790.5186   **Fax:** 787.790.5186
Email: *giameza@coqui.net*
Member Type: Designee

Maria Oquendo
Maria Judith Oquendo
P.O. Box 9065262
San Juan 00906
Phone: 787.449.1393   **Fax:** 787.282.7011
Email: *mjoa@coqui.net*
Member Type: Designee

Texas

Alston Boyd
Boyd & Boyd Properties
14607 Bear Creek Pass
Austin, TX 78737
Phone: 512.306.9966   **Fax:** 512.301.8382
Email: *alston@boyd2.com*
Member Type: Designee

Harlan Cooper
Cooper REALTORS®
1900 Plumbrook Dr.
Austin, TX 78746
Phone: 512.327.6600   **Fax:** 512.327.4344
Email: *cooper@aTexas.com*
Member Type: Designee

Wayne Stroman
Stroman Realty, Inc.
14500 Highway 105 West
Conroe, TX 77304
Phone: 936.588.4444   **Fax:** 936.588.4884
Email: *wayne@stroman.com*
Member Type: Designee

Lawrence Young
RE/MAX Metro Properties
5242 Holly Rd., PO Box 6729
Corpus Christi, TX 78466
Phone: 361.994.0330   **Fax:** 361.994.0340
Email: *lawryoung@aol.com*
Member Type: Designee

Melvin Simpson
TEAM 1 DFW Properties
1647 Bar Harbor Dr., PO Box 222246
Dallas, TX 75222
Phone: 214.371.1848   **Fax:** 214.371.0965
Email: *simpson@team1dfw.com*
Member Type: Designee

Brian Smith
Ellen Terry REALTORS®
6025 Luther Lane
Dallas, TX 75225
Phone: 972.588.8300   **Fax:** 214.522.8644
Email: *countryconnection@airmail.net*
Member Type: Designee

John Stone
John M. Stone Company
6060 N. Central Expressway, Ste. 512
Dallas, TX 75206
Phone: 214.368.7133   **Fax:** 214.265.8100
Email: *jmstone@johnmstone.com*
Member Type: Designee

Ghitta Torrico
Ebby Halliday REALTORS®
7601 Campbell Rd., Ste. 700
Dallas, TX 75248
Phone: 972.248.8800   **Fax:** 972.248.6872
Email: *ghitta@ebby.com*
Member Type: Designee

Sally Aubin
Aubin Realty
10637 Candlewood Ave.
El Paso, TX 79935
Phone: 915.591.5277   **Fax:** 915.590.0250
Email: *realtorsa@aol.com*
Member Type: Designee

Ward Arendt
Marilyn Arendt Properties
12414 Stafford Springs Dr.
Houston, TX 77077
Phone: 281.493.0155   **Fax:** 281.493.1686
Email: *ward@castle2sell.com*
Member Type: Designee

Bruce Binkley
Houston Community College System
3100 Main, MC 1748
Houston, TX 77002
Phone: 713.718.5240   **Fax:** 713.718.5336
Email: *alex.binkley@hccs.edu*
Member Type: Candidate

Sharon Brier
Greenwood-King Properties
1616 South Voss Rd., Ste. 900
Houston, TX 77057
Phone: 713.914.8727   **Fax:** 713.784.0968

Email: *cosmicsher@aol.com*
Member Type: Designee

Edna Corona
RE/MAX Alliance
5629 FM1960, Suite 121
Houston, TX 77069
Phone: 281.444.4848 Fax: 281.655.0367
Email: *ednacorona@sbcglobal.net*
Member Type: Designee

Richard Miranda
Keller Williams Realty
8300 FM 1960 West, Ste. 310
Houston, TX 77070
Phone: 281.807.1874 Fax: 281.894.1302
Email: *richardmiranda@kw.com*
Member Type: Designee

Cynthia Montero
Stewart Title
1990 Post Oak Blvd., Ste. 100
Houston, TX 77056
Phone: 713.625.8661 Fax: 713.629.2321
Email: *cmontero@stewart.com*
Member Type: Designee

John Partridge
Partridge Properties
3230 Yoakum
Houston, TX 77006
Phone: 713.528.1184 Fax: 713.528.2646
Email: *todd@toddpartridge.com*
Member Type: Designee

Luke Romero
Cameron & Tate Properties
3229 Houston Ave.
Houston, TX 77009
Phone: 713.426.3200 Fax: 713.426.3201
Email: *luke.romero@camerontate.com*
Member Type: Designee

Mariana Saldana
Uptown Real Estate Group Inc
5065 Westheimer, Ste. 640
Houston, TX 77056
Phone: 713.622.7771 Fax: 713.629.7773
Email: *uptownhtn@aol.com*
Member Type: Designee

Kimberly Clay
Prime Sterling Prop/GMAC Real Estate
22028 Highland Knolls, Ste. B
Katy, TX 77450
Phone: 281.395.1500 Fax: 281.395.1540

Email: *kimclay@pspgmac.com*
Member Type: Designee

Adrian Amaga
AAA Real Estate & Investments
PO Box 720838
McAllen, TX 78504
Phone: 956.682.1111 Fax: 956.682.2222
Email: *adrian@aaare.com*
Member Type: Designee

Becky Faust
RE/MAX Fine Properties
4500 Highway 6 South
Sugar Land, TX 77478
Phone: 281.265.5533 Fax: 281.494.5537
Email: *becky@beckyfaust.com*
Member Type: Designee

Consuelo Zubizarreta
Prudential Gary Greene REALTORS®
2323 Town Center Dr.
Sugar Land, TX 77478
Phone: 281.980.5050 Fax: 281.980.5426
Email: *zubic@garygreene.com*
Member Type: Designee

Raul Giorgi
Prudential Gary Green REALTORS®
9000 Forest Crossing
The Woodlands, TX 77381
Phone: 713.854.1519 Fax: 281.367.7027
Email: *homes@main.com*
Member Type: Designee

Larry Jackson
Jackson REALTORS®, INC.
9628 Jimmark Circle
Waco, TX 76712
Phone: 254.235.9972 Fax: 254.235.9973
Email: *larry@jacksonrealtors.com*
Member Type: Designee

Beth Mikulin
Kelly REALTORS®
8004 Woodway Dr., Ste. 400
Waco, TX 76712
Phone: 254.741.6500 Fax: 254.741.6505
Email: *bmikulin@kellyrealtors.com*
Member Type: Designee

Utah

Patsy Zubizarreta
Chilson & Associates Real Estate Co.
605 Main St., PO Box 2130
Park City, UT 84060
Phone: 435.645.9644 **Fax:** 419.858.4203
Email: *patsy@chilsoninternational.com*
Member Type: Designee

Bjoern Koch
Chilson & Associates Real Estate Co.
605 Main St., PO Box 2130
Park City, UT 84060
Phone: 435.645.9644 **Fax:** 435.649.1048
Email: *bjorn@chilsoninternational.com*
Member Type: Designee

Virginia

Mary Anthony
Long and Foster REALTORS®
3242 Sleepy Hollow Rd.
Falls Church, VA 22042
Phone: 703.750.2800 **Fax:** 703.750.2997
Email: *m.anthony@longandfoster.com*
Member Type: Designee

Washington

Donald LeMaster
Equity Management Group, Inc.
PO Box 10
Hoodsport, WA 98548
Phone: 360.877.6160 **Fax:** 3608776158
Email: *heloplt@aol.com*
Member Type: Designee

William Witting
Fine Real Estate Advice For Money
8441 282nd St. NW
Stanwood, WA 98292
Phone: 360.961.7603
Email: *billw@billwitting.com*
Member Type: Designee

Wisconsin

Stephen Beers
Keefe Real Estate, Inc.
751 Geneva Pkwy., PO Box 460
Lake Geneva, WI 53147
Phone: 414.248.4492 **Fax:** 414.248.9539
Email: *sbeers@keeferealestate.com*
Member Type: Candidate

Members of the National Association of Realtors Specializing in Mexico— Residing Outside the United States

Argentina

Carlos Rodriguez
Rodriguez Sanduay Propiedades
Montevideo 1985, 8th Floor, Apt. #48 • Buenos Aires C1021AAG
Phone: 54.114.816.3428
Fax: 54.114.816.3428
Email: *crs97@hotmail.com*
Member Type: International

Brazil

Jose Carlos Pellegrino
Pellegrino e Associados
Rua Dr. Rodrigo Silva No. 70-19 Andar
2398 East Camelback Rd., Suite 900
Sao Paulo 01501010

Phone: 55.113.105.1915
Fax: 55.113.107.9740
Email: *pellegrino@terra.com.br*
Member Type: Designee

Canada

Ursula Morel
RE/MAX of Whistler
4333 Skiers Approach
Whistler, BC V0N 1B4
Phone: 604.935.3635 **Fax:** 604.932.1140
Email: *ursula@ursulamorel.com*
Member Type: Designee

Judy Shaw
Noble House Real Estate Company
7033 Nesters Rd., Unit 2

Whistler, BC V0N 1B7
Phone: 604.932.6202 Fax: 408.547.9767
Email: *judi@noblehousecompany.com*
Member Type: International

Dianne Stickney
Coldwell Banker Peter Benninger Realty
508 Riverband Dr.
Kitchener, ON N2K 3S2
Phone: 519.742.5800 Fax: 519.742.5808
Email: *dianne-stickney@coldwellbanker.ca*
Member Type: International Realtor
Member

Guatemala
Sara Lois Siegel
Siegel B. Representaciones
Monterrey S.A. Ave. Reforma 10-00 Zona
9, Penthouse Edif. Condominio Reforma
Guatemala City 01009
Phone: 502.334.5233 Fax: 502.331.5214
Email: *slsiegel@intelnet.net.gt*
Member Type: International

Realtors Specializing in Mexico— Residing in Mexico

Acapulco, Guerrero
Raul Figuerola
Compasa 39690
Phone: 52.744.481.0070
Email: *compasa@prodigy.net.mx*
Member Type: CIPS Designee

Leon Borenstein Braun
Radisson Resort Acapulco 39850
Phone: 52.744.463.4259
Email: *corp0001@aol.com*
Member Type: International Realtor
Member

Ron Borenstein Braun
Ron Lavender & Asociados
Bienes Raices 39690
Phone: 52.744.484.7000
Email: *ron@ronlavender.com*
Member Type: International Realtor
Member

Federico Barton Guajardo
J.Q. Bienes Raices 39690
Phone: 52.744.484.4440
Email: *acapulco@jqrealestate.com.mx*
Member Type: International Realtor
Member

Aguascalientes
Jose de Jesus Lopez Soto
Habitat Desarrollos S.A. de C.V. 20000
Phone: 52.449.915.2257

Email: *jjlopezsoto@aol.com*
Member Type: International Realtor
Member

Ajijic, Jalisco
Manuel Hernandez Ontiveros
Hernandez Realty Group 45920
Phone: 52.376.766.2103
Email: *hernandezrg@laguna.com.mx*
Member Type: CIPS Designee

Lelia Riggs
Hernandez Realty Group 45920
Phone: 52.376.766.2103
Email: *lriggs@prodigy.net.mx*

Beverly Hunt
Laguna Real Estate 45920
Phone: 01.376.766.1174
Email: *lagunarealty@prodigy.net.mx*
Member Type: CIPS Designee

Margaret Britton
Ajijic Real Estate 45920
Phone: 52.376.766.2077
Email: *thebrittons@laguna.com.mx*
Member Type: CIPS Designee

Thomas Britton
Ajijic Real Estate 45920
Phone: 52.376.766.2077
Email: *thebrittons@laguna.com.mx*
Member Type: CIPS Designee

Jaime Niembro Montemayor
Ajijic Real Estate 45920
Phone: 52.376.766.2077
Email: *jaime@ajijic.com*
Member Type: CIPS Designee

Lynda MacMahon
International Realty 45920
Phone: 52.376.766.5122
Email: *lynda@mexicodreamhome.com*
Member Type: CIPS Designee

Arturo Garcia
Lakeside Homes Real Estate 45920
Phone: 52.376.766.5423
Email: *arturo_lakeside@prodigy.net.mx*
Member Type: International Realtor
Member

Bahia Kino, Sonora

Irma Patricia Martinez
Nieblas   Bahia Kino Bienes Real Estate 83348
Phone: 662.242.0037
Email: *kinobayrealestate@prodigy.net.mx*
Member Type: International Realtor
Member

Bahias De Huatulco, Oaxaca

Maria De Jesus Garcia Juarez
Data Habitat Bienes Raices 70989
Phone: 01.958.587.0218
Email: *datahabitat@yahoo.com.mx*
Member Type: International Realtor
Member

Bucerias, Nayarit

Fay Sloane
El Grupo Bienes Raices 63732
Phone: 52.329.298.1212
Email: *fbsloane@move2mexico.com*
Member Type: CIPS Designee

Cabo San Lucas

Ted Downward
Century 21 Paradise Properties 23450
Phone: 52.624.143.1101
Email: *paradise1@paradiseproperty.com*
Member Type: CIPS Designee

Judy Fabiani-Lujan
Pisces Real Estate 23400
Phone: 619.819.5080
Email: *judy@piscesrealestate.com*

Member Type: International Realtor
Member

Nita Bryson
Prudential California Realty Cabo Gold 23410
Phone: 52.624.104.3225
Email: *nbryson@homesinloscabos.com*
Member Type: International Realtor
Member

Stanley Patenaude
23450
Phone: 52.624.143.0852
Email: *stanley@cabotel.com.mx*
Member Type: International Realtor
Member

Jay West
Cabo Realty 23410
Phone: 206.347.3325
Email: *West@CaboRealty.com*
Member Type: CIPS Designee

Rene Billard Bayle
Cabo San Lucas Properties 23410
Phone: 52.624.143.3262
Email: *clsprops@cabonet.net.mx*
Member Type: International Realtor
Member

Teena Jones
Cabo Realty 23410
Phone: 206.347.3325
Email: *caboteena@yahoo.com*
Member Type: CIPS Designee

James Gladgo
Century 21 Paradise Properties 23450
Phone: 52.624.143.1110
Email: *jim@paradiseproperty.com*
Member Type: International Realtor
Member

Tim Vanni
Chilson & Associates International Real Estate 23410
Phone: 52.624.143.1778
Email: *tim@chilsoninternational.com*
Member Type: International Realtor
Member

Barbara Smith Cooperman
Coldwell Banker 23410
Phone: 52.624.151.5675
Email: *cabocoop@yahoo.com*
Member Type: International
Realtor Member

Joan Feinstein
Coldwell Banker Riveras 23410
Phone: 52.624.143.0202
Email: *feinstein.joanie@cbriveras.com*
Member Type: International
Non-CIPS Designee

Penelope Lash
Coldwell Banker Riveras REALTORS®
23410
Phone: 52.624.143.0202
Email: *lash.penny@pedregal.com*
Member Type: International
Realtor Member

Pierre Morel
Grupo Morel Internacional SA De CV
23450
Phone: 52.624.105.0611
Email: *morel@prodigy.net.mx*
Member Type: International
Realtor Member

Mark Nieman
Inmobiliaria Suenos del Sol, S.A. de C.V.
23410
Phone: 52.624.143.2797
Email: *cabosol@cabonet.net.mx*
Member Type: International
Realtor Member

Reyna Houston
Los Cabos Properties 23410
Phone: 52.624.143.1164
Email: *reynah@loscabosproperties.com*
Member Type: International
Non-CIPS Designee

Linda Miller
Property Solutions Real Estate Sales 23451
Phone: 52.624.143.1688
Email: *cabolinda@cabotel.com.mx*
Member Type: International
Realtor Member

Debra Dobson
Prudential California Realty – Cabo Gold
23410
Phone: 52.624.104.3226
Email: *debra@prucabogold.com*
Member Type: International
Realtor Member

Shane Kavanagh
Realty World Baja REALTORS® 23410
Phone: 619.819.5081
Email: *shane@realtyworldbajarealtors.com*

Member Type: International
Realtor Member

Cheryl Miller
Realty World Baja REALTORS® 23410
Phone: 52.044.624.1222
Email: *cheryl@realtyworldbajarealtors.com*
Member Type: International
Realtor Member

Clint Suveges
Realty World Baja REALTORS® 23410
Phone: 619.819.5081
Email: *clint@realtyworldbajarealtors.com*
Member Type: International
Realtor Member

Leticia Tolosa
Realty World Baja REALTORS® 23410
Phone: 619.819.5081
Email: *info@realtyworldbajarealtors.com*
Member Type: International
Realtor Member

William Stein
Zoe International de Construcciones 23410
Phone: 310.941.4614
Email: *bill@mexicovillarentals.com*
Member Type: International
Realtor Member

Cancun

Carmen Eichhorn
Carmen Bianca Real Estate 77500
Phone: 52.998.884.3462
Email: *carmenbianca@hotmail.com*
Member Type: International Realtor
Member

Victor Ivan Ebergenyi
Costa Realty S.A. de C.V. 77500
Phone: 52.998.885.1551
Email: *ieberganyi@costarealty.com.mx*
Member Type: International
Realtor Member

Jorge Casares
Flora Castellanos Bienes Raices – Real
Estate 77500
Phone: 52.998.887.5555
Email: *jorge@mrcancun.com*
Member Type: CIPS Designee

Luis Ornelas Reyes
International Realty Group 77500
Phone: 52.998.883.3962

Email:
luisornelas@internationalrealtygroup.com
Member Type: CIPS Designee

Luis R. Arce Lara
Century 21 Arce International
Phone: 52.998.884.1144
Email: *larce@century21cancun.com*
Website: *www.century21cancun.com*

Ricardo Barraza
Ricardo Barraza & Associates 77500
Phone: 52.998.884.0434
Email: *ricardojbarraza@yahoo.com*
Member Type: International
Realtor Member

Chapala, Jalisco

Pedro Arellano Arroyo
Arellano Corporation Group 45900
Phone: 52.376.766.3055
Email: *pedroarellano@laguna.com.mx*
Member Type: International
Realtor Member

Cristina Rojas Vargas
Century 21 Vistas Realty 45900
Phone: 52.376.766.2614
Email: *rojascristi@laguna.com.mx*
Member Type: International
Realtor Member

Garza, Garcia

Cesar Paredes
Global Commercial & Investment
Real Estate 66220
Phone: 52.818.400.0660
Email: *cparedes@att.net.mx*
Member Type: CIPS Designee

Hermosillo, Sonora

Margarita Castillo
Long Realty 83280
Phone: 52.662.217.3234
Email: *mcastillo@longrealty.com*
Member Type: International
Realtor Member

Mirna Torua
Long Realty 83280
Phone: 52.662.217.3234
Email: *mirnat@longrealty.com*
Member Type: International
Realtor Member

Carlo Alessi
Long Realty 83280
Phone: 52.662.217.3234
Email: *calessi@longrealty.com*
Member Type: International
Realtor Member

Kyoshi Monge
Kotake Long Realty 83280
Phone: 52.662.217.3234
Email: *yoshi@longrealty.com*
Member Type: International
Realtor Member

Adrian Loustaunau Pellat
Loustaunau & Asociados 83000
Phone: 52.662.215.2224
Email: *adrian@loustaunauyasociados.com*
Member Type: International
Realtor Member

La Paz

Enrique Angulo Marquez
Consultoria Y Gestoria Inmobiliaria 23060
Phone: 52.612.125.1470
Email: *eangulo@prodigy.net.mx*
Member Type: International Realtor
Member

Gordon Herpst
Omni Services S.A. de C.V. 23000
Phone: 52.612.123.4888
Email: *omni@osmx.com*
Member Type: International
Non-CIPS Designee

John Glaab
The Settlement Company 23000
Phone: 877.214.4950
Email: *john.glaab@settlement-co.com*
Member Type: CIPS Designee

Linda Neil
The Settlement Company 23000
Phone: 52.612.123.5056
Email: *linda.neil@settlement-co.com*
Member Type: International
Realtor Member

Leon, Guanajuato

Hector Obregon Serrano
Century 21 Obregon & Obregon 37160
Phone: 52.477.773.3477
Email: *hmobregon@aol.com*
Member Type: CIPS Designee

Los Cabos

Marco Ehrenberg
Ehrenberg & Associates/Pisces Real Estate
23410
Phone: 52.624.143.1588
Email: *marco@piscesrealestate.com*
Member Type: International
Non-CIPS Designee

Mazatlan, Sinaloa

Armando Castro Penna
Marca Inmobiliaria S.A. De C.V. 82010
Phone: 52.669.981.1295
Email: *arcastro@red2000.com.mx*
Member Type: International
Realtor Member

Merida, Yucatan

Vicente Gonzalez
Century 21 Maya Real 97133
Phone: 52.999.948.0900
Email: *vgonzalez@mayareal.com*
Member Type: International
Realtor Member

Mexicali, Baja California

Enrique Guadiana Machado
Promotora Azteca 21280
Phone: 52.686.566.2133
Email: *e_guadiana@hotmail.com*
Member Type: International
Realtor Member

Mexico City

Luis Diaz-Infante De La Mora
Aavan Pro, Corporacion para la
Construcion 01340
Phone: 52.555.635.3563
Email: *fagas@aavanpro.net*
Member Type: International
Realtor Member

Luis Madariaga Audiffred
Century 21 Wallsten 11830
Phone: 555.276.0200
Email: *luis_madariaga@terra.com.mx*
Member Type: International
Realtor Member

Jaime Barrios Knight
Jaime Barrios Y Asociados, S.C. 06500

Phone: 525.533.4533
Email: *jbarrios@prodigy.net.mx*
Member Type: International
Realtor Member

Salvador Rodriguez Lopez
Rodriguez Llerenas y Asociados, S.C.
11510
Phone: 555.557.9867
Email: *rodriguezlleren@infosel.net.mx*
Member Type: International
Realtor Member

Javier Martinez-Campos
Administracion Corporativa Inmobiliaria
11560
Phone: 52.555.531.2966
Email: *javier.martinez3@worldnet.att.net*
Member Type: International
Non-CIPS Designee

Duane Martinez-Campos
Century 21 Mexico 11930
Phone: 52.555.251.6700
Email: *irfcsb@aol.com*
Member Type: CIPS Designee

Maty Feldman-Bicas
Enlace Inmobiliario – REALTORS®
Link 11570
Phone: 52.555.203.6210
Email: *matyvida2@yahoo.com*
Member Type: CIPS Designee

Felipe Alvarez-Icaza Longoria
Grupo Define, S.A. de C.V. 03100
Phone: 52.555.559.1459
Email: *gdefine@prodigy.net.mx*
Member Type: CIPS Designee

Jorge Philippe R.
Habitat 11700
Phone: 52.555.251.1521
Email: *habitat@quality.com.mx*
Member Type: CIPS Designee

Jaime Quiroz
J.Q. Bienes Raices 03810
Phone: 52.555.669.4730
Email: *jqbr@prodigy.net.mx*
Member Type: CIPS Designee

Adolfo Kunz Bolanos
Kunz Y Asociados S.A. 06500
Phone: 52.555.553.5575

Email: *kasa@kunz.com.mx*
Member Type: International
Non-CIPS Designee

Ari Feldman
MIHC/REIT Mexicana S.A. de C.V 06700
Phone: 718.715.0410
Email: *afeldman@mihc.com.mx*
Member Type: CIPS Designee

Luis Madariaga
Real Solutions S.C. 01330
Phone: 52.555.442.9999
Email: *gante@prodigy.net.mx*
Member Type: CIPS Designee

Rodrigo Madariaga Barrilado
Real Solutions S.C. 01330
Phone: 52.555.442.9999
Email: *rmadariaga@randompartners.com*
Member Type: CIPS Designee

Isaac Holoschutz
Zenix 11560
Phone: 52.552.554.545
Email: *isaac@data.net.mx*
Member Type: International
Non-CIPS Designee

Monterey

Alejandro Erhard Lozano
RE/MAX Py V 64986
Phone: 01.818.317.8283
Email: *aerhard@pyv.com.mx*
Member Type: International
Realtor Member

Naucalpan

Enrique Blazquez Guerrero
Grupo GB Construcciones & Inmobiliaria 53150
Phone: 52.553.634.048
Email: *grupogb@prodigy.net.mx*
Member Type: International
Realtor Member

Isaac Podbilewicz Tenenbaum
Libra Administraciones y Promociones 53330
Phone: 52.555.360.3455
Email: *isaac@librabienesraices.com*
Member Type: International Realtor Member

Sergio Gomez Rabago
Arkidinamica 53100
Phone: 52.555.393.2770
Email: *arkidinamica1967@hotmail.com*
Member Type: CIPS Designee

Oscar Batiz Jam
Century 21 Batiz y Cia. 53119
Phone: 555.343.8287
Email: *c21batiz@prodigy.net.mx*
Member Type: CIPS Designee

Maria Gaxoet Bravo
Century21 Batiz y Cia 53119
Phone: 52.553.431.555
Email: *bgaxoet@prodigy.net.mx*
Member Type: CIPS Designee

North Puerto Vallarta, Nayarit

Heidi Byrd
RE/MAX Bahia 63732
Phone: 52.329.298.0044
Email: *heidi@remaxbahia.com*
Member Type: International
Realtor Member

Nuevo Laredo, Tamaulipas

Rodolfo Pena Rosas
Grupo Pecasa – Bienes Raices 88000
Phone: 52.867.713.6600
Email: *grupopecasa62@msn.com*
Member Type: International
Realtor Member

Gloria Cruz Vazquez
Tierra Cruz Bienes Raices 88270
Phone: 52.714.7985
Email: *gloriatierracruz@hotmail.com*
Member Type: International
Realtor Member

Oaxaca

Enrique Cantu Garza Gallardo
CIMA Inmobiliaria 68050
Phone: 52.951.502.5072
Email: *cimainmobiliaria@prodigy.net.mx*
Member Type: International
Realtor Member

Playa Del Carmen

Wael Gamaly
Premier Properties Group S De R.L. 77710

Phone: 52.984.873.0996
Email: *wael@premierproperties.net*
Member Type: International
Non-CIPS Designee

Luis R. Arce Lara
Century 21 Reef
Phone: 52.984.879.4858
Toll-Free US and Canada: 1.866.978.4615
Fax: 52.984.879.4859
Email: *sales@century21reef.com*
Website: *www.century21reef.com*

Puerto Aventuras

Teresa Gutierrez Valles
Caribbean Realty 77750
Phone: 52.984.873.5098
Email: *rental@cancun.com.mx*
Member Type: International
Realtor Member

Puerto Peñasco

Charlie Salem
Oceano
PO Box 577
Lukeville, AZ 85341
Phone: 52.638.383.5413
Fax: 928.569.0051
Email: *chuck@oceano-rental.com*

Jonni Francis
Coldwell Banker Rock Point
PO Box 177
Lukeville, AZ 85341
Phone: 52.638.383.4699
Email: *jonnifrancis@cbrockypoint.com*

Norm Oliver
Sonora Consulting
PO BOX 723, Lukeville, AZ 85341
Phone: 52.638.382.8026
Email: *nboliver2002@yahoo.com*

Steve Schwab
Realty Executives – First Mexican
Investments
PO Box 800
Lukeville, AZ 85341
Phone: 52.638.383.5856
Fax: 52.638.383.5003
Email: *steves@realtyexecs-mexico.com*

Esthela Hernandez
Realty Executives – First Mexican
Investments
PO Box 800

Lukeville, AZ 85341
Phone: 52.638.383.5856
Fax: 52.638.383.5003
Email: *estelahalmada@hotmail.com*

Dee Brooks
Twin Dolphins Real Estate
PO Box 116
Lukeville, AZ 85341
Phone: 52.638.383.3919
Email: *dbrooks@twindolphinsrealty.com*

Grant MacKenzie Jr.
REMAX
PO Box 1200
Lukeville, AZ 85341
Phone: 638.383.1425 Fax: 480.452.0634
Email: *jr.legacy@starband.net*

Grant MacKenzie S.
REMAX
PO Box 1200
Lukeville, AZ 85341
Phone: 52.638.383.1425 Fax: 480.452.0634
Email: *beachmagic@starband.net*

Ing. Jorge A. Lopez L.
Century 21 – Sun and Sand
Jose Alcanta 1
Phone: 52.638.388.1295
Fax: 52.638.388.1298
Email: *jorge@century21penasco.com*

Frank H. Jackson
Sandy Beach Resorts
Cholla Bay Road Km. 3.7
Rocky Point
Phone: 52.638.383.0600
Fax: 52.638.383.0601
Email: *ParadiseSandsMX@Aol.com*

Reyel Taylor
Sandy Beach Resorts
Cholla Bay Road Km. 3.7
Rocky Point
Phone: 52.638.383.0600
Fax: 52.638.383.0601
Email: *cholla@prodigy.net.mx*

Fayth Moody
Cholla Bay – Beachfront Community
Homesites
Phone: 52.638.382.5050
Fax: 52.638.382.5051
Email: *fayth@rockypointnetwork.com*

Linda S.C. Decker
Proaset Real Estate
Blvd. Freemont & Chiapas St.
Phone: 52.638.383.4404

Fax: 52.638.383.3411
Email: *jorge@century21penasco.com*

Patricia Perez
Mexico Bonito Realty
Apod. 73 PTO.
Phone: 52.638.383.5737
Email: *patricia@mexicobonitorealty.com*

Kent Cossey
The Costal Group
Phone: 52.638.383.1336
Fax: 52.638.383.7704
Email: *kent@tcgpenasco.com*

Scott Poturalski
The Costal Group
Phone: 52.638.383.1336
Fax: 52.638.383.7704
Email: *scott@tcgpenasco.com*

Jon Mirmelli
Las Palomas – Seaside Golf Community
Sandy Beach
Phone: 52.638.383.8090
Fax: 602.532.7742
Email: *jon@lpsgc.com*

John Hibbert
Las Palomas – Seaside Golf Community
Sandy Beach
Phone: 52.638.383.8090
Fax: 602.532.7742
Email: *john@lpsgc.com*

Tab Gray
Las Palomas – Seaside Golf Community
Sandy Beach
Phone: 52.638.383.8090
Fax: 602.532.7742
Email: *tab@lpsgc.com*

Guillermo Valencia Navarro
Las Palomas – Seaside Golf Community
Blvd. Kino # 1110
Col. Pitic
Hermosillo
Puerto Peñasco, Sonora, México
Phone: 52.662.214.43.10 ext. 247
Fax: 52. 662.215.17.25
Email: *gvalencia@vallegrande.com.mx*

Puerto Vallarta, Jalisco

Sandra Spence
Alpha Sphere Group S.A. de C.V.
48390
Phone: 52.322.221.5266

Email: *spence1sandra@yahoo.com*
Member Type: CIPS Designee

Wayne Franklin
Tropicasa Realty 48380
Phone: 52.322.222.6505
Email: *franklin@tropicasa.com*
Member Type: International
Realtor Member

Harriet Cochran Murray
Cochran Real Estate 48300
Phone: 52.322.228.0419
Email: *harriet@pvnet.com.mx*
Member Type: CIPS Designee

Silvia Elias A.
P.V. Realty, S.A. de C.V. 48350
Phone: 52.322.222.4288
Email: *silvia@pvre.com*
Member Type: CIPS Designee

David Pullan A.
P.V. Realty, S.A. de C.V. 48350
Phone: 52.322.222.4288
Email: *david@pvre.com*
Member Type: CIPS Designee

Teresa Kimball
Prudential California Realty Vallarta
Division 48300
Phone: 52.322.294.1612
Email: *tere.kimball@prurealtypv.com*
Member Type: CIPS Designee

M. Thomas Yablonsky
RE/MAX Exotic Realty 48354
Phone: 52.322.221.2377
Email: *exoticrealty@hotmail.com*
Member Type: International
Realtor Member

Michael Green
Tropicasa Realty 48380
Phone: 52.322.222.6505
Email: *michael@tropicasa.com*
Member Type: International
Realtor Member

Marla Hoover
Tropicasa Realty 48380
Phone: 52.322.222.6505
Email: *marla@tropicasa.com*
Member Type: International
Realtor Member

Donna Machovec
Tropicasa Realty 48380
Phone: 52.322.222.6505
Email: *donna@tropicasa.com*
Member Type: International
Realtor Member

Carmen Vargas
Tropicasa Realty 48380
Phone: 52.322.222.6505
Email: *carmen@tropicasa.com*
Member Type: International
Realtor Member

Queretaro

Manuel de la Torre
Alianza Realty, S.C. 76040
Phone: 52.442.213.8811
Email: *alianzarealty@televicable.net.mx*
Member Type: International
Realtor Member

Rogelio Ledesma Torres
Promociones Mercadeo y Servicios 76160
Phone: 52.442.212.8077
Email: *rledesma@promesa.com.mx*
Member Type: International
Realtor Member

Roberto Flores Fernandez
Promociones Mercadeo y Servicios 76160
Phone: 52.442.212.8077
Email: *promessa@infosel.net.mx*
Member Type: International
Realtor Member

San Jose Del Cabo

Connie Poirrier
Prudential California, Cabo Gold 23400
Phone: 52.105.2666
Email: *conniebreck@yahoo.com*
Member Type: International
Realtor Member

Janet Jensen
Snell Real Estate 23400
Phone: 52.624.142.4873
Email: *janetj@snellrealestate.com*
Member Type: International
Realtor Member

Susanne Giraud
Prudential California, Cabo Gold 23400
Phone: 619.819.8638

Email: *seascape4u@hotmail.com*
Member Type: International
Realtor Member

Robert Brown
Baja Properties 23400
Phone: 52.624.142.1910
Email: *escaped5555@hotmail.com*
Member Type: International
Realtor Member

Michael Schaible
Baja Properties 23400
Phone: 52.624.142.0988
Email: *broker@bajaproperties.com*
Member Type: International
Realtor Member

Paul Geisler
Dream Homes of Cabo S.A. de C.V. 23401
Phone: 800.403.6597
Email: *pgeisler@prodigy.net.mx*
Member Type: International
Realtor Member

Paul Clark
Eastcapehomes.com 23400
Phone: 52.624.147.0111
Email: *eastcape@starband.net*
Member Type: International
Realtor Member

Julie Kershner
Prudential California, Cabo Gold 23400
Phone: 619.819.8638
Email: *julie@juliekershner.com*
Member Type: CIPS Designee

Evelyn Pepper
RE/MAX Los Cabos 23400
Phone: 52.624.142.0716
Email: *pepper@remaxloscabos.com*
Member Type: International
Realtor Member

Jan Aldredge
Snell Real Estate 23400
Phone: 52.624.144.5470
Email: *jan@snellrealestate.com*
Member Type: International
Realtor Member

Gwen Chambers
Snell Real Estate 23400
Phone: 52.624.144.5200

Email: *gwen@snellrealestate.com*
Member Type: International
Realtor Member

Greg Filard
Snell Real Estate 23400
Phone: 52.624.144.5200
Email: *greg@snellrealestate.com*
Member Type: International
Realtor Member

Jordan Gardenhire
Snell Real Estate 23400
Phone: 52.624.145.8226
Email: *jordan@snellrealestate.com*
Member Type: International
Realtor Member

Robin Hamilton
Snell Real Estate 23400
Phone: 52.624.145.8226
Email: *robin@snellrealestate.com*
Member Type: International
Realtor Member

Al Kairis
Snell Real Estate 23400
Phone: 52.624.144.5470
Email: *al@snellrealestate.com*
Member Type: International
Realtor Member

Will Kendall
Snell Real Estate 23400
Phone: 52.624.142.4873
Email: *will@snellrealestate.com*
Member Type: International
Realtor Member

David Liles
Snell Real Estate 23400
Phone: 52.624.144.5200
Email: *david@snellrealestate.com*
Member Type: International
Realtor Member

Chuck Lohrman
Snell Real Estate 23400
Phone: 52.624.144.5200
Email: *chuck@snellrealestate.com*
Member Type: International
Realtor Member

April Martin
Snell Real Estate 23400
Phone: 52.624.144.5200
Email: *april@snellrealestate.com*
Member Type: International
Realtor Member

Dana Matzen
Snell Real Estate 23400
Phone: 52.624.144.5470
Email: *dana@snellrealestate.com*
Member Type: International
Realtor Member

Flemming Nielsen
Snell Real Estate 23400
Phone: 52.624.145.8226
Email: *flemming@snellrealestate.com*
Member Type: International
Realtor Member

Erin Ortiz
Snell Real Estate 23400
Phone: 52.624.145.8210
Email: *erin@snellrealestate.com*
Member Type: International
Realtor Member

Bryan Pacholski
Snell Real Estate 23400
Phone: 52.624.144.5200
Email: *bryan@snellrealestate.com*
Member Type: International
Realtor Member

Tad Snell
Snell Real Estate 23400
Phone: 52.624.151.5201
Email: *tad@snellrealestate.com*
Member Type: International
Realtor Member

Chris Snell
Snell Real Estate 23400
Phone: 52.624.142.4873
Email: *snell@snellrealestate.com*
Member Type: International
Realtor Member

Julie Swanzy
Snell Real Estate 23400
Phone: 52.624.144.5200
Email: *julie@snellrealestate.com*
Member Type: International
Realtor Member

Randy Thompson
Snell Real Estate 23400
Phone: 52.624.142.4873
Email: *randy@snellrealestate.com*
Member Type: International
Realtor Member

Cliff Wilson
Snell Real Estate 23400
Phone: 52.624.144.5470
Email: *cliff@snellrealestate.com*
Member Type: International
Realtor Member

Wendy Straumann-Knapp
W.F.R. Cape S de RL de CV 23400
Phone: 52.624.144.0288
Email: *wendy@rionda-knapp.com*
Member Type: International
Realtor Member

Santa Fe

Bernardo Noriega
Noriega y Asociados Bienes Raices 01330
Phone: 52.555.442.9999
Email: *bnoriega@na.com.mx*
Member Type: CIPS Designee

Santiago de Queretaro

Raul Martin Salamanca Riba
Sayro Bienes Raices, S.A. de C.V. 76030
Phone: 01.442.215.0102
Email: *sayrobr@prodigy.net.mx*
Member Type: International
Realtor Member

Tijuana

Maria Del Carmen Galindo Rodriguez
Zuksa Bienes Raices 22440
Phone: 664.621.1113
Email: *zuksa@telnor.net*
Member Type: International
Realtor Member

Tlalnepantla

Maria Antonia Flores Morales
Grupo Inmobiliaria Vincent S.A. de C.V.
54060
Phone: 52.555.365.6046
Email: *vincentt@avantel.net*
Member Type: International
Realtor Member

Mario Aviles Barroso
Opcion Avil, S.A. de C.V. 54055
Phone: 52.555.361.6061
Email: *avil2000@hotmail.com*
Member Type: CIPS Designee

Uruapan, Michoacan

Luis Moreno Valencia
Century 21 Cupatitzio 60080
Phone: 52.452.523.0321
Email: *cnt21upn@prodigy.net.mx*
Member Type: International
Realtor Member

Villa Hermosa, Tabasco

Reyna Leon-Aguilera
Century 21 Terranova 86000
Phone: 52.933.312.0628
Email: *c21terranova@prodigy.net.mx*
Member Type: International
Realtor Member

Reyna Veronica Juarez Leon
Century 21 Terranova 86000
Phone: 52.993.312.0628
Email: *verojuarez2002@hotmail.com*
Member Type: International
Realtor Member

APPENDIX B

U.S. Embassy and Consulates in Mexico

The U.S. Embassy is located in Mexico City at Paseo de la Reforma 305, Colonia Cuauhtemoc; telephone from the United States: 011.52.55.5080.2000; telephone within Mexico City: 5080.2000; telephone long distance within Mexico: 01.55.5080.2000. You may also contact the Embassy by e-mail at—*ccs@usembassy.net.mx*. The Embassy's Internet address is *www.usembassy-mexico.gov*.

In addition to the Embassy, there are several U.S. Consulates and Consular Agencies located throughout Mexico:

Consulates

Ciudad Juarez
Avenida Lopez Mateos 924-N
Phone: 52.656.611.3000

Guadalajara
Progreso 175
Phone: 52.333.268.2100

Monterrey
Avenida Constitucion 411 Poniente
Phone: 52.818.345.2120

Tijuana
Tapachula 96
Phone: 52.664.622.7400

Hermosillo
Avenida Monterrey 141
Phone: 52.662.289.3500

Matamoros
Avenida Primera 2002
Phone: 52.868.812.4402

Merida
Paseo Montejo 453
Phone: 52.999.925.5011

Nogales
Calle San Jose
Nogales, Sonora
Phone: 52.631.313.4820

Nuevo Laredo
Calle Allende 3330,
Col. Jardin
Phone: 52.867.714.0512

Consular Agencies

Acapulco
Hotel Continental Emporio
Costera Miguel
Aleman 121—Local 14
Phone: 52.744.484.0300
or 52.744.469.0556

Cabo San Lucas
Blvd. Marina Local C-4
Plaza Nautica
Col. Centro
Phone: 52.624.143.3566

Cancun
Plaza Caracol Two
Second Level
No. 320-323
Boulevard Kukulcan
km. 8.5, Zona Hotelera
Phone: 52.998.883.0272

Ciudad Acuna
Ocampo # 305
Col. Centro
Phone: 52.877.772.8661

Cozumel
Plaza Villa Mar en El Centro
Plaza Principal,
(Parque Juarez between
Melgar and 5th Ave.)
2nd floor
Locales #8 and 9
Phone: 52.987.872.4574

Ixtapa/Zihuatanejo
Hotel Fontan
Blvd. Ixtapa
Phone: 52.755.553.2100

Mazatlan

Hotel Playa Mazatlan
Playa Gaviotas #202
Zona Dorada
Phone: 52.669.916.5889

Oaxaca

Macedonio Alcala No. 407
Interior 20
Phone: 52.951.514.3054
or 52.951.516.2853

Piedras Negras

Prol. General Cepeda
No. 1900
Fraccionamiento
Privada Blanca
Phone: 52.878.785.1986

Puerto Vallarta

Zaragoza #160
Col. Centro

Edif. Vallarta Plaza
Piso 2 Int.18
Phone: 52.322.222.0069

Reynosa

Calle Monterrey #390
Esq. Sinaloa
Colonia Rodriguez
Phone: 52.899.923.9331

San Luis Potosi

Edificio "Las Terrazas"
Avenida Venustiano
Carranza 2076-41
Col. Polanco
Phone: 52.444.811.7802/7803

San Miguel de Allende

Dr. Hernandez Macias #72
Phone: 52.415.152.2357
or 52.415.152.0068

Mexican Consulates in the United States

Arizona

Douglas
1201 F Avenue
Douglas, AZ 85607
Phone: 520.364.3142
Fax: 520.364.1379

Nogales
571 N. Grand Ave.
Nogales, AZ 85621
Phone: 520.287.2521
Fax: 520.287.3175

Phoenix
1990 W. Camelback
Suite 110
Phoenix, AX 85015
Phone: 602.242.7398
Fax: 242.2957

Tucson
553 S. Stone Ave.

Tuscon, AZ 85701
Phone: (520) 882-5595
Fax: (520) 882-8959
E-mail: *contucmx@mindspring.com*

California

Calexico
331 W. Second St., Calexico, CA 92231
Phone: .760.357.3863
Fax: 760.357.6284

Fresno
2409 Merced St.
Fresno, CA 93721
Phone: 559.233.3065
Fax: .559.233.4219
Email: *consulado@consulmexfresno.net*

Los Angeles
2401 W. Sixth St.
Los Angeles, CA 90057
Phone: 213.351.6800
Fax: 213.389.9249

Oxnard
201 E. Fourth St.
Suite 206-A
Oxnard, CA 93030
Phone: 805.483.4684
Fax: 805.385.3527

Sacramento
1010 8th St.
Sacramento, CA 95814
Phone: 916.441.3287
Fax: 916.441.3176
Email: *consulsac1@quiknet.com*

San Bernadino
532 North D St., San Bernadino, CA
92401
Phone: 909.889.9837
Fax: 909.889.8285

San Diego
1549 India St.
San Diego, CA 92101
Phone: 619.231.8414
Fax: 619.231.4802
E-mail: *info@consulmexsd.org*

San Francisco
532 Folsom St.
San Francisco, CA 94105
Phone: 415.354.1700
Fax: 415.495.3971

San Jose
540 North First St.
San Jose, CA 95112
Phone: 408.294.3414
Fax: 408.294.4506

Santa Ana
828 N. Broadway St., Santa Ana, CA
92701-3424
Phone: 714.835.3069
Fax: 714.835.3472

Colorado
Denver
48 Steele St.
Denver, CO 80206
Phone: 303.331.1110
Fax: 303.331.1872

District of Columbia
Washington
(Embassy of Mexico)
1911 Pennsylvania Ave. N.W.
Washington, D.C. 20006
Phone: 202.736.1000
Fax: 202.234-4498
Email: *consulwas@aol.com*

Florida
Miami
5975 Sunset Dr.
South Miami, FL 33143
Phone: 786.268.4900
Fax: 786.268.4895
Email: *conmxmia@bellsouth.net*

Orlando
100 W. Washington St. Orlando, FL 32801
Phone: 407.422.0514
Fax: 407.422.9633

Georgia
Atlanta
2600 Apple Valley Rd
Atlanta, GA 30319
Phone: 404.266.2233
Fax: 404.266.2302

Illinois
Chicago
300 N. Michigan Ave., 2nd Fl.
Chicago, IL 60651
Phone: 312.855.1380
Fax: 312.855.9257

Louisiana
New Orleans
World Trade Center Building
2 Canal St., Suite 840
New Orleans, LA 70115
Phone: 504.522.3596
Fax: 504.525.2332

Massachusetts
Boston
20 Park Plaza, Suite 506
Boston, MA 02116
Phone: 617.426.4181
Fax: 617.695.1957

Michigan

Detroit
645 Griswold Ave., Suite 1700
Detroit, MI 48226
Phone: 313.964.4515
Fax: 313.964.4522

Missouri

Kansas City
1600 Baltimore, Suite 100
Kansas City, MO 64108
Phone: 816.556.0800
Fax: 816.556.0900

Nebraska

Omaha
3552 Dodge St.
Omaha, NE 68131
Phone: 402.595.1841
Fax: (402) 595-1845

New Mexico

Albuquerque
1610 4th Street NW
Albuquerque, NM 87102
Phone: 505.247.4177
Fax: 505.842.9490

New York

New York
27 East 39th. St.
New York, NY 10016
Phone: 212.217.6400
Fax: 212.217.6493

North Carolina

Charlotte
P.O. Box 19627
Charlotte, NC 28219
Phone: 704.394.2190

Raleigh
336 E. Six Forks Rd,
Raleigh, NC 27609
Phone: 919.754.0046
Fax: 919.754.1729

Oregon

Portland
1234 S.W. Morrison

Portland, OR 97205
Phone: 503.274.1450
Fax: 503.274.1540

Pennsylvania

Philadelphia
111 S. Independence Mall E
Suite 310
Bourse Building
Philadelphia, PA 19106
Phone: 215.922.3834
Fax: 215.923.7281

Texas

Austin
200 E. Sixth St., Suite 200
Austin, TX 78701
Phone: 512.478.2866
Fax: 512.478.8008

Brownsville
724 E. Elizabeth St.
Brownsville, TX 78520
Phone: 956.542.4431
Fax: 956.542.7267

Corpus Christi
800 N. Shoreline Blvd.
Suite 410, North Tower
Corpus Christi, TX 78401
Phone: 512.882.3375
Fax: 512.882.9324

Dallas
8855 N Stemmons Freeway
Dallas, TX 75247
Phone: 214.252.9250
ext. 123
Fax: 214.630.3511

Del Rio
300 E. Losoya
Del Rio, TX 78841
Phone: 830.775.2352
Fax: 830.774.6497

Eagle Pass
140 Adams St.
Eagle Pass, TX 78852
Phone: 830.773.9255
Fax: 830.773.9397

El Paso
910 E. San Antonio St.
El Paso, TX 79901
Phone: 915.533.3644
Fax: 915.532.7163

Houston
4507 San Jacinto St.
Houston, TX 77004
Phone: 713.271.6800
Fax: 713.271.3201

Laredo
1612 Farragut St.
Laredo, TX 78040
Phone: 956.723.6369
Fax: 956.723.1741

McAllen
600 S. Broadway Ave.
McAllen, TX 78501
Phone: 956.686.0243
Fax: 956.686.4901

Midland
511 W. Ohio, Suite 121
Midland, TX 79701
Phone: 915.687.2334
Fax: 915.687.3952

San Antonio
127 Navarro St.
San Antonio, TX 78205
Phone: 210.271.9728
Fax: 210.227.7518

Utah

Salt Lake City
230 West 400 South, 2nd Floor
Salt Lake City, Utah 84047
Phone: 801.521.8502
Fax: 801.521.0534

Washington

Seattle
2132 Third Ave.
Seattle, WA 98121
Phone: 206.448.3526
Fax: 206.448.4771

British Colombia

Vancouver
710-1177 West Hastings St.
Vancouver, B.C. V6E 2K3
Phone: 604.684.1859
Fax: 604.684.2485

Ontario

Ottawa
(Embassy of Mexico)
45 O'Connor, Suite 1500
Ottawa, Ont. K1P 1A4
Phone: 613.233.8988
Fax: 613.235.9123

Toronto
199 Bay St., Suite 4440
Commerce Court West
Toronto, Ont. M5L 1E9
Phone: 416.368.1847
Fax: 416.368.8141

Quebec

Montreal
2000 Mansfield St.
Suite 1015
Montreal, Que. H3A 2Z7
Phone: 514.288.2502
Fax: 514.288.8287

Getting into Mexico
Provided by the U.S Department of State

The Government of Mexico requires that all U.S. citizens present proof of citizenship and photo identification for entry into Mexico. While U.S. citizenship documents such as a certified copy of a U.S. birth certificate, a Naturalization Certificate, a Consular Report of Birth Abroad or a Certificate of Citizenship are acceptable, the U.S. Embassy recommends traveling with a valid U.S. passport to avoid delays or misunderstandings. U.S. citizens have encountered difficulty boarding onward flights in Mexico without a passport. U.S. citizens boarding flights to Mexico should be prepared to present one of these documents as proof of U.S. citizenship, along with photo identification. Driver's permits, voter registration cards, affidavits and similar documents are not sufficient to prove citizenship for readmission into the United States.

Tourist cards

U.S. citizens do not require a visa or a tourist card for tourist stays of 72 hours or less within "the border zone," defined as an area between 20 to 30 kilometers of the border with the United States., depending on the location. U.S. citizens traveling as tourists beyond the border zone or entering Mexico by air must pay a fee to obtain a tourist card, also known as an FM-T, available from Mexican consulates, Mexican border crossing points, Mexican tourism offices, airports within the border zone and most airlines serving Mexico. The fee for the tourist card is generally included in the price of a plane ticket for travelers arriving by air.

The tourist card is issued upon presentation of proof of citizenship, such as a U.S. passport or a U.S. birth certificate, plus a photo I.D., such as a driver's license. Tourist cards are issued for up to 90 days with a single entry, or if you present proof of sufficient funds, for 180 days with multiple entries.

Upon entering Mexico, retain and safeguard the traveler's copy of your tourist card so you may surrender it to Mexican immigration when you depart. You must leave Mexico before your tourist card expires or you are subject to a fine. A tourist card for less than 180 days may be revalidated in Mexico by the Mexican immigration service (*Instituto Nacional de Migración*).

Tourists wishing to travel beyond the border zone with their car must obtain a temporary import permit or risk having their car confiscated by Mexican customs officials. To acquire a permit, one must submit evidence of citizenship, title for the car, a car registration certificate and a driver's license to a *Banjercito* branch located at a Mexican Customs office at the port of entry, and pay a processing fee. Mexican law also requires the posting of a bond at a Banjercito office to guarantee the departure of the car from Mexico within a time period determined at the time of the application. For this purpose, American Express, Visa or MasterCard credit card holders will be asked to provide credit card information; others will need to make a cash deposit of between $200 and $400, depending on the age of the car. In order to recover this bond or avoid credit card charges, travelers must return to any Mexican Customs office immediately prior to departing Mexico. Disregard any advice, official or unofficial, that vehicle permits can be obtained at checkpoints in the interior of Mexico. Avoid individuals outside vehicle permit offices offering to obtain the permits without waiting in line. If the proper permit cannot be obtained at the Banjercito branch at the port of entry, do not proceed to the interior where travelers may be incarcerated, fined and/or have their vehicle seized at immigration/customs checkpoints. For further information, inquire with Mexican Customs offices about appropriate vehicle permits.

Know before you go

As you travel, keep abreast of local news coverage. If you plan a stay in one place for longer than a few weeks, or if you are in an area where communications are poor, or that is experiencing civil unrest or some natural disaster, you are encouraged to register with the Department of State. The web page for Americans to register with us is *travelregistration.state.gov/ibrs.*

You can register your entire itinerary on the website. Alternately, after you have arrived in Mexico, you can register at the U.S. Embassy in Mexico City or one of the U.S. consulates.

Registration takes only a few moments, and it may be invaluable in case of an emergency.

Other useful precautions are:

- Leave a detailed itinerary and the numbers of your passport or other citizenship documents with a friend or relative in the United States.

- Bring either a U.S. passport or a certified copy of your birth certificate and current, valid photo identification.

- Carry your photo identification and the name of a person to contact with you in the event of serious illness or other emergency.

- Keep photocopies of your airline or other tickets and your list of traveler's checks with you in a separate location from the originals and leave copies with someone at home.

- Leave things like unnecessary credit cards and expensive jewelry at home.

- Bring travelers checks, not cash.

- Use a money belt or concealed pouch for passport, cash and other valuables.

- Do not bring firearms or ammunition into Mexico without written permission from the Mexican government.

Upon arrival in Mexico, business travelers must complete and submit a form (Form FM-N 30 days) authorizing the conduct of business, but not employment, for a 30-day period. Travelers entering Mexico for purposes other than tourism or business or for stays of longer than 180 days require a visa and must carry a valid U.S. passport. If you wish to stay longer than 180 days, or if you wish to do business or conduct religious work in Mexico, contact the Mexican Embassy or the nearest Mexican consulate to obtain a visa or permit. Persons conducting religious work on a tourist card are subject to arrest and deportation.

Visitors intending to participate in humanitarian aid missions, human rights advocacy groups or international observer delegations should contact the nearest Mexican consulate or Embassy for guidance on how to obtain the appropriate visa before traveling to Mexico.

In an effort to prevent international child abduction, many governments have initiated procedures at entry and exit points, including requiring documentary evidence of relationship and permission of the parent(s) or legal guardian not present for the child's travel. Parents of minor children (under 18 years old) should carefully document legal custody prior to traveling to Mexico. If a minor child is traveling with only one parent, the absent parent should provide notarized consent. If only one parent has legal custody, that parent should be prepared to provide such evidence to airlines and Mexican authorities. In cases in which a minor child is traveling to Mexico alone or in someone else's company, both parents (or the sole, documented custodial parent) should provide notarized consent. If a child traveling to Mexico has a different last name from the mother and/or father, the parents should be prepared to provide evidence to airlines and Mexican authorities, such as a birth certificate or adoption decree, to prove that they are indeed the parents. Mexican entry regulations require Spanish translations of all legal documents, including notarized consent decrees and court agreements. Enforcement of this provision is not always consistent, however, and English-language documents are almost always sufficient.

Residing or retiring in Mexico

If you plan to live or retire in Mexico, consult a Mexican consulate on the type of long-term visa required. As soon as possible after you arrive in the place you will live, it is a good idea to register with the U.S. Embassy or the nearest U.S. consulate or consular agent. You may register on line at *travelregistration.state.gov*. If you wish to register in person, bring your passport or other identification with you. Registration makes it easier to contact you in an emergency. (Registration information is confidential and will not be released to inquirers without your express authorization.)

For further information concerning entry and visa requirements, travelers may contact the Embassy of Mexico at 1911

Pennsylvania Ave. NW, Washington, DC 20006, phone 202. 736.1000, Internet site: *portal.sre.gob.mx/usa* or any Mexican consulate in the United States.

Returning to the United States

Make certain that you can return to the United States with the proof of citizenship that you take with you. Although some countries may allow you to enter with only a birth certificate, U.S. law requires that you document both your U.S. citizenship and identity when you re-enter the United States.

The best document to prove your U.S. citizenship is a valid U.S. passport. Other documents that establish U.S. citizenship include an expired U.S. passport, a certified copy of your birth certificate, a Certificate of Naturalization, a Certificate of Citizenship, or a Report of Birth Abroad of a U.S. citizen. To prove your identity, either a valid driver's license or a government identification card with a photo is acceptable.

The following frequently-cited documents are NOT sufficient proof to enter the United States: US driver's license alone, Social Security Card, US military ID, a noncertified photocopy of a US birth certificate, a notarized Affidavit of Citizenship signed at the airport in the U.S. or even a voter's registration card. Travelers with only these documents may not be able to enter the United States.

Without proof of both identity and citizenship, the traveler will not be allowed to board an airplane to the United States. The airline faces a fine of $3,300 if a passenger that the airline boarded is not admitted to the United States, and, in addition, the airline must bear the cost of flying the passenger back to the point of departure. Because of these penalties, most airlines will not board anyone—including probable U.S. citizens—without proof of citizenship and identity.

Internet

The most convenient source of information about travel and consular services is the Consular Affairs home page. The web site is *travel.state.gov*.

Telephone

Consular Information Sheets and Travel Warnings may be heard any time by dialing the office of American Citizens Services at 888.407.4747 from a touchtone phone.

Mexico Buyer's Checklist

❑ Obtain the advice and services of a U.S or Mexican attorney, a registered Mexican real estate agent, a title insurance company and/or an appraiser.

❑ Understand and follow the Mexican law concerning real estate purchases.

❑ Obtain a property disclosure statement from the seller, as available.

❑ Obtain a copy of existing public deed *(escritura pública)* complete with recording information and a current copy of the lien certificate *(certificado de libertad de gravámen)*.

❑ Request a copy of any existing commitment for title insurance on the subject property. Obtain a current commitment for title insurance on your specific property.

❑ When dealing with residential developments advertised in the United States, obtain a public report from that state. For example, in Arizona, obtain an Arizona Public Report.

❑ Obtain a copy of applicable Mexican state/municipal development authorizations.

❑ Obtain a copy of any Covenants, Conditions, or Restrictions for the property and any homeowners' association bylaws, budget, and financial statements.

❑ Analyze all risks associated with purchasing property where any infrastructure, building or other improvements have not been fully completed.

❑ Analyze all risks associated with seller financing.

❑ Estimate closing costs associated with your purchase.

❑ Complete due diligence, including investigations of title and value, prior to committing to purchase, or make purchase contract contingent on those investigations.

❑ Enter into a written purchase contract (in Spanish and English) that defines the details and contingencies of the agreement with the seller.

❑ Place all deposits in a neutral, third party escrow account, pursuant to a fully executed escrow agreement.

❑ Obtain title through a Mexican notary public, and title insurance, at the time of full payment.

❑ Ensure proper recording of the title transfer with all applicable municipal and federal registries at time of title transfer.

Source: The Arizona-Mexico Commission

Basic Spanish Phrases

¡Buenos días!
(bway-nohs dee-ahs)
Hello!/Good morning!

¡Buenas tardes!
(bway-nahs tard-ays)
Good afternoon!

¡Buenas noches!
(bway-nahs noh-chays)
Good evening!/
Good night!

¡Hola!/¡Chao!
(oh-lah/chow)
Hi!/Bye!

Adiós.
(ah-dee-ohs)
Good bye.

Por favor.
(por fah-bor)
Please.

Hasta la vista/Hasta luego.
(ah-stah lah vees-tah/ah-stah loo-ay-go)
See you/See you later.

Hasta pronto.
(ah-stah prohn-toh)
See you soon.

Hasta mañana.
(ah-stah mahn-yahn-ah)
See you tomorrow.

(Muchas) Gracias.
((moo-chahs) grah-see-ahs)
Thank you
(very much).

De nada.
(day nah-dah)
You're welcome.

Bienvenidos
(byen-veh-nee-dohs)
Welcome

Lo siento
(loh see-ehn-toh)
I'm sorry

Con permiso/Perdón
(kohn pehr-mee-soh/pehr-dohn)
Excuse me/Pardon

¡Vamos!
(bah-mohs)
Let's go!

¿Cómo está usted?
(koh-moh ay-stah oo-sted)
How are you?
(formal)

¿Cómo estás?
(koh-moh ay-stahs)
How are you?
(informal)

¿Qué tal?
(kay tahl)
How's it going?

Bien/Muy bien
(bee-ehn/moy bee-ehn)
Good/Very good

Mal/Muy mal/Más o menos
(mahl/moy mahl/mahs oh may-nohs)
Bad/Very bad/OK

Sí/No
(see/noh)
Yes/No

¿Cómo se llama usted?
(koh-moh say yah-mah oo-sted)
What is your name?
(formal)

¿Cómo te llamas?
(koh-moh tay yah-mahs)
What is your name?
(informal)

Me llamo...
(may yah-moh)
My name is...

Mucho gusto./Encantado.
(moo-choh goo-stoh/en-cahn-tah-doh)
Nice to meet you.

Igualmente.
(ee-guahl-mehn-tay)
Same here.

Señor/Señora/Señorita
(sayn-yor/sayn-yor-ah/sayn-yor-ee-tah)
Mister/Mrs./Miss

¿De dónde es usted?
(day dohn-day ehs oo-sted)
Where are you from? (formal)

¿De dónde eres?
(day dohn-day eh-rehs)
Where are you from? (informal)

Yo soy de…
(yoh soy day)
I'm from…

¿Cuántos años tiene usted?
(quahn-tohs ahn-yohs tee-ay-nay oo-sted)
How old are you? (formal)

¿Cuántos años tienes?
(quahn-tohs ahn-yohs tee-ayn-ays)

How old are you? (informal)

Yo tengo _____ años.
(yoh tayn-goh _____ ahn-yohs)
I am _____ years old.

¿Habla usted español?
(ah-blah oo-sted eh-spahn-yol)
Do you speak Spanish? (formal)

¿Hablas ingles?
(ah-blahs een-glehs)
Do you speak English? (informal)

(No) Hablo…
(noh ah-bloh)
I (don't) speak…

¿Entiende usted?/¿Entiendes?
(ehn-tyen-deh oo-sted/ehn-tyen-dehs)
Do you understand? (formal/informal)

(No) Entiendo.
(noh ehn-tyen-doh)
I (don't) understand.

Yo (no lo) se.
(yoh noh loh seh)
I (don't) know.

¿Puede ayudarme?
(pweh-deh ah-yoo-dar-meh)
Can you help me?

Claro que sí
(klah-roh keh see)
Of course

¿Cómo? *(koh-moh)*
What? Pardon me?

¿Dónde está/Dónde están…?
(dohn-deh eh-stah/dohn-deh eh-stahn)
Where is…/Where are…?

Aquí *(ah-kee)*
Here.

Hay/Había… *(eye/ah-bee-ah)*
There is/are…/There was/were…

Cómo se dice _____ en español?
(koh-moh seh dee-ceh _____ on eh-spahn-yol)
How do you say _____ in Spanish?

Qué es esto?
(keh ehs ehs-toh)
What is that?

¿Qué te pasa?
(keh teh pah-sah)
What's the matter (with you)?

No importa.
(noh eem-por-tah)
It doesn't matter.

Qué pasa?
(keh pah-sah)
What's happening?

**No tengo
ninguna idea.**
*(noh tehn-goh neen-
goo-nah ee-deh-ah)*
I have no idea.

**Estoy cansado/
enfermo.**
*(eh-stoy kahn-sah-
doh/ehn-fehr-moh)*
I'm tired/sick.

Tengo hambre/sed.
*(tehn-goh ahm-
breh/sed)*
I'm hungry/thirsty.

Tengo calor/frío.
*(tehn-goh kah-lohr/
free-oh)*
I'm hot/cold.

Estoy aburrido.
*(eh-stoy ah-boo-
ree-doh)*
I'm bored.

No me importa.
(noh meh eem-por-tah)
I don't care.

No se preocupe.
*(noh seh preh-oh-
koo-peh)*
Don't worry

Está bien.
(ehs-tah bee-ehn)
That's alright.

Me olvidé.
(meh ohl-vee-deh)
I forgot.

Tengo que ir ahora.
*(tehn-goh keh
eer ah-oh-rah)*
I must go now.

¡Salud!
(sah-lood)
Bless you!

¡Felicitaciones!
*(feh-lee-see-tah-
see-oh-nehs)*
Congratulations!

¡Buena suerte!
(bweh-nah swehr-teh)
Good luck!

Te toca a ti.
(teh toh-kah ah tee)
It's your turn.
(informal)

¡Callate!
(kah-yah-teh)
Shut up!

Te amo.
(tay ah-moh)
I love you.
(informal
and singular)

Helpful Property Terms

Abogado: Attorney

Alquiler: Rent

Arrendamiento: Lease

Avalúo: Appraisal

Certificación: Certificate*

Comprador: Purchaser, Buyer

Corredor: Real estate agent, Broker

Costo: Cost

Depósito: Deposit

Déposito de confianza: Escrow*

Escritura notarial: Contract

Escritura de compraventa notarial:
Purchase contract

Fideicomiso: Trust

Finca: Farm, property

Firma de escritura de compraventa: Closing*

Gastos: Expenses

Hipoteca: Mortgage

Impuestos: Taxes

Impuesto de traspaso: Transfer tax

Notario: Notary

Opción de compra: Purchase option

Plazo: Duration, Time term

Precio: Price

Propiedad: Property, tract of land

Registro: Registry

Sociedad: Corporation

Testimonio: Copy of the escritura sent to the registry for registration.*

Timbres or Timbres fiscales: Stamp taxes

Topógrafo: Surveyor

Traspaso: Transfer

Vendedor: Seller

There is no exact translation.

Index

INDEX

INDEX

preventive notice to public registry of
property, 50
PRI *see* Institutional Revolutionary Party
price-earnings ratios for rental property,
138–39
primary residence
determining tax residency, 256, 258–61
losses on sale of, 250
and Mexican rules, 245–47, 255,
258–59
not under tax-deferred exchange, 252
and US rules, 248, 249, 250–51
Princesa (condominium), 170
principal residence *see* primary residence
private property, 166–67
determining if property is *ejido*, 57–58
and *ejido* property, 55–56
see also ejido property
steps to privatize *ejidos*, 56–58
processing fees, 206
Procuraduría Federal de Consumidor see
PROFECO
PROFECO, 174, 195
prohibited zone *see* restricted zone
Prohibition era, 20
Promise to Trust Agreement
100% payment up front, 47
partial upfront payment, 50
promissory agreement, 36
property appraisal, 48
property comparison, 137–40
property managers, 162, 163–64, 254–55
property ownership policy and Mexican law,
242
property regularization, 190
property taxes, 105, 179, 256
certificate of no tax liability, 35
tax deductibility of, 121, 254
property transfer cost, 50–51
property, types of in Mexico, 166–67
public deeds, 48, 50, 171, 208, 239, 242
see also deeds
public notary *see notario publico*
public property, 166–67

Public Registry of Property and Commerce,
168, 171, 178, 212, 214
Puerto Escondido, 110, 113
Puerto Loreto, 113
Puerto Peñasco, xviii, 20–22, 107
efforts to educate and protect buyers,
191–99
problems with legal titles, 165–72
Puerto Vallarta, xviii, 102–3
Punta Banda, 60–63
Punta Camarón, 15
Punta Colonet, 107–8
Punta Mita, 24–27
purchase price
100% with Promise to Trust
Agreement, 47, 49
vs. declared value, 206–7, 246–47
purchase-sale agreement, 34, 36, 38, 48,
177, 178
PV *see* photovoltaics

— Q —

"qualified residence" *see* primary residence,
determining tax residency
Quantum Advisors, 223
Quintana Roo (state), 115–16

— R —

railroads, 6
rates of return, 238
real estate agent registry, 176, 192, 195–96,
238
real estate IRAs, 220–24
real estate licenses, none in Mexico, 46, 176
real estate registry law (of Sonora), xxi
Real Estate Task Force, xxi, 172
real estate transaction process, 30
identifying desirable location, 139–40
protecting investment, 49–50, 51–53
real estate transfer tax, 50–51
real estate trust agreement, 36, 40, 51
cost of, 180
see also fideicomiso

327

INDEX

Order Form

Crabman Publishing

Online Orders: *www.tomkelly.com*
Fax Orders: 206-855-0605
Telephone Orders: 206-842-0877
E-mail Orders: *orders@tomkelly.com*
Postal Orders: Crabman Publishing
P.O. Box 4719
Rolling Bay, WA 98061

Cashing In On a Second Home in Mexico $19.95

Quantity: _____

Price: $_____

Subtotal: $_____

Sales Tax: Please add 8% for books shipped to
Washington state addresses: $_____

Shipping: In the U.S., please add $5 for first
book, $3 for each additional book.
Outside the U.S., please add $10 for
first book, $6 for each additional book. $_____

TOTAL: $_____

Shipping Address:

Name: _____

Address: _____

City: _____State: _____ Zip:_____

Telephone: _____

E-mail address: _____

Payment: ❑ Check enclosed   ❑ VISA   ❑ MasterCard

Card number:_____ Exp. Date: _____

Signature: _____

Name on card: _____

Sales and distribution to the book trade facilitated by:
Partners Publishers Group, Inc., 2325 Jarco Drive, Holt, MI 48842.
Phone: 800-336-3137. **Fax:** 517-694-0617